DEVOTIONS®

January

Therefore, as God's chosen people, holy and dearly loved, clothe yourselves with compassion, kindness, humility, gentleness and patience.

— Colossians 3:12

Gary Wilde, Editor   **Margaret Williams,** Project Editor   Photo Zoonar | Thinkstock®

DEVOTIONS® is published quarterly by Standard Publishing, Cincinnati, Ohio, www.standardpub.com. © 2013 by Standard Publishing. All rights reserved. Topics based on the Home Daily Bible Readings, International Sunday School Lessons. © 2012w by the Committee on the Uniform Series. Printed in the U.S.A. All Scripture quotations, unless otherwise indicated, are taken from the *HOLY BIBLE, NEW INTERNATIONAL VERSION®. NIV®.* Copyright © 1973, 1978, 1984, 2011 by Biblica, Inc.®. Used by permission of Zondervan. All rights reserved. The *New King James Version* (NKJV). Copyright © 1982 by Thomas Nelson, Inc. *King James Version* (KJV), public domain.

Painful Witness

"The harvest is plentiful, but the workers are few. Ask the Lord of the harvest, therefore, to send out workers into his harvest field" (Luke 10:2).

Scripture: Luke 10:1-11
Song: "Lord of the Harvest, Hear"

Henry Ward Beecher once said: "Troubles are often the tools by which God fashions us for better things." We need to believe that! After all, every one of us faces a certain amount of adversity in our lives—and every Christian knows the challenges that come with a faithful witness.

But there are people around the world working in the harvest field, spreading the gospel, who face truly severe persecution, far beyond what we experience. Some face death every day. And though we may not know their names, they are brothers and sisters in the Lord.

God has called such brave souls to serve Him in supremely difficult circumstances. Yet their suffering isn't in vain, for the persecuted church is growing.

Today, let's join together in asking God to strengthen and protect our fellow believers who face daily persecution. Let's support ministries that take an active role in upholding their work. And let's simply follow the example of sharing the gospel with those around us, whenever we have the opportunity.

Lord, I pray for my brothers and sisters around the world. Give them the courage to keep serving You amidst great difficulty. Through Christ, amen.

January 1–4. **Deborah Christensen,** of Addison, Illinois, is a writer and editor for Lighthouse Christian Products. She loves to cook and spend time with family and friends.

God's Care Never Fails

Look at the birds of the air; they do not sow or reap or store away in barns, and yet your heavenly Father feeds them. Are you not much more valuable than they? (Matthew 6:26).

Scripture: Matthew 6:25-34
Song: "God Sees the Little Sparrow Fall"

Carl called his family to a dinner table set with plates and silverware. But there were no steaming bowls of food there as they sat down to pray. Carl was my grandfather, and it was just one evening in the era of the Great Depression.

My father, born on the day the stock market crashed, lived in a family that struggled. His dad took whatever job he could to provide for his family. But sometimes it wasn't enough.

The day came when there was simply no food in the house. Yet my grandparents continued to trust in God's gracious care. They knew He would provide for them. So Grandma set the table, and Grandpa called everyone to sit down.

While they were praying, they heard a knock. Upon opening the door, they found a basket of food sitting there on the front step. They never discovered who'd left it, but they knew that, ultimately, it was God's hand at work.

Dad told us that story, and I think about it every time God meets my needs. Every time someone tells me, "the Lord brought you to my mind for prayer, Deborah," I think about the legacy of God's care for my family, down through the years.

Lord, You care for me with an infinite depth of love. Help me remember how You've poured Your goodness into my family through the generations—so You're not going to leave me without help. I thank You, in Jesus' name. Amen.

Hold Me!

The law of their God is in their hearts; their feet do not slip (Psalm 37:31).

Scripture: Psalm 37:27-34
Song: "O That the Lord Would Guide My Ways"

"Yay!" we cheered from the stands as we watched the games. My family had come together to cheer for my niece and nephew as they participated in a multi-church competition. We celebrated their victories and encouraged them through every defeat.

As we sat down, I peeked over as my 3-year-old nephew, Jeff, played with a friend further down the stands. He was oblivious to the games.

When the event was over and we headed downstairs, a blast of cold air hit us as the auditorium doors opened. I grabbed Jeff's hand, and we started to run to the parking lot. The wind whipped against us as we slid over the ice and snow.

"Hold me," a little voice said. "Hold me." I stopped and swooped Jeff into my arms and carried him the rest of the way to the car.

God cares about me more than I care about my little nephew? Hard to believe, but true! When I live for Him, He keeps my feet from slipping. No matter how hard the winds of difficulty blow or how slippery the ice of life becomes, He's there.

The Lord also puts people into my life who encourage me. He guides me through His Word and shows me how to grow closer to Him. All of this, while keeping my feet on solid ground.

Lord, I know You are the one who keeps me walking forward on the slippery path of life. I sense Your presence even now. Bless Your holy name! Through Christ, amen.

First, Change Me

"So I say to you: Ask and it will be given to you; seek and you will find; knock and the door will be opened to you" (Luke 11:9).

Scripture: Luke 11:1-13
Song: "Have You Prayed It Through?"

"Lord, I need a new job, and these are the things I want it to include . . . " As I prayed, I stated all my criteria for a good job. And I prayed that prayer for two years! Yet nothing happened, and I became more desperate to leave my current position.

Eventually, though, my praying began to change. "Lord, I'll do anything, even if it means I have to clean bathrooms. Please help me." Two weeks later, I had a new job. It wasn't what I had wanted, but it helped me transition from where I was.

I only stayed there for a few months. I found another "help wanted" listing and decided to interview. As I sat in the waiting room and read over the job description, I realized that everything on the list had been on my original criteria list. My heart started beating faster.

I connected with the man who would become my boss—and I stayed with that company for 18 years. And it was that boss who encouraged me to begin freelance writing.

God didn't bring all of this to me when I demanded it. He waited until I came to a point of submission to His leading. Before changing my circumstances He needed to change *me* first.

Heavenly Father, I know You want what's best for me. Therefore, You don't always give me what I want but what I need. Thank You that prayer changes things—especially the one who is praying. In the name of Jesus, amen.

Observing Misery: Belief!

They believed. And when they heard that the LORD was concerned about them and had seen their misery, they bowed down and worshiped (Exodus 4:31).

Scripture: Exodus 4:27-31
Song: "God Will Make a Way"

Numerous operations and monthly treatments: this was the life that Lucas and James, two young brothers, would live— without any hope of relief from their shared medical condition. The boys knew the Lord in a special way because they had experienced suffering at such an early age. They prayed sweet, innocent prayers, fully believing God heard them. But the years of difficulty continued to unfold.

The Lord wasn't absent, though. Nor did He ignore their pain and suffering. And together, Lucas and James came to that unshakable realization. They acknowledged with great confidence that in sickness or in health God cared deeply for them. Thus their lives testified to friends, family, and the medical staff surrounding them on their journey.

In the months and years to come, Lucas and James, along with their many caregivers, grew keenly aware of the Lord's presence. They sensed the one who was ever present and compassionate in every circumstance of life. Could it be that God is using a painful circumstance in your own life in just this way?

Lord, may the difficulties in my life cause Your goodness to shine more brightly. And through the comfort You give, may I extend mercy to others. In Jesus' name, amen.

January 5–11. **Kathleen Wilson-Dowdy** lives in Sarver, Pennsylvania, where she and her husband enjoy serving the Lord. She has written for several Christian publications over the years.

Be Careful Little Eyes

How can a young person stay on the path of purity? By living according to your word (Psalm 119:9).

Scripture: Psalm 119:9-16
Song: "Create in Me a Clean Heart"

The phone rang just before midnight, causing my stomach to knot up. Our young son was staying overnight at a friend's house, making the call all the more ominous. It's amazing how so many thoughts can pass through one's mind in the span of a few telephone rings.

It was indeed Tyler. He needed us to come right away, giving us no clear reason for the urgent call for rescue. My husband dressed quickly, wasting no time in bringing him home. We tucked him back into his own bed and assured him that he was now home and safe.

The next morning we continued to reel with curiosity, since it had never been in Tyler's nature to get homesick. As we talked with him, we discovered that he felt he had to leave for reasons we never imagined.

As protective parents, we limited what the children watched on television at home. But had our words of explanation really taken root? Apparently so! During his overnight stay, Tyler certainly couldn't control what his friends chose to watch on television, so he removed himself in order to "stay on the path of purity." Isn't it wonderful how a child can teach us?

Holy Father, I struggle with temptations to see and do things that would not please You. Help me to realize that You are worthy of my very best—and that means controlling my thoughts and actions. In Jesus' name, amen.

Guide Your Children

"Jehonadab son of Rekab ordered his descendants not to drink wine and this command has been kept. To this day they do not drink wine, because they obey their forefather's command. But I have spoken to you again and again, yet you have not obeyed me" (Jeremiah 35:14)

Scripture: Jeremiah 35:12-17
Song: "Have Thine Own Way, Lord"

For some strange reason, society makes allowances for the younger generation so they can "find themselves" by experimenting with all kinds of behaviors and beliefs. For example, it isn't uncommon to hear parents say that they will let their children decide what faith they want to follow, if any at all. And many young people go on an extended self-discovery tour, checking out what might feel good or bring the most pleasure.

This was not true for my friend Crystal. She simply wanted to live for God. Growing up, Crystal was lovingly mentored by her family and church. She didn't need to discover herself because she already knew who she was and that her purpose as a creature came from loving and obeying the Creator. Today, Crystal cares for the forgotten and discarded children of Africa, and she keeps her faith tradition alive in each child.

God has taught me a lot through Crystal's life. I need to claim my identity in Him and impress the same upon my children.

Father God, I am reminded today that my life isn't a self-discovery tour or a popularity contest. It is all about my desire to know and serve You. May my faithfulness influence my family. May they learn to know You deeply and hear Your special calling for them. In Jesus' name I pray. Amen.

Even If It Hurts

He cuts off every branch in me that bears no fruit, while every branch that does bear fruit he prunes so that it will be even more fruitful (John 15:2).

Scripture: John 15:1-11
Song: "The True Vine"

The Hampton Court Palace grapevine in England was listed in the *Guinness World Records 2005* as the largest grapevine in the world. The Great Vine, planted in 1769, has a base trunk 12 feet in diameter with some branches extending over 120 feet long. It has a rich history to tell as it produced grapes solely for the royal family until it was sold to the public.

The Great Vine at Hampton Palace depends on the work of a full-time gardener who has tended the vine for 23 years. Part of this gardener's job is to know when to prune the vine so that it stays healthy and continues to produce fruit. The gardener prunes for two main reasons: so the fruit will be tasty and so the branches won't become too heavy and break off. The gardener knows exactly how and what to prune.

In our own lives the Father tends to our growth and care. Pruning hurts, but it makes us better and more fruitful with vibrant life. Sometimes we aren't producing fruit—other disciples—and we need the gardener's touch of rejuvenation. At other times we reach too far, and our leaves become sparse and dry. In every case, the solution is to remain intimately connected to the source of all life, Jesus the true vine.

Father, You know exactly what I need, even when I don't. I want to remain closely connected to You through every pruning and harvest! Through Christ, amen.

Beautifully Finished!

I have brought you glory on earth by finishing the work you gave me to do (John 17:4).

Scripture: John 17:1-5
Song: "O God, Who Didst Thy Will Unfold"

This past summer, my husband and I decided to remodel our kitchen. We shopped around, planned, counted the cost, and prepared ourselves for the whole do-it-yourself process. When our supplies arrived, we knew the task would be monumental as we sat amidst 296 boxes of all shapes and sizes. *What did we get ourselves into?*

One thing we learned very early: We had to follow carefully every detail as written by the designer. The slightest departure from the plan would cause colossal failure.

We didn't allow ourselves to do anything that would alter the designer's vision—and our potential for success. At times we felt our ideas might work better, and shortcuts could even speed up the process. But we knew better than to take the chance. Finally, our new kitchen was completed—the most laborious and exhausting project we'd ever tackled. What a relief!

And what a blessing! When those myriad boxes arrived, they held a great mystery for us. But the designer knew what had to happen. The discipline of following every instruction gave us the desired outcome. The kitchen was beautiful.

Father, thank You for Your instructions. I pray that I complete the tasks ahead of me just as You have designed. Help me to love and serve You, even if it becomes difficult, even when I want to quit or do things my way. And when the task is accomplished, may I give You the glory. In the holy name of Jesus I pray. Amen.

Let Me Introduce You

"Righteous Father, though the world does not know you, I know you, and they know that you have sent me. I have made you known to them, and will continue to make you known in order that the love you have for me may be in them and that I myself may be in them" (John 17:25, 26).

Scripture: John 17:22-26
Song: "I Have Decided to Follow Jesus"

With the acceptance of a new job, John was confident God had answered his prayers. As a faithful man, he desired that wherever God placed him, he'd live an upright life that reflected well upon His Lord. His past had its challenges, but he was committed.

In getting to know his new crew, John soon discovered that the majority of his coworkers didn't know God, let alone bring Him honor with their words and actions. John wasn't one to loudly broadcast he was a Christian or preach to them during the lunch hour; instead, his contrasting lifestyle simply evoked a curiosity in those around him.

It wasn't easy! But John's manner of life allowed others to get a glimpse of the Lord God who dwelt within him.

Not so very long ago I worked alongside this man. Knowing him led me to know the love and grace of the God he brought to work with him everyday. I'm glad John didn't hide any of this. Because I knew John, I now know God.

Heavenly Father, may I bring You glory and honor, through my words and deeds. You are a righteous God, and the world needs to know You. May I remember, though, that I may be the only "Jesus" some people ever see. Help me, in His name. Amen.

Standing on My Knees

My prayer is not that you take them out of the world but that you protect them from the evil one (John 17:15).

Scripture: John 17:6-21
Song: "How Firm a Foundation"

OK, I'll admit it. I was a thoroughly protective parent. Just ask my kids! It's not that I smothered them or didn't give them room to exercise their own personalities. I just cared deeply about their spiritual well-being and the choices they made. Sometimes they needed direction, . . . and sometimes I needed to trust them more.

My number one priority was to train my children in the ways of the Lord and to encourage them in faithful discipleship. My prayer life consisted mainly of asking God to protect them from temptation and the tricks of Satan. I prayed they would be so deeply rooted in the Word that nothing could shake their faith.

This all seemed to work pretty well until my children all chose a college that was eight driving hours from home. Until then I'd been with them daily. What would happen now?

Saying good-bye to each of them over the years held its pain for me. But over time I learned to let go and trust just a little more. My prayers continued as my children faced the good and evil sides of the world. They were not immune to the temptations that tested their stability from time to time, but they knew they could count on God . . . and the prayers of their mother.

Heavenly Father, it is difficult to give back to You what is most precious to me. Forgive me for holding on so tightly, even to my own children. For they too are gifts on loan from You! In the name of Jesus, amen.

In the Redemption Business

Who gave Himself for us, that He might redeem us from every lawless deed and purify for Himself His own special people, zealous for good works (Titus 2:14, *New King James Version*).

Scripture: Titus 2:11-15
Song: "I've Been Redeemed"

Like women in other households, I comb the newspaper each week, faithfully clipping coupons to redeem at the grocery store. It helps me save money for extras, stretching the family budget.

Jesus uses His own process of redemption to build His family. People who enter the fold receive His saving grace and then learn to practice good deeds, just as He did. His kingdom abounds with all sorts of individuals, called to exercise all manner of gifts and talents to glorify His name.

As for savvy shoppers, they know that the best kind of coupons are those with "No Expiration Date" written on their faces. So it is with Jesus. Having already paid the price for us at Calvary, He remains the same yesterday, today, and forever. His atonement is eternally effective, and redeeming grace is always available to us.

Are you a smart coupon shopper? You're in good company. God has been in the redemption business since the beginning of time.

Thank You, Heavenly Father, for the redeeming work of Your Son in my life and for preparing me each day to serve others. In Jesus' name, amen.

January 12–18. **Jill Davis** lives in Eugene, Oregon, with her husband and Muggles the cat. When she's not writing, she enjoys scrapbooking, needlepoint, and beading.

No Contract Needed

Whoever keeps His word, truly the love of God is perfected in Him. By this we know that we are in Him (1 John 2:5, *New King James Version*).

Scripture: 1 John 2:1-6
Song: "Lord, Keep Us Steadfast in Your Word"

My mother grew up in the 1930s, an era when a person's word was her bond. Her parents bought their household goods at the local general store. Every month they agreed to pay for their purchases by the first of the following month. Only a handshake with the store owner was needed to seal the deal. And the owner honored their word, because they always paid on time.

Back then many people often did business the way my grandparents did. With few exceptions, most of them paid their debt as promised. Today it's the same concept, but with loans and credit cards. Banks expect customers to pay off monthly balances in a timely fashion.

When believers practice God's commandments, His love is exchanged like currency. Men and women who follow Jesus make trustworthiness a top priority, following through on what they say they will do.

The Word of the Lord, being a sacred trust, is not to be taken lightly. And the best part of it all: With the Lord, our lifesaving contract was "signed" with precious, eternal blood.

Almighty and most merciful God, keep Your words on my lips and also keep me mindful of speaking the truth as I live day by day. May I always do what I say I will do. Thankfully, in this way I can contribute to Your own reputation in the world. In the name of the Father and of the Son and of the Holy Spirit, I pray. Amen

Home Sweet Home

Christ is faithful as the Son over God's house. And we are his house, if indeed we hold firmly to our confidence and the hope in which we glory" (Hebrews 3:6).

Scripture: Hebrews 3:1-6
Song: "How Blest a Home — The Father's House"

I tried running away from home as a youngster. I loaded up my red wagon and made it about three, maybe four blocks. Then I suddenly felt tired and hungry. So I trudged back home to wait for another day. Growing up, I still felt like leaving home sometimes, but that day didn't come until I was truly ready.

We can run all we want, but God knows where to find us. Our bodies are temples of the Holy Spirit and serve as our earthly house. Our heart, where Jesus resides, is home. So, in a sense, running is no longer an option.

Some people choose to defile their temples with countless forms of self-destructive behaviors, some obvious and others quite subtle. Such forms of escape are tempting, and being comfortable in one's own skin isn't always easy — especially when we face significant inner pain. Ultimately, though, running away doesn't bring peace.

Thankfully, God has provided a path for me. Really knowing Him does bring peace, and loving myself and others gives me comfort. The master designer built this place where I live. And I must admit — there's nothing shabby about living in a temple.

Dear Father in Heaven, thank You for providing me with a comfortable home here on earth where I am loved by You. Only know that I anxiously look forward to occupying my heavenly mansion! In Jesus' name, amen.

Are You Tempted?

When He came to the place, He said to them, "Pray that you many not enter into temptation" (Luke 22:40, *New King James Version*).

Scripture: Luke 22:39-46
Song: "With Jesus in Temptation"

When Jesus asked His disciples to simply support Him while He prayed in the garden, what did they do? They caved to temptation and fell asleep. Of course! None of them committed to an all-nighter, even though Jesus (humanly speaking) seemed to need them that night more than ever.

I'm no better when it's time to enter into serious prayer. The problem? My mind is always awash with thoughts. This serves me well as a writer, but when seeking God's face, I can't seem to keep Him on my radar for more than a few minutes.

My mind is too active, jumping from what I want for breakfast the next morning to what I'll buy on my next shopping trip. My thoughts zigzag everywhere, as I'm constantly giving in to a wandering mind. It's as if I've left Jesus back in Gethsemane to intercede for me.

Praying aloud, writing prayers down, or reading the psalms does help keep me on course. But keeping those random thoughts on a different frequency while I pray? It can be just as hard as fighting sleep. Thank God, He stays tuned to me, regardless.

Father, forgive me for giving into temptation instead of staying in direct communication with You. I often squander opportunities to pray, but You still step in to pray on my behalf by the indwelling Holy Spirit. Thank You, in Jesus' name. Amen.

All Points Bulletin!

Then they cried out to the LORD in their trouble, and He delivered them out of their distresses (Psalm 107:6, *New King James Version*).

Scripture: Psalm 107:1-15
Song: "Cry Out to Jesus"

The children of Israel sure let their sin and stubbornness sidetrack them in the wilderness. I too have a penchant for straying. The route to the promised land is already mapped out, but I'm like a distracted driver, failing to keep my eyes on the road.

Yes, I often insist on running my own life rather than follow God's plan. If I'd seek Him first, it would be like using a GPS or an atlas. Instead, I barrel ahead, giving no heed to directions. No wonder I'm scared in unfamiliar territory. That's when it's necessary to put out an all points bulletin for my Savior.

Preparation makes a trip more pleasurable. Yet I don't always use foresight as I should. In fact, I'm usually impatient as I wait for God's leading, ready to make a beeline for any shortcut that looks attractive. Thankfully, just about the time I'm hopelessly lost, God puts on the brakes with His tender mercies.

My attitude could use an overhaul regularly. I guess I'm a little too much like God's beloved Israelites when they strayed. I've found, though, that letting God do the navigating saves a great deal of time and heartache, thereby easing my distress.

Dear Heavenly Father, I know You always listen to me and that Your hand is outstretched to pluck me from every bad decision. When You speak, may I have ears to hear. Thanking You in advance. Through Christ, amen.

Taking on the World

We have boldness and access with confidence through faith in Him (Ephesians 3:12, *New King James Version*).

Scripture: Ephesians 3:7-13
Song: "Arise, My Soul, Arise"

Sometimes when I wake before dawn, I feel my way through the living room and into the kitchen in my bare feet. There's no need to turn on any lights. My hands guide me to the rug where the cat sleeps.

I'm so familiar with the cabinet that guards her food that, even though I can't see it, I know its telltale creak when it opens. I deliver her food to its exact destination without incident. Morsels never fall to the floor.

Once the cat's satisfied, I search for my own treat. The light in the refrigerator gives off just enough illumination so I can pour a glass of juice. Done there, I find my way back to bed in the darkness. There I sip my drink, say my prayers, and wait for a new day to arrive.

When the sun begins filtering through the slats in my blinds and peeks through the skylight, I am thankful there's really no need to just *feel* my way through life. Jesus is always here to guide me. With His help, I manage matters large or small with certainty and boldness. The Lord is my lamp as I forge ahead into a future He's prepared for us together.

Thank You, **Heavenly Father,** for lighting up my life with Your Son, the light of the world. I desire to walk by faith and follow Him with all my heart, for He gives me immediate access into daily fellowship with You. In the name of Jesus, who lives and reigns with You and the Holy Spirit, amen.

Modeling Obedience

Though He was a Son, yet He learned obedience by the things which He suffered (Hebrews 5:8, *New King James Version*).

Scripture: Hebrews 4:14–5:10
Song: "My Heart Says Amen"

While our family lingered over angel food cake in my aunt's kitchen, my cousin's wife recounted their story of painful losses. She had miscarried, my cousin lost his job, and the family dog was run over by a car. All of these tragedies happened within a few months of each other!

When I opened my mouth to express my sympathy, she stopped me mid-sentence. A year had passed, and she was pregnant again. My cousin had landed an even better job. And, though they certainly missed their beloved canine family member, they'd decided to adopt a new border collie named Sam.

This family, I think, could deeply relate to the idea that comes through in our verse today—that in some mysterious way even our sufferings can contribute to our desire to obey the Lord of all. And what an opportunity for them to witness to their faith in God and His goodness. Though my cousin and his wife mourned their losses, they never complained or looked back on their misfortunes. Instead, they sought what they might learn in the midst of their trials, and they kept moving forward.

Almighty God, I thank You for the times when my sorrow turns to joy. Teach me obedience in all the circumstances that come my way, that my faith may grow stronger, no matter how long I may need to endure. I realize that this is not the best of all possible worlds and that I am not home yet. Through Christ I pray. Amen.

Do We Display the True Lord?

We will go with you: for we have heard that God is with you (Zechariah 8:23, *King James Version*).

Scripture: Zechariah 8:18-23
Song: "God Be with You Till We Meet Again"

Ever wonder why a person chooses to "follow" another person on Twitter? Even if you've never used the popular social media program that lets one communicate a brief message to his or her followers, you probably "follow" someone by reading his book or listening to her talk show. You may share a common interest or outlook on life. Such key influencers in our lives can make quite a difference in how we think or act.

Why would people from other nations want to follow the Jews? Because they had heard that a great god was with them, and they wanted that god to be with them too. After all, if you become a follower of a powerful god, you'd presumably enjoy his protection and provision.

Followers of the one Lord almighty shared in the benefits of knowing Him, of being identified with Him. And in Zechariah's day, people of all nations came to the Jews of Jerusalem to find this Lord of all. In those days, you could identify who knew this God by what they wore! Today, finding followers of God may take more effort—unless our lives and our churches openly shine bright with the presence of God.

Lord, help me live each day as a true follower of You. Let my life attract others to You as I seek to glorify Your holy name. Amen.

January 19-25. **Carol McLean** is a publishing consultant living in Venice, Florida, with her husband, Gary, who ministers there full-time.

Really Want Guidance?

That the LORD thy God may shew us the way wherein we may walk, and the thing that we may do (Jeremiah 42:3, *King James Version*).

Scripture: Jeremiah 42:1-6
Song: "Where He Leads Me"

Every day you and I make decisions on where we will go and come, whether it's to work or school, to run errands, or simply to stay home. Such decisions don't usually need a lot of thought, except to find your keys and wallet! But what about those big, life-changing decisions—whom do I marry, what job do I take, and where will our next move take us? Those kinds of decisions require careful consideration, and often we turn to God for His input before we act.

Of course, we may hope that God agrees with us! Such is the case of the people who asked Jeremiah to pray that God would show them the right way to go.

At least that's what they *said* they wanted. This war-torn, frightened remnant of Judah declared their intention to "obey the voice of the Lord our God" (v. 6). They hoped to hear that God agreed with them, that they should escape the Babylonian invasion of Jerusalem, and run to the safety and security of Egypt.

Jeremiah warned them that God had another plan, one that would require them to stay put and live through the terror with God by their side.

Lord, I need to remember Jeremiah's words the next time I ask You for guidance. Whatever Your answer, help me to obey. In the name of Jesus, amen.

It's Worth It to Persevere

That ye may be counted worthy of the kingdom of God, for which ye also suffer (2 Thessalonians 1:5, *King James Version*).

Scripture: 2 Thessalonians 1:5-12
Song: "It Is Well with My Soul"

"No pain, no gain" is a popular saying among athletes. Yes, it may hurt to work your body hard, to reach your physical goals. But the saying reminds us with each push, pull, bend, or press that reward awaits those who sweat it out in the gym each day.

Whether the goal is to make the Olympic team or simply to burn a few calories, only those who persevere enjoy the benefits. And according to Paul's letter to the Thessalonians, the same holds true for them spiritually. He encourages them, prays for them, and soberly reminds them that even Christians will experience pain and suffering.

At the time of Paul's writing, Thessalonian believers faced persecution from the wicked society around them, just because they trusted in God. They would suffer injustice from the unrighteous, and yet be proven "worthy of this calling" (v. 11). They would glorify God simply by persevering through the pain.

Yes, bad things happen to good people. Yes, we will experience pain and suffering as Christians, perhaps even to the level that the Thessalonians experienced. Yes, we must persevere in trials. But we will also reap the rewards of faith, hope, and love as we support each other in prayer as Paul and the Thessalonians did 2,000 years ago.

O Lord, help me reach the goal of maturity in Christ. Give me the perseverance I need to keep training in Your will and ways. Through Christ, amen.

Just Call

Thou hast heard my voice: hide not thine ear at my breathing, at my cry. Thou drewest near in the day that I called upon thee: thou saidst, Fear not (Lamentations 3:56, 57, *King James Version*).

Scripture: Lamentations 3:52-58
Song: "Turn Your Eyes upon Jesus"

Often these days we hear about children being bullied by other children for no reason, "without cause." Like the author of Lamentations, they may feel chased, cut off, overwhelmed in flowing waters, struggling for a breath, and wondering who will hear their cries.

Abused spouses, harassed employees, fearful victims of crime or prejudice—they all experience suffering for no reason, "without cause." Each and every one of us who experiences loss, seemingly for no good reason, can relate; we understand, and we cling to the hope of this passage.

It's the hope of a good ending, even when we face smothering isolation or life-threatening circumstances. Help is on the way; the Lord hears our voice crying from the pit. He's right by our side and will redeem our life.

Though today you may feel as if you're living in a dungeon, you have unequaled hope in the one who hears when you call. So move past your anxiety. And, yes, call on Him.

Almighty and everlasting God, thank You for hearing my cry today and for drawing close to me. There is no one like You! In the name of Jesus, who lives and reigns with You and the Holy Spirit, one God, now and forever, amen.

Fine Example of Faithfulness

God forbid that I should sin against the LORD **in ceasing to pray for you: but I will teach you the good and the right way** (1 Samuel 12:23, *King James Version*).

Scripture: 1 Samuel 12:19-25
Song: "Great Is Thy Faithfulness"

Ever feel like just giving up on someone? You've prayed and prayed, tried to give guidance and support, but they just keep choosing the wrong way. If so, you can relate to Samuel as he once again addressed the sinful people of Israel.

At this crucial point in their history, the people demanded to have a king to rule over them, after decades of claiming only the Lord God as their king. Now standing before Samuel, the people wanted God's stamp of approval on their actions.

Samuel could have easily turned his back on them. He could have wiped his hands of the whole situation. Instead, he faithfully chose prayer on their behalf. No matter how many times they sinned, he encouraged them to choose the right way, to honor the Lord, and to "serve him in truth with all your heart" (v. 24).

Prayer gives us the opportunity to come before the Lord, our king, in an attitude of dependence as we thank Him, ask forgiveness for sin, or simply express a need. God promises to hear our prayer and guide our ways. This is the case, even when we fall, even when we'd rather just walk away and let the consequences of sin take their toll.

O Lord and Father, I pray that Samuel will be my example of faithfulness today. Help me never give up on prayer, knowing that it attaches me to the power of the omnipotent and all-loving Lord of all. In the name of Your Son, amen.

Stand Together to Win

Grudge not one against another, brethren, lest ye be condemned (James 5:9, *King James Version*).

Scripture: James 5:1-12
Song: "Victory in Jesus"

Whether in war or office politics, one rule stands golden: "divide and conquer." For example, the great warriors of Sparta, standing in one huge formation, shields surrounding each other as one giant wall which no arrows could penetrate, knew the secret to survival in battle. Keep in formation, keep the shields high, protect one another's back. Don't get separated. The moment those soldiers would break formation and scatter, the enemy gained the advantage.

James knew this secret too. In the face of injustice and persecution because of their faith in Christ, fellow believers must not let the enemy "divide and conquer."

Yes, the rich who took advantage of the poor would be punished, their silver and gold would turn to rust. The undeserved suffering of the believers would come to an end, just as Job's did. But in the meantime, until the Lord comes again, James instructed us all to "be patient" like the farmer who waits for the "early and latter rain" (v. 7) before a fruitful harvest.

James knew how hard it was to wait, to endure suffering patiently. And he understood how important it was to stand together, undivided, while vulnerable to attack. If we turn on one another, then the enemy wins!

Lord, help me and my fellow believers to keep our relationships pure and our unity strong, no matter how long or hard the battle. Through Christ, amen.

Find an Accountability Partner

Confess your faults one to another, and pray one for another, that ye may be healed (James 5:16, *King James Version*).

Scripture: James 5:13-18
Song: "And Must I Be to Judgment Brought?"

Science and medical research today indicates a real connection between our overall health and this: what we do and how we think. And in this key instructional passage, James also shows the links between "confessing your faults one to another . . . pray . . . be healed."

He gives us specific tasks to follow when sickness falls, some of which we have no problem following. But how many of us actually confess our faults to one another before we pray? How countercultural, how vulnerable, how embarrassing! Yet, James again leads us in the Lord's way for health and wellness, that we may be healed.

While many Christians agree that confession leads to forgiveness and prayer in faith brings spiritual healing, some question the physical healing process. Yet James clearly tells us that prayer is a part of healing. And if we want to continue to live well, here's what we are to do: "confess your faults."

Prayer sessions like this require trust between believers, to keep in confidence what we hear in confession. And the cleansing of our thoughts in confession clears the way for fervent prayers of faith that can change sickness into health. "So that you may be healed," so that I may be healed.

O Lord, I know You want to cleanse our hearts, our minds, and our sicknesses. Please help me find a trusted accountability partner today. In Jesus' name, amen.

Burning Brightly . . . Again!

Zeal for your house consumes me, and the insults of those who insult you fall on me (Psalm 69:9).

Scripture: Psalm 69:5-18
Song: "Revive Us Again"

He was raised in church and attended Bible college, but Darrin's life had spun out of control. He'd been shoplifting pills to feed a painkiller addiction. Then, seemingly overnight, the desire for drugs vanished, replaced by a burning desire for God. Soon Darrin was preparing for a mission trip. He spoke earnestly in his church about the need for total commitment to Christ.

Naturally, he was met by some skepticism. Was such a quick turnaround possible? And, even if this was genuine renewal, wouldn't it be wise for Darrin to spend plenty of time within his congregation building credibility once again?

As I tried to encourage him, I was reminded that Jesus encountered His strongest opposition from the religious authorities and leaders of His day. Unfair—since Jesus came to them with a spotless history of righteous living.

Yes, God forgives our sins and converts us, sometimes quite suddenly. (Remember Saul, on the road to Damascus? See Acts 9:26.) Our faith can become rock solid in no time. But it will take time to build confidence once again within those who have observed the destructive effects of our past poor decisions.

Thank You, **God,** for eternal forgiveness by the cross. And help me and every Christian, seek to repair the temporal consequences of our sins. Through Christ, amen.

January 26–31. **Dan Nicksich** is senior minister of the Northland Church of Christ in Grant, Michigan. He and his wife, Donna, are still adjusting to the empty nest.

Anticipating His Deliverance

Let them know that it is your hand, that you, LORD, have done it (Psalm 109:27).

Scripture: Psalm 109:21-27
Song: "Blessed Be Your Name"

I think one of the most heart-wrenching questions in all of Scripture must be when Isaac asks his father Abraham, "Where is the lamb for the burnt offering?" (Genesis 22:7). Knowing God had commanded him to offer his son as the sacrifice, Abraham nevertheless responds, "God himself will provide the lamb for the burnt offering, my son" (v. 22:8).

Testimonies are easy to give when God has blessed us. Far more compelling are testimonies about the *other* times—when we're still waiting for anticipated deliverance in tough times.

In this psalm David prays for deliverance from serious distress. His words suggest a potent mixture of physical, spiritual, and emotional pain.

We do know his heart is wounded. Spiritually and emotionally, he's hurting. But David doesn't merely pray for deliverance. He prays that his enemies will see God at work in his life. In other words, he wants *God* to receive the blessing.

Do you realize that you will never receive a better opportunity to praise God than during times of trial and suffering? It's during those times of hardship that your testimony prior to deliverance will show others that God has done this.

Lord, I have known both times of joy and times of trial in this world. Whenever difficulties cloud my days, I pray that all will hear words of praise as I look forward to Your deliverance in this life or the next. In Jesus' name I pray. Amen.

Two Models of Prayer

"I tell you that this man, rather than the other, went home justified before God. For all those who exalt themselves will be humbled, and those who humble themselves will be exalted" (Luke 18:14).

Scripture: Luke 18:9-14
Song: Search Me

During a heated argument, Harry bet his brother Jack that he couldn't repeat the Lord's Prayer. With $100 hanging in the balance, Jack took a deep breath and timidly began, "Now I lay me down to sleep . . . "

"OK, you win," Harry said, tossing a hundred dollars on the table. "But I'm shocked that you knew it."

These two could stand a lesson or two on prayer! But do you want to learn about prayer? Jesus proposes a stunning teacher: not a noted religious leader, but a sinful tax collector. As Jesus told it, two men went into the temple to pray. One man bragged about his adherence to religious law and couldn't stop telling God how good he was. The other man prayed about his sin with a broken heart. Guess which man went home forgiven.

As you read our Bible passage today, did you notice how many times the Pharisee spoke of himself—his good deeds and religious acts? Do you see the contrast of the humbled tax collector who understood his need before God? Which will be your model and mine, as we seek to grow deeper in prayer?

Lord, I am humbled that I, a sinful man, can come into Your presence, through the power and blood of Jesus Christ. My sin is always before me—but how precious is the saving forgiveness You provide! Through Christ, amen.

Acts of God?

If my people, who are called by my name, will humble themselves and pray and seek my face and turn from their wicked ways, then I will hear from heaven, and I will forgive their sin and will heal their land (2 Chronicles 7:14).

Scripture: 2 Chronicles 7:11-18
Song: "If My People's Hearts Are Humbled"

Insurance companies classify natural disasters as "acts of God." However, they don't do it in order to render praise to the Almighty. Their motive is to avoid paying off potential claims.

Though certain "laws of nature" govern the natural order and, as Matthew 5:45 tells us, God sends the rain on good and bad alike, apparently the Lord has sometimes intervened to create drought, plagues, or storms. His purpose may be to call people, or even a nation, to repentance. We see this particularly in Old Testament history.

Some have come to see terrorist attacks and the severe storms we often face as this same kind of divine intervention. While it's foolish to brand every such disaster or attack as the direct hand of God reaching down in judgment, we can easily agree that our nation has turned away from our Lord in grievous ways.

God's calls to repentance frequently center in promises of blessing. It's a familiar refrain from Him: you've done wrong; turn away, and you will be blessed. It's a simple formula. Repentance precedes blessing. Faithfulness insures His favor.

Thank You, **Lord,** that Your calls to repentance include a promise of blessing. In each decision I face today, help me choose the right one. In all humility I pray I don't miss out on any of the promises You give so generously. In Jesus' name, amen.

Praying for the Leaders

Because you humbled yourself before me and tore your robes and wept in my presence, I have heard you, declares the LORD (2 Chronicles 34:27).

Scripture: 2 Chronicles 34:24-33
Song: "For You I Am Praying"

I love the great painting of George Washington kneeling in the snow and praying while his army struggled to survive a bitterly cold winter at Valley Forge. Washington surely sensed providential leading in the fight for independence that forged a new nation. He stands as an example of the difference a godly leader can make in the survival of a cause or nation.

In ancient times, Josiah came to the throne at 8 years of age, when the land of Judah had lost sight of God. But during his reign, workmen discovered a book while remodeling the temple. It turned out to be the book of the Law, God's Word. Upon reading it, Josiah was moved to repentance, and this godly leader led the nation in turning back to God.

One godly leader can make a difference. Disaster was delayed until after Josiah's lifetime.

Some fear America is headed for a similar time of judgment and disaster. But will we find leaders to turn our nation back to its foundations of individual liberty and personal moral responsibility? The Scriptures call us to pray for our current leaders. Perhaps we should also be praying for future leaders, as well.

Lord, thank You for those who dedicate themselves to national leadership. Please raise up godly leaders as You did in the days of Josiah. And when it comes to strengthening the moral foundations—start with this one citizen. In Christ, amen.

Bad Company and Good Character

Jesus said, "It is not the healthy who need a doctor, but the sick. But go and learn what this means: 'I desire mercy, not sacrifice.' For I have not come to call the righteous, but sinners" (Matthew 9:12, 13).

Scripture: Matthew 9:9-17
Song: "People Need the Lord"

They say that bad company corrupts good character. Apparently Jesus didn't agree. He was rebuked by the Pharisees for eating with tax collectors and sinners.

Tax collectors were known to be cheats. They manipulated scales, weights, and tax rates. Most would see no distinction between tax collectors and "those sinners."

Jesus often confronted what might be considered conventional wisdom. His teaching was sometimes the opposite of what we'd expect. For example, in this case, it's not avoiding those of corrupt character that's important. It's redeeming them.

As we see folks who may be out of step with God, it's important to remember: God might want to use us as instruments of His redeeming love. Bad company need not corrupt good character. Rather, the character of Jesus, dwelling in us, can influence the "company" He attracts as we go through each day.

It's easy to write off those who seem to be sinners. But that leaves many sitting at the tax collector's booth, ready to follow Jesus if we would only issue the invitation.

Merciful God, I have passed by some of those who sit at the tax collector's booth. It's difficult to minister to those whose sin seems so obvious, but I pray You will give me the words to share. For my own sin is ever before me. Through Christ, amen

DEVOTIONS®

FEBRUARY

> Do not worry about tomorrow, for tomorrow will worry about itself. Each day has enough trouble of its own.
>
> —*Matthew 6:34*

Gary Wilde, Editor   **Margaret Williams,** Project Editor

Photo iStockphoto | Thinkstock®

DEVOTIONS® is published quarterly by Standard Publishing, Cincinnati, Ohio, www.standardpub.com.
© 2013 by Standard Publishing. All rights reserved. Topics based on the Home Daily Bible Readings,
International Sunday School Lessons. © 2012 by the Committee on the Uniform Series. Printed in
the U.S.A. All Scripture quotations, unless otherwise indicated, are taken from the *HOLY BIBLE,
NEW INTERNATIONAL VERSION®. NIV®.* Copyright © 1973, 1978, 1984, 2011 by Biblica, Inc.®.
Used by permission of Zondervan. All rights reserved. The *Revised Standard Version of the Bible
(RSV),* copyright 1946, 1952 [2nd edition, 1971] by the National Council of the Churches of Christ
in the United States of America. Used by permission. All rights reserved.

For God or Man?

So that it will not be obvious to others that you are fasting, but only to your Father, who is unseen; and your Father, who sees what is done in secret, will reward you (Matthew 6:18).

Scripture: Daniel 1:5, 8-17; Matthew 6:16-18
Song: "Take My Life and Let It Be"

"Is Scott sick?" the man asked. "He's lost so much weight that his clothes look like they're about to fall off."

"No, he's not sick," I said. "It's just a combination of exercise, healthy eating, and spiritual disciplines."

I didn't want to specifically mention fasting, since Scott doesn't make a big deal out of his spiritual practices. Some would think he's overdoing it since he has, at times, fasted over a number of days and lost quite a bit of weight. But I have to appreciate Scott's adherence to the words of Jesus. He's one of those rare individuals who lives simply for the Lord. There's no pretension or superiority complex. He does all that he does to enhance his ability to love and serve the Lord.

We may prefer different ways to enhance our spiritual lives. But would we consider an occasional time of fasting as well? I'm going to try a half day to start and skip a meal or two for the purpose of prayer. While Scott's regimen is too demanding for most of us, let's be sure to hold onto the words of Jesus and seek only to please God rather than win the praise of others.

Lord, I give You my life. My prayer, Heavenly Father, is simply that You would help me in those times I'm tempted to take it back. In Jesus' name, amen.

February 1. **Dan Nicksich** is senior minister of the Northland Church of Christ in Grant, Michigan. He and his wife, Donna, are still adjusting to the empty nest.

Give It All

"All these I have kept," the young man said. **"What do I still lack?"** (Matthew 19:20).

Scripture: Matthew 19:16-22
Song: "Jesus, Priceless Treasure"

Climbing big steps to enter a brick building through heavy wooden doors . . . That may not sound like something a 5-year-old would enjoy, but I couldn't wait to enter. My Sunday school teacher, Miss Winnie, had huge teeth, lots of white hair, and a funny voice that sounded like she spoke through a tunnel. I loved her. She greeted us each week with a smile and taught us songs and Bible stories. She taught us to pray too and helped us put our quarters in the offering cup.

Miss Winnie was as different from the young man who approached Jesus as night is different from day. His type A personality caused him to check off every commandment as "done." But his heart still longed for peace; hence his question to Jesus. The man thought he had nailed the holiness angle. Then Jesus challenged him to give more than he ever had—and possibly more than he could—by giving up all his wealth.

Miss Winnie never had much money, as I learned years later. Instead, she gave her time, energy, and knowledge for years in teaching children about God. She chose to honor God by doing what she could . . . and letting Him take care of the rest.

Almighty Father, today remind me of my need for a huge heart of giving to Your people, then help me to overflow with generosity. In Christ I pray. Amen.

February 2–8. **Kayleen Reusser**, of Bluffton, Indiana, has written children's books and periodical articles for years. She and her husband, John, have three fantastic grown children.

Whatever the Future: Trust

Speak and act as those who are going to be judged by the law that gives freedom (James 2:12).

Scripture: James 2:8-13
Song: "I Surrender All"

The slender, young woman with black, shoulder-length hair and dark eyes sitting across from me didn't look like a murderer. As editor of the jail's chaplaincy newsletter, I interviewed a person for each issue who had been helped by our program. The chaplain had set me up with this woman convicted of killing her baby.

During the interview, Carla (not her real name) said she had been raised in a church-going family. A few months after she'd delivered a baby boy, her husband found their son lying in his crib, apparently not breathing. A call to 911 for help was too late. The baby died, allegedly strangled with a telephone cord.

Based on evidence at the scene, Carla was arrested and later convicted. But Carla began reading the Bible given to her by a jail volunteer chaplain. She also attended weekly Bible studies and was baptized in a jail chapel service. Nevertheless, her husband divorced her and friends abandoned her. "My future is uncertain," she told me. "I rely on God for everything."

She had killed her baby and seemed to have no future. Yet Carla rested in knowing God forgave and loved her. I pray that I too may trust God so completely amidst every circumstance that my future may hold.

God, help me to understand and appreciate fully the extent of Your love and forgiveness for me. Help me to love sincerely every fellow sinner. Through Christ, amen.

Hold Fast to Him

Be very careful to keep the commandment and the law that Moses the servant of the LORD gave you: to love the LORD your God, to walk in obedience to him, to keep his commands, to hold fast to him (Joshua 22:5).

Scripture: Joshua 22:1-6
Song: "We Have an Anchor"

In the mid-1970s, my husband was 20 years old and a new Air Force recruit, assigned to MacDill Air Base in Tampa, Florida. Having been raised on a dairy farm in the Midwest, where the chances for free time were rare, he was tempted to spend all of his off-hours at the gulf beaches.

But John had always attended church with his family, and he chose not to slough off his religious upbringing. He read the Bible and attended church in Tampa on his own.

Upon being honorably discharged, John found a church to attend at home. His parents accompanied him. He and I met there and were married a few years later. We raised our three children at this same church, taking them to worship services every Sunday.

I'm thankful for John's dedication to the Lord because of his Christian roots. My goal was to marry a strong Christian man, and he has always been that. As we sought to obey the Lord, He has blessed us with a strong marriage and loving family and friends. For all of this, I have profound gratitude for the goodness that flows from the gracious hand of my heavenly Father.

Lord, I am blessed in following Your leading in my life. Thank You for the influence of other faithful people to keep me holding fast to You. In Jesus' name, amen.

Sharing the Wealth in Obedience

Not looking to your own interests but each of you to the interests of the others (Philippians 2:4).

Scripture: Philippians 2:1-5
Song: "Give of Your Best to the Master"

She could have kept the information to herself, and my life would have possibly never changed. "If you've never written a children's book before," said my writing class instructor, "you might want to contact this editor. She likes to give new writers a chance." Since my instructor had written books for that publisher, I figured she knew what she was talking about.

A few weeks later, I e-mailed the children's book editor a letter of interest. After receiving samples of my work, she assigned me to write a book. Then another. And another. Within three years I had written nine books for that company.

Being a children's book author opened new worlds for me. I was asked to speak to schools, libraries, civic groups, churches. It even helped me obtain a job as library aide in a public middle school library. There I have the opportunity to influence young lives about the importance of reading.

Since many of those students and I attend the same church, we talk about their walks with God and how to minister to other students at school. My instructor had no way of knowing what path her words of encouragement would take, but I'll be forever thankful she shared them.

Gracious Father, thank You for people who unselfishly help others. Help me to be just as generous with my knowledge and experience whenever I encounter someone who could use my helping hand. I pray in the name of Christ my Lord. Amen.

The Test of Life

One of them, an expert in the law, tested him with this question: "Teacher, which is the greatest commandment in the Law?' (Matthew 22:35, 36).

Scripture: Matthew 22:34-40
Song: "Brighten the Corner Where You Are"

I work in the library of a public middle school. I am not a teacher but I do have a huge respect for what they do, especially when it comes to giving national tests to students. This is done several times each year, because there are many required academic tests for students.

The rules for administering certain tests are finely tuned. In fact, teachers must watch a video to learn the correct procedures. They must sign a form verifying their efforts to administer the test within its guidelines, and they must read the directions to students, word for word. And here's the point: the purpose of the tests is not to trick the students, but to help them find their strengths and weaknesses in certain subjects.

Jesus was constantly tossed "trick questions" by the spiritual leaders of His day. They wanted to trip Him up so He'd look foolish. Unsurprisingly, our Lord always had a ready answer filled with heavenly wisdom.

In the Scripture for today, He tells us that obedience to God can be boiled down to the simple basics: loving God and His people. If a life task or a test results in my showing love to God and His people, then He gives me the letter grade of A.

Father, as I test the purposes and goals of my life, help me remember: every activity should focus on honoring You and helping Your people. In Jesus' name, amen.

From Pain, Service

You, my brothers and sisters, were called to be free. But do not use your freedom to indulge the flesh; rather, serve one another humbly in love (Galatians 5:13).

Scripture: Galatians 5:10-17
Song: "In the Hour of Trial"

I recently interviewed a nurse for a trade magazine who told me an amazing story of how she became interested in nursing. Her first baby, a boy, was only 9 months old when he was diagnosed with a brain tumor. Experimental treatments failed and he died at 17 months of age.

The mother, Kelly, said she grieved for her baby for many weeks but finally came to a resolution. "I knew what it felt like to watch my sick baby lay in a hospital bed and eventually die," she said. "I thought that if I became a nurse, I could help others in similar situations through their own pain."

Within months of her baby's death, Kelly enrolled in a nursing college. She graduated a few years later and has worked on the Neonatal Intensive Care unit of a children's hospital for many years. She helps not only babies but their families as they struggle to adjust to the difficult schedule of hospital visits and expenses. Close relationships have developed over the years; in fact, Kelly often attends birthday parties for former patients.

Kelly showed me the positive result of a deep grief. She could have wallowed in her sadness to the point of despair. Instead, she focused her energies on serving families in difficult times.

Lord, You are the master of creativity. Help me see ways to help others when I'd rather focus on helping myself through a painful situation. In Jesus' name, amen.

Help, One by One

He went to him and bandaged his wounds, pouring on oil and wine. Then he put the man on his own donkey, brought him to an inn and took care of him (Luke 10:34).

Scripture: Luke 10:25-37
Song: "God Will Take Care of You"

My heart ached for Madelyn, whose daughter had just lost a stillborn baby. As my coworker told of each family member holding the tiny infant whose heart valves had not formed properly, I wished there was something I could do to comfort her.

"The nurse provided a pink crocheted gown for baby Helen," said Madelyn. "She said it was made by people for just this type of situation. Can you imagine how comforting that has been to us—to have strangers caring for us in such a way?" Her eyes filled with tears.

"I work with a group that crochets things for people," I told her, touching her shoulder. "When a nurse told our volunteers of the need for those gowns, our group wanted to make them. They pray for comfort to the recipient's family with every stitch."

"Please tell your volunteers how much it helped us," Madelyn murmured. I assured her I would do so.

Jesus called us to love God and love people, with the good Samaritan as prime example. Needy people surround you and me. We can't help everyone, but we can reach out with our particular gifts, talents, and personalities to do what we can for the one who comes before us at the moment.

Heavenly Father, I don't know why people hurt and go through tragedies, but may I see needs around me and be willing to help as I can. In Jesus' name, amen.

Sky Action

"Therefore keep watch, because you do not know on what day your Lord will come" (Matthew 24:42).

Scripture: Matthew 24:37-44
Song: "Days of Elijah"

Little wind blew as I walked my dog Rocky in the early morning. It was shortly after 7:00 a.m., with the slightest breeze for a balmy dawn. It was the calm before the storm.

The hurricane tracker on my smart phone showed we'd at least experience a tropical storm as the hurricane made its way up through the Gulf of Mexico. I looked up at the sky, admiring the beautiful painting God had created.

I smiled, a snippet of a song running through my mind. Would I see Jesus today? The clouds slowly moved clockwise, and as I turned the corner the clouds switched direction, rotating counterclockwise. The first outer-bands, I said to myself. How awesome! The sky became alive with action as clusters of blackbirds and pairs of sand cranes noisily flew overhead.

Matthew 24:30 says, "They see the Son of Man coming on the clouds of heaven, with power and great glory." Revelation 1:7 says, "Look, he is coming with the clouds," and "every eye will see him." When Christ returns, the time for any last-minute repentance will be over. Now, let's look toward the sky and listen for the loud trumpet. Be ready.

Precious Lord Jesus, while I wait to see that action in the sky, I ask that You mold me into the person You want me to be. In Your name I pray. Amen.

February 9–15. **Shirley J. Conley** is a freelance writer living in Oviedo, Florida. She enjoys writing devotionals and creative nonfiction. Her hobbies are gardening and sewing.

Don'ts to Live By

"Do not steal. Do not lie. Do not deceive one another. Do not swear falsely by my name and so profane the name of your God" (Leviticus 19:11, 12).

Scripture: Leviticus 19:9-15
Song: "Open Mine Eyes"

What if God included "Do not be impatient" as one of the commands of the Old Testament? Well, I for one could not pass that test! No matter how much I try and how much I pray, I find myself growing more and more impatient. Two things can throw me into this frame of mind: incompetence and noise, with noise topping my list. Lawn mowers, weed eaters, leaf blowers, tree trimmers, hammers, and loud music can cause my patience to wane. (In my defense, I can patiently wait in line at the grocery store, even motioning others to go in front of me. I don't mind the line of cars at the bank's drive-up window. And even the slowest traffic gives me time to reflect.)

What should I do to improve in this area? As I search for an answer, to my relief, I find that at least I'm not alone in suffering this defect. The Israelites became thoroughly impatient with Moses, who was leading them in the wilderness. Job believed he had a right to be impatient with his well-meaning friends.

But the prophet Micah asks, "Does the Lord become impatient?" (Micah 2:7).

Hmmm. I wonder if God is impatient with me.

Father, You know I'm not perfect, but I'll keep trying to become the holy person You want me to be, out of pure gratitude for Your grace. I pray that You will never become impatient with me as I seek more patience with others. Through Christ, amen.

Share the Cup

There will always be poor people in the land. Therefore I command you to be openhanded toward your fellow Israelites who are poor and needy in your land (Deuteronomy 15:11).

Scripture: Deuteronomy 15:7-11
Song: "Cups of Cold Water"

A dirty, tattered woman cautiously approached our vehicle as we prepared to leave the restaurant's parking lot. With tears in her eyes, she told her sad story of needing milk and bread for her daughter who was sick at their campsite. From the backseat, my granddaughters' eyes widened as they watched their dad take two bills from his wallet and hand them to her.

We see economic hardship in every country in the world. The homeless sleep in cars or doorways in cities and camp in the woods. They search dumpsters for food or line up at soup kitchens. Children attend school hungry. But churches and individual Christians do try to help.

When I think of the many generous people I know, my eldest son tops the list. For example, I've known him to make payments on a vehicle for an elderly man, to mentor a young man throughout high school, and to give to many families in need. His outpouring of God's love goes on and on. In fact, without his help, I too might be homeless.

Father, nothing can separate me from You. In what can sometimes be a bleak world, You give me hope and a desire to help others. Let Your love flow through me to bring comfort to those less fortunate. Let them know the grace and mercy of a loving God. In the name of Jesus I pray. Amen.

Joyful Turnabout

He wrote them to observe the days as days of feasting and joy and giving presents of food to one another and gifts to the poor (Esther 9:22).

Scripture: Esther 9:19-23
Song: "We've a Story to Tell to the Nations"

In Esther, the Jews faced destruction. But when they finally triumphed over their enemy, they celebrated Purim—a holiday of joyous rest after a threat of harm has passed. The people of God celebrated with a feast and shared gifts of special food with family, friends, and the poor. They happily gave to others a portion of what their Lord had given them.

What a turnabout this was! The people had come full circle from potential destruction to heartfelt celebration. It makes me think about the roundabouts that many cities use to handle their road traffic—circular intersections. As we circle a roundabout, we must make a decision. We could continue circling round and round, getting nowhere, or we can choose to exit at the right or wrong juncture.

Life's journey is much like the roundabout. We might spin out of control, not knowing which way to turn. Our choice could take us into harm's way and everything connected with it—anxiety, fear, pain. Or, we may choose another juncture. We can walk with God, placing our destiny in His all-knowing hands. God can turn a wrong choice around. It is then that we can celebrate in joyous rest.

God, I often make wrong choices, even spinning out of control in some instances. But I know when those hard days pass I will be resting in joy. In Jesus' name, amen.

Endless Prayers

You, LORD, hear the desire of the afflicted; you encourage them, and you listen to their cry, defending the fatherless and the oppressed, so that mere earthly mortals will never again strike terror (Psalm 10:17, 18).

Scripture: Psalm 10:12-18
Song: "Crown His Head with Endless Blessing"

The Scriptures call us to pray continuously. But how? I couldn't seem to stay focused in prayer for even a few minutes. So I end my prayers and grab the television's remote control.

Morning news fills the screen. First comes the local bad news: clerk killed, teen stabbed to death, apartment shooting kills two, neighbors can't believe it's happened in their neighborhood. Then the newscaster tells the bad news in the nation at large: the economy, the war, and the terrorists. And let us not forget the weather—blizzards and ice cause pileups on interstates, tornados tear off roofs . . . it goes go on and on. There's certainly enough on the news to keep me praying continuously throughout my waking hours with endless prayers.

David points to the condition of the world in his time and appeals to the Lord to act, believing He will do so. We too can appeal to God. He listens to our cries, and He's always with us. Pray for the accident victims holding up traffic. Pray for the hungry standing on corners. Pray for those who have lost their jobs. Pray for the perpetrators of crime. Pray endless prayers.

O God, help me to share my honest feelings with You when I pray. Hear my cries as I practice endless prayer for those in need of encouragement. Thank You for being with all who are in distress. In Jesus' name, amen.

Travel Light

Now, however, I am on my way to Jerusalem in the service of the Lord's people there (Romans 15:25).

Scripture: Romans 15:22-28
Song: "I'll Go Where You Want Me to Go"

I packed my bag . . . unpacked . . . and repacked. At last, I was headed for the adventure of my lifetime, and all I could think of was: travel light. A mix-up in luggage arrangements would remind me of that thought when I struggled to drag a heavy suitcase of donations behind me while trekking through the airport. Unlike my 10-day mission trip, the mission trips of Paul took years to complete. He traveled by foot, horse, and boat. I would be traveling mostly by car, bus, and plane, often just standing in long lines for hours on end.

I anxiously anticipated boarding the medical boat that would carry me up the Rio Negro to the unknown, at least unknown to me. Myriad emotions welled up in me. The excitement of at last going where God was leading! I wonder if the apostle Paul had the same emotions as he and Barnabas packed their bags and headed for Jerusalem.

Paul's journey from Pharisee to righteous follower of Christ shows our powerful redeeming God at work. My Lord can take an ordinary person, such as myself, and give me a passion to go where He leads, even into the unknown.

O God, the king of glory, let the Holy Spirit fill me with a desire and passion to carry out Your work, no matter how large or small the task. Keep me willing to go anywhere You want me to go and do whatever You want me to do. I pray this prayer in the name of Jesus, my Savior and Lord. Amen.

The Call to Care

I was hungry and you gave me something to eat, I was thirsty and you gave me something to drink, I was a stranger and you invited me in (Matthew 25:35).

Scripture: Matthew 25:31-46
Song: "Anywhere with Jesus"

I stared at the man resting under the bus stop canopy. He ran his left hand through a straggly beard; his other hand held a Bible. As he pushed up the sleeves of a dirty green jacket, I saw a wrinkled shirt hanging sloppily below it. A sweat-stained baseball cap kept his long hair from his eyes. At his feet lay a bedroll and shopping bag that must have held his worldly possessions. *He's different from other homeless men,* I thought. He sat quietly, never without the worn Bible.

A passerby handed the man a candy bar, and he carefully unwrapped it, took a bite, and placed the remainder in his bag. Someone else handed him a sandwich and a bottle of water. Slowly he ate the sandwich, savoring each bite, then leaned forward, elbows on knees and continued reading.

I wondered what twist of fate or accumulation of troubles or poor decisions had landed him on the streets. Mesmerized, I spent the lunch hour at the busy square in downtown Orlando and watched the man and observed those who fed him and those who walked on by without a nod.

What would my Lord want me to do?

Great Shepherd, I thank You for all the mercy You've poured into my life. Please help me to follow Your guidance when it comes to simple acts of mercy toward others. Remind me that there, but for the grace of God, go I. In Jesus' name, amen.

We Are More Than Flesh

"It is written, 'Man shall not live on bread alone'" (Luke 4:4).

Scripture: Luke 4:1-12
Song: "I Shall Not Want"

Teenagers from all regions of Liberia traveled in December 2012 to Passport Youth Camp. In a country recovering from civil war, the theme "Life Together" was very appropriate as students experienced deep fellowship and studied the biblical definition of community found in Christ.

During the week, several students began complaining about the food they were being served. Ironic, since just a few years earlier, many of them were struggling to find a meal a day. Now, most had enough to eat, and at camp they were receiving three meals a day. Like the Hebrews moving through the wilderness with Moses on their way to the promised land, these students had learned to complain, even though they had plenty to eat.

Whether we live in a third-world country or in America, it's human nature to focus on satisfying the flesh, which Jesus tells us is not enough to sustain us. We are more than flesh. If we neglect our spirit, that is, if we neglect communion with God and neglect building community within the body of Christ, we will walk around with undernourished souls. And that poses the serious risk of spiritual starvation.

Father in Heaven, I know that Jesus' food was to do Your will. May that be my special delicacy daily. In the name of Christ my Lord I pray. Amen.

February 16–22. **Michael Helms**, of Jefferson, Georgia, is a minister and president of the Bricks for Ricks Liberian Housing Foundation. He and his wife, Tina, have two adult sons.

Running into Danger

Early in the morning David left the flock in the care of a shepherd, loaded up and set out, as Jesse had directed. He reached the camp as the army was going out to its battle positions, shouting the war cry (1 Samuel 17:20).

Scripture: 1 Samuel 17:19-30
Song: "Glory to God, Whose Sovereign Grace"

Most people run from danger. However, policemen, firefighters, paramedics, and soldiers are trained to run toward it.

Perhaps no other day exemplified this more than September 11, 2001, as thousands of people fled the terrorist-blasted Twin Towers. Yet rescue personnel ran into the burning towers, pushing away fears of their own in an effort to save others.

David was a shepherd. He had known danger as he protected his sheep from wild animals, but he knew nothing about war. Yet he didn't hesitate to go check on his brothers who were engaged in battle with the Philistines. Nor did any natural fears keep him from inquiring about the giant who instilled such trembling in the Israelites that their army was immobilized.

Courage isn't the absence of fear; it's the ability to step forward in fearful situations, usually with shaky knees. As General Omar Bradley once said: "Bravery is the capacity to perform properly even when scared half to death." For us, in Christian service, courage often requires simply waiting for God, patiently, to lead us. And then, when He calls, we follow, step by step.

O God, the king of glory, who sent Jesus into a dangerous world, help me realize that fear is a natural reaction to danger—but give me the courage needed to help others in need. Through Christ I pray. Amen.

And the Lord Be With You

Saul said to David, "Go, and the LORD be with you"
(1 Samuel 17:37).

Scripture: 1 Samuel 17:31-39
Song: "Make Me a Blessing"

I never heard my grandfather give my father any words of
blessing or affirmation. My father often did things for my dis-
abled grandfather, but his father didn't seem to be able to find
a blessing for him. While there was never any abuse, there was
never a lot of warmth present either—no hugs, no affection.

But we human beings are so empowered by blessings! We are
affirmed by blessings. A blessing is itself a hug. When the blessing is spiritual in nature, we are wrapped in God's goodness and
God's grace.

Contrary to David's older brother—who ridiculed him for
having left his sheep to come to the battlefield—Saul saw something in David that he didn't see in the other men. He saw
promise. He saw a glimmer of hope. He saw someone whose
confidence was in God. So he blessed David. And Saul's blessing did far more to empower David than the king's armor, which
David laid aside.

Look around you. Who in your sphere of influence needs a
blessing from you? Who can you encourage to love God with all
his or her heart, soul, mind, and strength? (And, by the way—
might it be best to start with our own family?)

O Lord God, help me to be intentional in blessing those who need encouragement
to do your work. Remind me that a kind word can make all the difference. In the
name of Jesus I pray. Amen.

The Bigger They Are . . .

"Come here," he said, "and I'll give your flesh to the birds and the wild animals!" (1 Samuel 17:44).

Scripture: 1 Samuel 17:40-50
Song: "Sweet Humility"

One of the giants of collegiate football was Brian Bosworth, nicknamed "The Boz." He is listed among the top 100 players of all time. His pro career was rather brief, though, and some believe it really ended the night his team, the Seattle Seahawks, played the Los Angeles Raiders on Monday Night Football in 1987. That night, America had a chance to see the two-sport star, Bo Jackson, on prime time television.

The players were similar in size, strength, and high level of skill. However, the Boz was known for his outspokenness while Jackson approached football with a quiet confidence. Before the Monday night game, Bosworth made insulting comments about the Raiders' rookie running back and promised that he would keep Bo in check.

However, Jackson ran for 221 yards. And, to cap off the night, when Jackson and Bosworth met in a one-on-one clash at the goal line, Bo ran right over the Boz for one of his three touchdowns for the night.

Arrogance isn't attractive in any human being. It's especially unbecoming in Christians, who aspire to reflect the character of Christ. Nor does humility make one weak. David proved that.

Lord of heaven and earth, there is no better example of a strong person clothed in humility than Jesus. Help me to use my strengths in ways that are humble, as did Jesus. Let His beautiful nature shine forth in me. In His name I pray. Amen.

Debt of Love

Let no debt remain outstanding, except the continuing debt to love one another, for whoever loves others has fulfilled the law (Romans 13:8).

Scripture: Romans 13:8-14
Song: "At the Cross"

According to CardTrak.com, the average American household carries nearly $10,000 in credit card debt. At 18% interest per year, that comes to $1,800 a year in payments.

In his audio course through Financial Peace University, Dave Ramsey teaches people how to become debt free (owing nothing except a house mortgage). This gives them the financial freedom to be more benevolent, experience less stress associated with money, and enjoy greater freedom to save for retirement and future needs.

In warning the church at Rome about the dangers of debt, the apostle Paul reminds them of one kind of debt they should always aspire to have: the debt of love. Regardless of how much they do for each other, they could never bank enough love that they could stop loving each other.

Suppose we took up this attitude in the most practical ways, throughout the church? What if we gave as if we were always in debt to one another? What if we took this approach even toward those we don't like or those who don't like us? What a revival would ensue!

Heavenly Father, I can never repay the debt I owe You. However, You have asked me to love others. So, when I love others I will try to remember that it is a form of worship offered to You. In the name of Jesus I pray. Amen.

A Different Kind of Wardrobe

As God's chosen people, holy and dearly loved, clothe yourselves with compassion, kindness, humility, gentleness and patience (Colossians 3:12).

Scripture: Colossians 3:12-17
Song: "Clothed in Righteousness"

As we drove into the outskirts of a small town in Bomi County, Liberia, about 100 people were in the street. They were yelling, beating drums, and waving sticks at a man who was wearing a mask and was clothed in colored rags. He looked like some kind of evil character.

I asked our driver what was going on, and he said, "They are driving the devil out town. The two guys with the devil are collecting money from the people who want the devil driven out of town. It's just a way for these guys to make money." One of the guys knocked on the window of our car, wanting money, but our driver refused. As we rode away, I watched the "devil" in my rearview mirror making his way out of town.

Paul had a much better way of getting rid of the devil! He told the Romans to clothe themselves with God's own character. Just as light and darkness cannot coexist, the evil one can't live in a community where people clothe themselves in goodness. He much prefers to live where people's lives are ragged with sin.

Take a look at your wardrobe today. Where can you replace ragged clothes of sin with clothes of compassion and kindness?

O God, too often I'm paying a price for my own sinfulness, my own poor decisions when temptation hits. Clothe me, Lord, in Your mercy and grace, and help my inner character, more and more, match what's on the outside. In Jesus' name, amen.

As the Battle Continues . . .

Put on the full armor of God, so that when the day of evil comes, you may be able to stand your ground, and after you have done everything, to stand (Ephesians 6:13).

Scripture: Ephesians 6:10-20
Song: "O God, Our Help in Ages Past"

When our son John served in Afghanistan, he was stationed at Camp Leatherneck. There he trained Afghans to become policemen. He was also responsible for accompanying high-ranking officers from the base to the airport. These trips were always dangerous, for hidden roadside bombs were frequent sources of casualties for Marines and soldiers.

What a blessing that we were able to communicate with John through the Skype audiovisual computer phone. Some mornings, as John prepared for one of his missions, he would be putting on his gear. I was amazed to see how much protection he had to wear, about 55 pounds of body armor in all.

For him, the daily battle was his entire focus. But for us, it can be easy to forget that there's a spiritual battle taking place constantly. If we fail to put on our spiritual armor, we put ourselves at risk for Satan's "shrapnel" to lodge in our minds or our hearts.

As you read Paul's advice to the Ephesians, can you identify where you might have a chink in your spiritual armor? I have to ask myself: *Where's the weakness in me, this day, as I face the powers of this dark world?*

O Lord, I am grateful that You do not leave me defenseless against the wiles of the tempter. Thank You for the belt of truth and the rest of the armor You've provided me! May I use it well! I pray through Christ, my victorious Savior. Amen.

Whose Agenda, Anyway?

Pharaoh asked them, "Can we find anyone like this man, one in whom is the spirit of God?" (Genesis 41:38).

Scripture: Genesis 41:38-43
Song: "Savior, Like a Shepherd Lead Us"

I arose early, with a clear agenda. I faced an important writing project for a Christian publication, and the editor's deadline rapidly approached. Then, everything began to unravel.

Our next door neighbor called. They would be away all day. "Would you come over and let Duke out about noon and again at supper time?" Duke is their big golden retriever — big enough that my wife cannot handle his playfulness.

Martha was coming home from the rehab unit, and my wife had prepared a meal for Martha and her husband. "Would you help me deliver the food and visit them for a while?" she asked. "They never have much company."

Late that night, I'm in bed thinking, *So much for my good intentions. I'm trying to do God's work by getting this writing assignment e-mailed to the editor, and these interruptions scuttled my plans. Another wasted day.*

As I closed my eyes, a new thought hit me: *Was it really wasted? I had not accomplished what I had set out to do, but wasn't I doing God's work in other ways? Could I just close my eyes and be thankful?* Sometimes the distractions *are* the agenda.

Dear God, let me fill my day with Your business, led by Your Holy Spirit. Today, by the Spirit's power, Your agenda is my agenda. In Jesus' name, amen.

February 23–28. **Drexel Rankin** served the Christian Church (Disciples of Christ) as an ordained minister for more than 35 years in Indiana, Alabama, and Kentucky. .

Shaping Something Beautiful

Then the LORD said to Moses, "See, I have chosen Bezalel son of Uri . . . and I have filled him with the Spirit of God, with wisdom, with understanding, with knowledge and with all kinds of skills" (Exodus 31:1-3).

Scripture: Exodus 31:1-6
Song: "We Plow the Fields and Scatter"

My wife will tell you that I am not a handyman, and fixing things around the house is not one of my strengths. Occasionally, I'll stumble onto a solution, but usually I have no idea how I actually fixed the problem.

God is quite aware of the talents that He has given to me. Each gift is the correct one for the circumstance. Many times throughout my life, God has given me the wisdom, ability, and expertise to do something that needed doing.

God gives gifts to all of us and chooses which gifts to give to each person. Some have a gift of musical ability; others are workers of wood or metal; some are gifted speakers. God gives knowledge, skill, ability, and craftsmanship—all for the purpose of building up the church. The wonderful thing is that God, in His wisdom, gives each of us exactly the creative gifts that, when joined with another's gifts, shape something beautiful.

I don't want to miss the opportunity of a lifetime. So, I receive those gifts that are part of my being, accept them with thanksgiving, and use them to the best of my ability.

Giving Lord, You choose and assign gifts to each of us to complete our calling with excellence. Help me to discover and use these creative, wonderful gifts that I may enrich the lives of others, and that You will be glorified. In Jesus' name, amen.

One to Trust

The LORD answered Moses, "Is the LORD's arm too short? Now you will see whether or not what I say will come true for you" (Numbers 11:23).

Scripture: Numbers 11:11-25
Song: "In Heavenly Love Abiding"

My son had chosen cute little Viking as his 12th birthday present. Greg was drawn to this particular puppy as it cowered near the back of a cage at the local Humane Society. He brought the puppy home, cared for him, and watched him mature. We all grew to love Viking because he was friendly with adults, loved to chase a tennis ball, and always seemed to be by our sides.

But Viking scurried under the bed during thunderstorms; he hid behind the couch when children wanted to play with him; occasionally, he would even nip at people if he felt cornered. At such times, we remembered that Viking seemed just so fearful when we first saw him.

So, during those fearful times, we would draw Viking a little closer. One of us would speak to him in a quiet voice telling him: "It's OK, Viking. Don't be afraid. I'm right here." His ears would relax, and his trembling would cease.

It's good to have a master whom we can trust—to have one to whom we can always draw close, one who eases our worries and comforts us when we are afraid. He's the one who says, "It's all right. I'm here. Trust me. I'm the Lord of the universe."

Thank You, **Dear God,** for the pledge of Your presence, Your promise never to leave me, and Your assurance of blessings. I can trust any promise given by an omnipotent being—and there is only one of those! Praise You, through Christ. Amen.

Growing in the Light

Moses replied, "Are you jealous for my sake? I wish that all the LORD's people were prophets and that the LORD would put his Spirit on them!" (Numbers 11:29).

Scripture: Numbers 11:26-30
Song: "Take My Life"

When I served as the interim minister at her church, I hardly knew Linda. She was retiring and shy; she was into the church and out quickly on Sunday mornings; she participated in no study groups or Sunday school classes.

So, my wife and I were surprised to see that Linda was still a member when, after retirement, we chose to join this church where I had been four years previously.

But something had changed her dramatically. Now, she was involved in leadership. Her creative talents had blossomed and were apparent both in groups and in personal leadership. She was currently helping to plan a memorial for a long-time member of the church who had recently died. In that kind of leadership, her talents shone brightly.

To this day, my wife and I are still not quite sure what happened to Linda during those intervening four years. Like Moses, empowered by God's Spirit, she served and led with effective result. Yes, in some profound way she had yielded to the Holy Spirit in her life. Thus God has gifted her and is using her in wonderful ways.

Nurturing God, thank You for making new life possible by Your indwelling Holy Spirit. Help me yield to Him completely and grow in love and service today. I pray in the precious name of Jesus the Lord. Amen.

A Personal Wilderness

He said, "I am the voice of one crying in the wilderness, 'Make straight the way of the Lord,' as the prophet Isaiah said" (John 1:23, *Revised Standard Version*).

Scripture: John 1:19-23
Song: "If You Will Trust in God to Guide You"

In recent weeks, I've found myself in my own personal wilderness. My life has felt cluttered—not full or abundant. If you walked into my study at home, you would know what I mean.

I've got to get rid of the disorder—the extreme untidiness—piles of paperwork, unanswered e-mails, junk scattered on the floor. I need to rid my life of unrealistic expectations, an overcrowded calendar, and things I said "yes" to when I should have said "no." God has a hard time entering my wilderness life when it is crowded with debris and disorder.

What clutter is pulling you down? What would it mean for you to get a new perspective on life—for God to really grab hold?

Wilderness is that place which is no place, where we lose our way, wander from the path, get lost, become enslaved to some false god, and sell out. Then again, maybe it's not that harsh for most of us. For most of us, we just forget—forget our identity in Christ and forget who called us to a higher life.

The solution? Listen again to our verse for today: "In the wilderness, 'Make straight the way of the Lord.'"

God of hope and love, in the wilderness of life, help me to rid myself of the clutter and junk that keeps me from coming closer to You. I seek Your face again, with open heart, and I know this prayer is one You always answer! In Jesus' name, amen.

In God's Time

He is the one who comes after me (John 1:27).

Scripture: John 1:24-28
Song: "Maker and Sovereign Lord"

We fished with determination. We were in charge of that day, of that lake, of those fish. Check out the rods and reels. Look at the tackle boxes filled with crack baits and spinners. We would have dominion over those fish.

But God, of course, is the only being in the universe who is actually "in charge." So . . . you have guessed already how the day turned out. Just when I think I've got it all under control, God comes along and says, "No." So it was empty hooks and cold cuts for dinner.

It was calm from the time we started out at an early hour right through the day. The breeze scarcely blew. The lake was still. The gulls just sat and bobbed. But the fish were still, not biting. In other words, it was a beautiful day, but not for fishing.

I discovered something that day, though. This was not a hollow stillness. It was full, not empty. More like a pause, a waiting. It was as if all creation were waiting, and we waited with it.

Most cycles of life are free from our control—times that will not be counted by our measures. A stillness that speaks.

For us, on that glorious day, it was a grand waiting that leaned upon and told of the providential care of God. Looking back, I wouldn't have wanted it any other way.

God of Creation, may I always look for signs of Your presence and be thankful for evidences of Your goodness, no matter the circumstances. In the name of the Father and of the Son and of the Holy Spirit, I pray. Amen.

My Prayer Notes

_____

_____

_____

_____

_____

_____

_____

_____

_____

_____

_____

_____

_____

_____

_____

_____

_____

_____

_____

_____

_____

_____

_____

My Prayer Notes

My Prayer Notes

DEVOTIONS®

MARCH

Be strong and take heart,
all you who hope in the LORD.

—Psalm 31:24

Gary Allen, Editor　　　**Margaret Williams,** Project Editor　　　Photo DesignPics | Thinkstock®

DEVOTIONS® is published quarterly by Standard Publishing, Cincinnati, Ohio, www.standardpub.com. © 2014 by Standard Publishing. All rights reserved. Topics based on the Home Daily Bible Readings, International Sunday School Lessons. © 2012 by the Committee on the Uniform Series. Printed in the U.S.A. All Scripture quotations, unless otherwise indicated, are taken from the *HOLY BIBLE, NEW INTERNATIONAL VERSION*®. *NIV*®. Copyright © 1973, 1978, 1984, 2011 by Biblica, Inc.® Used by permission of Zondervan. All rights reserved. *New American Standard Bible*®, (*NASB*) Copyright © 1960, 1962, 1963, 1968, 1971, 1972, 1973, 1975, 1977, 1995 by The Lockman Foundation. Used by permission. (www.Lockman.org). The *Revised Standard Version of the Bible* (*RSV*), copyright 1946, 1952 [2nd edition, 1971] by the National Council of the Churches of Christ in the United States of America. Used by permission. All rights reserved. The *Holy Bible, New Living Translation* (*NLT*). Copyright © 1996, 2004, 2007. Used by permission of Tyndale House Publishers, Inc., Wheaton, Illinois 60189. All rights reserved. *King James Version* (*KJV*), public domain. The *New King James Version* (*NKJV*). Copyright © 1982 by Thomas Nelson, Inc.

Sign of Anointing

Then John gave this testimony: "I saw the Spirit come down from heaven as a dove and remain on him" (John 1:32).

Scripture: John 1:29-34
Song: "Sweet Holy Spirit"

A trip to the Safari Park in San Diego was the order of the day when I visited my brother and his family. I was calm when we arrived at Lorikeet Landing and we bought tiny cups of food for the birds. "They'll land on you," I was told, over and over.

And land they did. But I nearly freaked out when the colorful birds—two at a time—winged down to my wrist. I'd never had a bird land on me before. I flashed to a memory of watching *The Birds,* a film directed by Alfred Hitchcock, where the neighborhood's ordinary winged creatures took on a more ominous presence. Yet watching my niece and nephew delight in the colorful parrots and hearing the birds' cheerful squeaks heartened me. Soon I could enjoy the brush of velvety feathers on my skin.

John the Baptist had a different mind-set when describing his belief in Jesus as the promised Messiah. The presence of the Holy Spirit, in the form of a dove, signified God's peace and anointing. Unlike the lorikeets who came and went after being fed, the heavenly dove remained with Jesus. Thanks to the death and resurrection of our Lord—and our identification with Him in baptism—the presence of the Holy Spirit remains in us.

Lord, I'm so grateful for the gift of Your Spirit. Please fill me with Your presence and grant me Your grace and peace this day. In Jesus' name, amen.

March 1-7. **Linda Washington** is a freelance writer living in Carol Stream, Illinois. She has written several books as well as curriculums.

Take the Cure

Is there no balm in Gilead? Is there no physician there? Why then has not the health of the daughter of my people been restored? (Jeremiah 8:22, *New American Standard Bible*).

Scripture: Jeremiah 8:18-22
Song: "There Is a Balm in Gilead"

I'm not one to run to a doctor whenever I become sick. But I finally reached a point, after coughing for two weeks and then experiencing facial swelling, where I realized I just wasn't getting better—even after much prayer. I admit that I had been ignoring the still voice inside telling me to go to the doctor.

"Why don't You just heal me, Lord?" I asked. Without medical insurance, I find my visits to the doctor's office quite costly. But to the doctor I went, after a nearly sleepless night. The morning was little better, as I struggled with the pain of irritated sinuses. Now I was grateful to get an early appointment! The diagnosis: severe sinus infection. And I definitely had to take the meds in order to get better.

The people of Judah had a "medical problem" in our Scripture today. Diagnosis: idol worship made them spiritually ill. Though Jeremiah's tender heart caused him to lament over their illness, the only cure was repentance. It would require a significant dose, but it was the only way. God exercised tough love by refusing to rush to their aid when enemies threatened to conquer. And though He was there for them, He couldn't help if they refused the cure.

Lord, I need the balm that only You can provide. But first, Lord, I need the humility to accept Your cure. In Christ's name I pray. Amen.

Relief for the Broken

LORD, see my anguish! My heart is broken and my soul despairs, for I have rebelled against you (Lamentations 1:20, *New Living Translation*).

Scripture: Lamentations 1:17-21
Song: "Cry Out to Jesus"

Frontal lobes develop over time. I can attest to that, judging by some of the decisions I made as a kid. Take the time my older brother and I decided to have a plate fight in the living room. We didn't touch the good china, but the everyday plasticware was fair game. We slung plates at each other like Frisbees. What a great time — until the sound of shattering glass that shattered the experience (and damaged our mother's prized vase).

"We can tape it back together," my brother suggested. But the only tape we could find was our father's black electrical tape. "Mom will never notice if we turn the crack to face the wall" was my brilliant suggestion. But Mom immediately noticed the black tape on her purple vase, which now was broken beyond repair. Our subsequent punishment lasted a couple of weeks.

Judah's punishment was longer lasting. The sin of idolatry led to exile. They were forced to watch the walls of Jerusalem shattered by enemy invaders. Jeremiah's lament mirrored the brokenness of the people. However, though their relationship with God was broken, it was not beyond repair. In God's time and way, by His grace, they would be restored.

Holy One, sometimes I don't want to admit to the wrongs that I do. I also fail to mourn my sin. Instead, I feel embarrassed at being found out. O God, forgive my pride and restore what is broken between us. Through Christ, amen.

Prepare the Way

A voice cries: "In the wilderness prepare the way of the LORD, Make straight in the desert a highway for our God" (Isaiah 40:3, *Revised Standard Version*).

Scripture: Isaiah 40:1-10
Song: "Prepare the Way"

Navigating the section of Lake Shore Drive in Chicago once known as the "S Curve" was always a nerve-racking challenge for me whenever I traveled downtown. The road was like a corkscrew. And it was extremely treacherous under icy conditions. You had to approach it cautiously to avoid skidding.

The whole idea behind the road's design was to allow motorists to experience the beauty of the lakefront and to easily reach the museums. Sadly, that beauty was often dimmed in the face of ugly traffic snarls and accidents. That's why many motorists breathed a sigh of relief when the curve-straightening construction got underway.

In Bible times, roads were cleared of debris before the arrival of a king. But Isaiah, and later John the Baptist (who quoted from this passage), meant these words metaphorically to help prepare the people's hearts for the coming Messiah (see Matthew 3:3). Repentance was the only way to clear the impediment of sin and allow for the Savior's smooth arrival in His new home: the human heart. Sin was a rock in the road that needed to be cleared. But the good news, according to Isaiah and John the Baptist, was that the king at last was coming!

Lord God Almighty, prepare my heart and take Your rightful place there. Come, Lord Jesus! In Your name I pray. Amen.

Comfort in Affliction

This is my comfort in my affliction: for thy word hath quickened me (Psalm 119:50, *King James Version*).

Scripture: Psalm 119:49-64
Song: "Safe in the Shepherd's Care"

With his 95 theses, the big priest and monk Martin Luther spurred a reform movement within the church that netted him a world of trouble. Luther spoke out against the church's system of indulgences—payments made for release (supposedly) from the punishment of sin. Instead, he firmly proclaimed: forgiveness comes only by the grace of God through the death of Jesus.

Opposition grew as a result of his stance. Branded a heretic, Luther was excommunicated in 1521. Having been ordered to recant his position—and refusing—he was arrested and sentenced to execution.

Yet, he escaped! Finding refuge in Wartburg Castle, Luther spent much of his time studying and translating the New Testament into German. While his status as an outlaw hadn't changed, his influence grew, despite opposition.

The writer of Psalm 119 was no stranger to the pain of opposition. Like Luther, he delved into the Word of God and found comfort and support in the Lord's unchanging promises.

Shoring up the inner man—that's the goal of Scripture study. Luther found it perfectly suited to just that purpose, and so can we.

Heavenly Father, I need Your strength. Truly those who oppose me speak with loud voices. Give me Your wisdom . . . and Your grace. In the name of Jesus, amen.

Quiet Waters

He makes me lie down in green pastures; He leads me beside quiet waters (Psalm 23:2, *New American Standard Bible*).

Scripture: Psalm 23
Song: "My Shepherd Will Supply My Need"

While vacationing in Jamaica, my college friend Kim and I wanted to go rafting. I wasn't quite ready for the hustle and bustle of extreme white-water adventures, however. So floating down on the Martha Brae River proved a lovely alternative.

At Falmouth in Trelawny, we boarded a long bamboo raft guided by a captain who stood at the bow and used a long pole. We sat in the stern on a comfortable seat and enjoyed the view. Three miles of calm water, with a backdrop of beautiful trees, passed like a dream. The only rough part of the experience was the sunburn! (But even that was worth it; all I had to do was sit back and enjoy the ride.)

Can you feel the atmosphere of that day? It's something like that in Psalm 23, the most well-known psalm of David in the Scriptures. Ironically, David's life was anything but peaceful. He remained on the run from the murderous Saul for over a decade. Yet this great king, a former sheepherder himself, knew the value of a good shepherd—the ultimate shepherd, God. God led David through still water and turbulence. He was the refuge David desperately needed while running for his life. He trusted God to keep him safe. Do you?

Father God, it's not always easy for me to surrender my life to Your control. But I trust You to lead me down the right paths for my life. Thank You for loving me enough to construct a beautiful plan for me. In Jesus' name, amen.

Just Like Jesus

They will treat you this way because of my name, for they do not know the one who sent me (John 15:21).

Scripture: John 15:18-26
Song: "We Are One in the Spirit"

It was 1:30 in the morning, and I was tired as I stood on Royal Street handing out gospel tracts. Laughter and other noise blared in the background. And I was face-to-face with an angry man who snatched the tract and threw it on the ground.

"What right have you to come down here and spoil my fun?" he asked. He went on and on about his right to attend Mardi Gras—to party and pursue pleasure. And here I was, a killjoy, handing him some Christian literature.

I had no rebuttal. For some reason the Holy Spirit kept my response to only a nod in acknowledgment of the man's words. But I could sense His presence in the softened look in the man's eyes and his admission that he'd always wanted God to speak to him in an audible voice. God chose not to do so; the man chose not to believe in Him. After that admission, the man hurried away, wrapping his anger around himself like a cloak.

Jesus told His followers that the world would have the kind of response the man in New Orleans had toward me. Jesus' own life proved that. He faced angry Pharisees, hecklers, and brutal Roman guards. He died the worst death imaginable. All for us. Now we must live for Him.

Lord, forgive me for the desire to live a life without suffering or opposition. You promised that I would have both in this world. Prepare my heart and provide the strength I need to endure. Through Christ I pray. Amen.

Helper and Reminder

The Helper, the Holy Spirit, whom the Father will send in My name, He will teach you all things, and bring to your remembrance all things that I said to you (John 14:26, *New King James Version*).

Scripture: John 14:15-26
Song: "Breathe on Me"

Executives, high-level government officials, and world travelers would agree that they'd miss plenty of meetings and important calls if they didn't check in with their assistants—they are not alone in forgetfulness! How often have you missed an appointment or forgotten to pick up an item at the grocery store? So many things demand our attention—kids, e-mails, phone calls—all disrupting our memory of where we left our keys, cell phones, or eyeglasses.

Thankfully, God understands how our minds handle distractions and that we may not remember His teachings without the help of an Assistant, a Helper, the Holy Spirit. He would help the apostles recall Jesus' teachings—and for us, He will bring "all things that I said" to mind right when we need to remember. Even when we're upset or hurting, He'll help us recall the Word. He'll remind us too that the Living Word is right there with us.

Yes, the more we study the Scriptures or listen to scriptural teaching, the more we may recall. But with the help of our official heavenly helper, the Holy Spirit, we're empowered to put into practice what we know.

O Lord, I often need to check my calendar for meeting and call times. But when it comes to spiritual things, I am so thankful for the Holy Spirit, who reminds me of my identity in Christ and the goodness of His teachings. In His name I pray. Amen.

It's Instructive, Too

Discipline your children, and they will give you peace; they will bring you the delights you desire (Proverbs 29:17).

Scripture: Proverbs 29:12-18
Song: "Lord, for the Gift of Children"

Corporal punishment was once a widespread practice in our public schools. These days most American schools and churches have strict rules that prohibit it and laws that require violations to be reported. Spanking children has become a controversial topic and an unpopular practice. Yet, whether we believe "the rod of discipline" (Proverbs 22:15) is to be taken literally or figuratively, we are all accountable to discipline our children in some fashion. We do it because we love them; our kids long for boundaries that show how much we value them.

It's important to remember that discipline isn't merely corrective; it is also instructive. Put another way, we must teach our children how to do right things and not merely correct them when they do wrong things. We must also take every opportunity to bring the gospel front and center.

After all, if you are a parent, wouldn't you agree that there is a peace we want more than well-behaved children? How about the peace of knowing our children are trusting in the Lord for their daily walk through life?

Father, teach me how to parent my children the way You parent me: with grace. Help me to discipline my children in such a way that correction occurs and wisdom is imparted. Most of all, teach me to delight in my children! Through Christ, I pray. Amen.

March 9–15. Steve Johnson is an ordained minister from Ruckersville, Virginia, currently working as a freelance writer/editor, supply preacher, and speaker.

Just Going Through the Motions?

These people come near to me with their mouth and honor me with their lips, but their hearts are far from me. Their worship of me is based on merely human rules they have been taught (Isaiah 29:13).

Scripture: Isaiah 29:8-14
Song: "Keep Silence, All Created Things"

My wife or son can observe me reading my Bible every morning. But they cannot gauge how sincerely I am seeking God. Reading the Bible and praying are good habits to develop, of course. But such activities aren't really *spiritual* disciplines unless they're Spirit-led. God is neither impressed nor fooled by our efforts to please Him in our own strength. In light of our Scripture today, we can conclude that worship which only *appears* outwardly proper is actually offensive to God! It's the old problem of merely going through the motions.

A famous church-planting minister once joked: "I love Jesus, I just don't like talking to Him." I have found, in my own life, that it is possible to hide behind a busy schedule of godly activities in order to avoid actually spending time with God. At those times I've had to ask myself: Am I willing to serve the Lord but unwilling to practice the spiritual discipline of solitude? Yes, I've needed to learn better what it means to "Be still, and know that I am God" (Psalm 46:10).

Lord, draw my heart near to You in this silence. Teach me how to worship you with sincere praise that flows from a blessed life and a glad heart. Stop me from going through the motions only. Help me to pray, praise, sing, and read Your Word in ways that bring You honor. In Christ's name I pray. Amen.

Know God, Not Just About Him

Now Samuel did not yet know the LORD: The word of the LORD had not yet been revealed to him (1 Samuel 3:7).

Scripture: 1 Samuel 3:1-10
Song: "Speak, O Lord"

I thought I was already a believer. I went to Sunday school and worship services every Sunday. My perfect attendance even earned me a large children's Bible as a fourth grader. As I finished elementary school, I remember that I believed that Jesus had died on a cross for sins and was raised from the dead on the third day. On a junior high retreat I responded by raising my hand after an emotional appeal—because I wanted to go to Heaven. My junior high youth group leaders were happy about my "response," but (like Samuel) I still "did not yet know the Lord."

It took a couple more years and many conversations with my youth minister before the Lord Jesus drew me into His fold. Likewise, Samuel knew *about* the Lord, but He didn't yet know the Lord in a personal relationship.

This is how it is for every one of us. We must undergo a spiritual awakening—conversion—before we will recognize God's call to us. In terms of his prophetic ministry, Samuel had never received a vision or heard the voice of God speak to him prior to this instance. But the Lord's adopted children can certainly expect to hear from Him.

Lord, as I participate in Bible studies and listen to sermons, lead me to actually know You. Speak to me though Your written Word, and reveal the plans You have to prosper me and to give me a hope and a future. In the name of Jesus. Amen.

Predictions That Never Fail

The LORD was with Samuel as he grew up, and he let none of Samuel's words fall to the ground (1 Samuel 3:19).

Scripture: 1 Samuel 3:11-21
Song: "Word of God, Across the Ages"

Samuel was regarded as a true prophet because the Lord made sure that whatever Samuel predicted came to pass. However, Christians are somewhat divided over how the spiritual gift of prophecy works in the church today. Some, who believe that the predictive aspect of the gift ceased when the canon of Scripture was completed, now restrict it to preaching the gospel. And that is certainly the most common way the word *prophesy* is used in the New Testament writings. And there is great agreement that the Lord will be with the preacher who restricts his preaching to the inspired words of Scripture!

Many of us are not preachers or teachers, but we all have our own spheres of influence. Whatever roles you have and whatever venues you have been placed in, the only words that the Lord promises to stand by are His own. As someone once said, if you are totally original in your Christian proclamation, you're probably flirting with heresy.

This doesn't mean we can't share our biblically informed opinions. But our words should never contradict the solid body of doctrine that has been handed down to us through the centuries.

Lord, help me to believe what You say in Your Word enough to share it with others. Lead me away from mere speculations and predictions—toward the certain hope of what You have prophesied in the Bible. In the name of Jesus I pray. Amen.

Certain Hope

Into your hands I commit my spirit; deliver me, LORD, my faithful God (Psalm 31:5).

Scripture: Psalm 31:1-8
Song: "In Thee, O Lord, I Put My Trust"

Today's Scripture comes from a Messianic psalm. It was written by King David, who prayed for God to deliver him from the people conspiring against him.

Sometimes our problems surround us like David's enemies surrounded him. Then we're tempted to give in to anxiety and loneliness. In fact, the crucible of suffering can drive us to despair or . . . toward a deeper faith in our sustaining Lord.

You may recognize the focal verse for the day as some of the final words that Jesus spoke to His heavenly Father after suffering for hours on the cross (see Luke 23:46). Though Jesus wasn't delivered from the distress of Gethsemane or the affliction of Golgotha, He was not abandoned to the grave. Indeed, Jesus trusted the Father with His spirit moments before He died. Moreover, Jesus was delivered from death on the third day, when God raised Him from the tomb.

We do not know when we will die, of course. But we can know, with a *certain* hope, that we'll be raised back to life on the final day. How do we know? Our risen Jesus has already led the way.

Father, I find my shelter in You and trust in Your righteousness alone. Hear my prayer for deliverance from evil, and guide me into all truth. I commit my soul into Your care, knowing that You are the only one who can save me from eternal death. Thanks for being such a faithful Lord! Through Christ, amen.

He Loves Even Us

God is spirit, and his worshipers must worship in the Spirit and in truth (John 4:24).

Scripture: John 4:21-26
Song: "Heart of Worship"

"I don't need to go to church; I can worship God anywhere." Heard it before? It's true that God's presence is no more limited to church buildings than it was to a mountain in Samaria. Yet many avid outdoorsmen have forsaken the assemblies in order to pursue their pastimes on the Lord's Day. Yet those of us still in the pews may only *appear* to be the kind of worshippers the Father desires.

We are to worship Him "in the Spirit and truth." We are also to offer not just our voices but our whole "bodies as a living sacrifice, holy and pleasing to God—this is your true and proper worship" (Romans 12:1).

These may seem like monumental challenges. How can we do it? By remembering who God is and who we are in relation to Him. I love how writer John Piper put it: "God created us for this: to live our lives in a way that makes him look more like the greatness and the beauty and the infinite worth that he really is. This is what it means to be created in the image of God."

We are creatures; He is the Creator. If we've got this perspective right, we can sincerely offer our praise and join our voices with others in worship. The almighty king of the universe has chosen to love and care for us!

Lord, You are God and worthy of my genuine worship. Help me worship You, not just on Sundays at church, but everywhere and every day. In Jesus' name, amen.

Why Jesus Left His Disciples

Very truly I tell you, it is for your good that I am going away. Unless I go away, the Advocate will not come to you; but if I go, I will send him to you (John 16:7).

Scripture: John 16:4b-15
Song: "For Your Gift of God the Spirit"

What if Jesus couldn't hear you? The very notion is unthinkable, since after the Day of Pentecost, His Spirit came to dwell within each believer. Yet when Jesus lived His human life, He subjected himself to the limitations of a human body. This meant He could only be in one place at one time. So there were times when His disciples might have wanted to speak to Jesus; for example, they might have been out in a boat on the sea while He was up on a mountain. They could call out for Him, but He was too far away to hear them.

Christ's abiding presence is just one of the many reasons it was for our good that He left earth. I sometimes wish I could have been one of the Lord's original disciples. I imagine being able to watch Him perform miracles before my very eyes!

Yet, as memorable as sharing a meal with Jesus may have been, His first disciples couldn't enjoy uninterrupted fellowship with Him the way we can now. Through His Spirit, we have an "Advocate," the promised Comforter, who is both *with* us here on earth and *for* us there in Heaven.

Lord Jesus, thank You for sending Your Spirit to guide me into all truth and empower me to do the work of Your kingdom. Help me to glorify You by trusting in Your righteousness alone. When I am discouraged, remind me that I have an Advocate before our heavenly Father. In Your precious name I pray. Amen.

On Guard!

"You must be on your guard. You will be handed over to the local councils and flogged in the synagogues. On account of me you will stand before governors and kings as witnesses to them" (Mark 13:9).

Scripture: Mark 13:5-11
Song: "A Shelter in the Time of Storm"

The security director's presentation to our company's leaders emphasized the increasing frequency of workplace violence. He recounted some gruesome details of several well-publicized national incidents where former employees had returned to the work site with evil intentions. "Frequently the person was someone nobody would ever have imagined doing such a thing," he pointed out. "Almost always their coworkers never noticed the warning signs of potential danger."

Jesus told us that the days would become increasingly evil as His return draws closer. He also promised that He would be with us always, giving us His peace. But we must stay alert—on guard!—to what is happening around us.

As we open our hearts to the Lord in prayer, fellowship, worship, and Scripture reading, His presence sustains us in all circumstances. Our part is to rely on Him for His loving care and guidance. And even if we are brought "before governors and kings," He will give us the words to say (see Matthew 10:19).

Father, I will not be dismayed nor distracted by the evil I see all around me. For You have promised me Your eternal presence in all situations. In Jesus' name, amen.

March 16–22. **Jeff Friend,** a big Baltimore Orioles fan, is an award-wining freelance writer and speaker who lives with his wife, Nancy, in Largo, Florida.

Nothing But the Truth

"We are witnesses of everything he did in the country of the Jews and in Jerusalem. They killed him by hanging him on a cross" (Acts 10:39).

Scripture: Acts 10:39-48
Song: "I Was There When It Happened"

It's a classic scene in many old television crime dramas. The prosecutor steadily builds the case against the wrongly accused man. He takes bits of information and weaves them together with theories of how the defendant supposedly carried out the crime. The jury members hang on every detail, trying to sort out the truth.

Then, just as the D.A. stands to make his final demand for a conviction, the back doors of the courtroom burst open, a woman strolls in, and the defense attorney jumps up and says, "Your Honor, we have a new witness. She was at the scene and saw everything!" After her testimony . . . case dismissed!

Why the sudden change? Because despite all the prosecutor's suppositions, once an actual witness told what she had personally experienced, all the theories of the crime became useless.

We have personally experienced the grace and forgiveness of Jesus Christ. We know our lives have been changed. Others may scoff or say we're deceived, but anyone who's witnessed firsthand the transforming power of Jesus knows it is definitely true. You and I are living testimonies every day of our lives.

Lord, I thank You that I have been a witness to Your forgiveness and mercy. I know You live within me, and nobody can make me doubt Your authenticity. Now give me an opportunity to testify of Your love to someone today. In Jesus' name, amen.

It's Not About Me

The Lord's hand was with them, and a great number of people believed and turned to the Lord (Acts 11:21).

Scripture: Acts 11:19-26
Song: "All Hail the Power of Jesus' Name"

I was scheduled to meet a famous athlete to conduct an interview for a sports magazine. I arrived early at the stadium, but apparently the athlete had forgotten to let the security guards know I'd be there. Several guards held me back, saying they couldn't verify my story. They also made it very clear they had no intention of contacting the team office and that I should leave. As I prepared to go, my celebrity interviewee drove up and parked his car. When he asked if everything was all right, I said, "Yes, except those guards won't let me in." He smiled and motioned for me to follow him. At the gate he simply said, "He's with me." The guards stepped aside, welcomed me, and apologized for my inconvenience.

Just three little words changed everything. Actually, it was not the words, but *who spoke them* that made the difference. The athlete had the power to change the situation.

In Acts 11, many people believed in the Lord because His hand was on the disciples. Let us remember, then, that it is not through our own abilities that God's will is accomplished. It is His presence in our lives that gives us victory.

Most Holy God, remind me that I am just a servant, and You are the one with all power and authority in Heaven and earth. Only by allowing You to work through me will I be able to make an impact for Your kingdom. All glory to You, in the name of Jesus, my merciful Savior and Lord. Amen.

All for One

Let us therefore make every effort to do what leads to peace and to mutual edification (Romans 14:19).

Scripture: Romans 14:13-19
Song: "Blest Be the Tie That Binds"

Our minister opened the meeting with the youth minister and the choir director by presenting the problem. "For too long I have heard complaints about our music. The teenagers want louder, faster songs. And the older folks demand we sing more hymns. Both sides are passionate about their desires, and it is causing bad feelings in our church. We need to decide how to reach a realistic solution."

The three leaders discussed several options before the choir director suggested, "Suppose we mixed in more of the old hymns but give them a more modern beat? We could try it this Sunday."

At the end of the service, several people—old and young alike—told the minister how much they enjoyed the new format. Some even offered ideas on other ways of merging the styles. In fact, a new bond developed between the old and the young.

Jesus calls His church to operate in unity and represent His kingdom to the world, and the apostle Paul echoes His Lord's desire. Let us commit to building up one another and uniting in love as we worship and serve our Savior.

Most holy God, I repent for the times I've tried to get my own way and caused discord among Your children. Help me build up and esteem others so Your church can function in love and unity for Your glory. In the name of Jesus, who lives and reigns with You and the Holy Spirit, one God, now and forever, amen.

In His Time

"It is not for you to know the times or dates the Father has set by his own authority" (Acts 1:7).

Scripture: Acts 1:4-8
Song: "'Tis So Sweet to Trust in Jesus"

Seven-year-old Billy asked his father one more time for the same birthday gift he had wanted for the last couple of years. "Daddy, can I please have a puppy?" Billy had been on his best behavior, trying to convince his parents of his willingness to care for a dog. "Son, I know this is very important to you, and I know you won't understand right now, but I am not getting you a puppy this year. I haven't forgotten your request, but for now the answer is no. There will be a time when you will be ready to properly care for an animal. But I will decide when that time will be. Until then, you must be patient."

We often wonder about God's timing. When will I be healed? When will this difficult time pass? When will my prayer be answered? It helps me to remember that God is sovereign, and He alone knows the future. (In fact, because He exists outside of time, our God somehow dwells in our past, present, and future all at once!) Like Billy, we must simply trust that our Father knows what is best for us in the total context of all things. He knows our requests and desires, but it is not for us to know the times or means of His actions. Let's be steadfast in our faith as we trust God's ways in our lives.

O God, the king of glory, sometimes it is hard to be patient and wait upon You! But I will trust You today and take comfort in knowing my life is in Your hands. I will seek to be still and wholly submit to Your will. In the name of Jesus, amen.

A Reflection of God

Be careful how you live. Don't live like fools, but like those who are wise (Ephesians 5:15, *New Living Translation*).

Scripture: Ephesians 5:15-21
Song: "Walking in the King's Highway"

Jerry had been trying to get Harold to attend church with him since Harold's family moved next door two months ago. As a Sunday school teacher, elder, and choir member, Jerry certainly impressed Harold with his dedication to the church. Harold often saw Jerry taking his family to some church event, and Jerry seemed so friendly to everyone. *Maybe I should check out that church sometime,* Harold thought. *Every time I see Jerry, he looks happy and he seems sincere. I think I'll tell him I'll go with him next Sunday.*

But as Harold was putting out the trash late that night, he heard a commotion next door. Moving closer to Jerry's house, he heard Jerry yelling loudly and cursing his wife. The kids seemed to be crying. Shaking his head, Harold thought, *I knew it was too good to be true. Just another hypocrite. He'll never see me at his church.*

Paul warned the Ephesians to be careful how they lived, but the same admonishment applies to Christians today. Are we fully following Christ's example, or do we act differently when we think nobody is watching us? Be careful. Let us reflect the glory and love of God at all times.

Forgive me, **Lord,** when my actions, words, or thoughts are not Christlike. I know that even when I think others may not be watching me, You always are. May my life be a true reflection of Your love, every minute of every day. In Jesus' name, amen.

Forever in His Presence

After he said this, he showed them his hands and side. The disciples were overjoyed when they saw the Lord (John 20:20).

Scripture: John 20:19-23
Song: "We Shall Behold Him"

As she waited in the outer office, Lori's mind drifted back to the events of 23 years ago. As a frightened teenager facing a life-altering choice, she finally decided to put her newborn child, Mary, up for adoption. Through the following years, not a day passed when she didn't think of her daughter. *Did I do the right thing?* Now, only moments remained before she'd see Mary again.

A private investigator had located Mary and arranged a meeting. *Will I even recognize her?* Lori wondered. *She's a grown woman now.* But as she watched Mary walk through the door, Lori had no doubt. What a happy, tearful embrace!

The disciples did not know if they would ever see Jesus again after His crucifixion. But when they saw him face-to-face, they were overjoyed.

Soon we will be overwhelmed with joy when we finally see the face of Jesus. Then all of our pains, sorrows, and regrets will fall away. Our Father awaits to welcome us home, and we will never be separated again.

Blessed Father, I long to look upon Your face and be in Your presence for eternity. I long to bow before You and praise You in person, along with that mighty chorus of the redeemed. But even now I will lift my voice in adoration to You. I await You with joy. In the name of Jesus, Lord and Savior of all, I pray. Amen.

God's Shining Face

May God be gracious to us and bless us and make his face shine on us — so that your ways may be known on earth, your salvation among all nations (Psalm 67:1, 2).

Scripture: Psalm 67
Song: "Shine on Me"

What does it mean for God's face to shine upon us? Can we correctly assume that this is vital to our relationship with Him? We can, as indicated by the above Scripture. Also note Psalm 34:16 to see when God's face *doesn't* shine on us: "The face of the Lord is against those who do evil, to blot out their name from the earth." Now that's a compelling reason not to do evil!

As the psalmist prays for all peoples, we too should pray unselfish prayers — that those who receive salvation as a result of our prayers may be able to sing for joy to the Lord: "May the nations be glad and sing for joy, for you rule the peoples with equity and guide the nations of the earth" (Psalm 67:4). How wonderful to know of God's tender mercies — and to want them for all persons.

The psalmist even mentions our crops in connection with God's blessings. While poor crops can occur for a number of reasons, and the sun shines — and the rain falls — on both the righteous and unrighteous, the writer speaks of one being more productive when fully serving God. Again, what grace!

Lord God Almighty, thank You for this opportunity to pray—not just for myself, but for all people. Please hear and send Your blessings! In Jesus' name, amen.

March 23–29. **Jimmy Oliver Fleming,** of Chester, Virginia, has written for several devotional magazines over the years. She recently moved to a new home with her husband, Joe, of 44 years.

Saved and Safe

Turn to me and be saved, all you ends of the earth; for I am God, and there is no other. But all the descendants of Israel will find deliverance in the LORD and will make their boast in him (Isaiah 45:22, 25).

Scripture: Isaiah 45:20-25
Song: "Sheltered in the Arms of God"

I am guilty, and perhaps you are too. I refer to serving idols. These are the false "gods" in our lives that sometimes crowd out our focus on the true Lord of all. Why? Maybe it's as simple as human nature. For example, think about this when you decide to "keep your fingers crossed" for a certain superstitious reason.

Again, we are only human—and certainly finite in our capacity to know and understand reality as it is. "Ignorant are those who carry about idols of wood, who pray to gods that cannot save" said the prophet (Isaiah 45:20). The words apply to people of any era. Sadly, modern knowledge makes no dent on ignorant worship.

I am so thankful that God, out of His great depth of love, constantly calls us to turn to Him for deliverance. If we've been walking far from Him, we simply need to reverse direction to start on our journey back. As the father ran to meet his returning prodigal son (see Luke 15:11-31), so the heavenly Father embraces us with loving arms as we let our idols fall to the ground.

Lord, I am up for this task because I know that You can loosen my grip on my disordered affections, the idols that sometimes seem so important. Deliver me, and satisfy my deepest longings in Christ. Through Him I pray. Amen.

Grumbling or Gratitude?

Do everything without grumbling or arguing, so that you may become blameless and pure, "children of God without fault in a warped and crooked generation." Then you will shine among them like stars in the sky (Philippians 2:14, 15).

Scripture: Philippians 2:9-16
Song: "I Won't Complain"

Since God is God and I'm just me, He knows for sure when my grumbling starts. Sometimes it never stops. Sometimes it seems I'm grumbling when I go to bed at night and doing the same when I open my eyes in the morning.

Do we ever stop the grumbling? Even when we don't verbally complain, our attitudes and actions might reflect a spirit of discontent.

Thankfully, if we follow Paul's advice in our Scripture today, we'll be well on our way to a grumble-free existence. Even better, we can encourage seekers through our joyful way of living with a basic, down-to-earth "attitude of gratitude."

And wouldn't it be wonderful to shine like stars in the sky? I certainly think so, and I want to seize the opportunity and act on it.

How? I can look up to God our Creator for strength. I can ponder the fact that in His great creative power, He made the stars that shine in the sky . . . well before He made me. (This was a wise decision indeed!)

O, Lord, my God, how great Thou art! Thank You for making me a part of Your creation. I truly want to be an example to others. When I look in the mirror and see Your handiwork, help me not to complain. In Christ's name I pray. Amen.

Mystery Solved

About that day or hour no one knows, not even the angels in heaven, nor the Son, but only the Father (Mark 13:32).

Scripture: Mark 13:30-37
Song: "I Want to Be Ready"

It's happened before and will happen again. What's more, it's probably happening even as you read these words: someone is predicting the end of the world. Yet we know what God's Word says about the subject. Not even Jesus knew for sure when that day would come.

I'm reminded of the time when my friend Crystal insisted that she was ready for the Lord to come and take her home to Heaven. "I'm fed up with all of this mess going on down here," she declared. "Completely fed up!"

Although I don't remember my exact words in response, I'm sure that I tried to offer some consoling words for my friend's anxiety. I may have even mentioned the Scripture verse for today.

Still, I know that Crystal got over her frustration. And recently we talked about it one Sunday morning. I mentioned that I hadn't heard such a complaint from her again.

No matter what, let us be thankful amidst our circumstances, just as they are. We aren't happy *for* the difficulties, but we can be joyful *in the midst* of them. For the Lord is right there with us. His presence now—and His fuller presence then—makes our every minute worthwhile.

Lord, thank You for this unpredicted rainy day. It is another great reminder that You control the world that You created, weather and otherwise. In Christ I pray. Amen.

Framed!

[They] . . . were looking for evidence against Jesus so that they could put him to death . . . Many testified falsely against him, but their statements did not agree (Mark 14:55, 56).

Scripture: Mark 14:55-62
Song: "Were You There?"

It has been said, "the more things change, the more they stay the same." Since the earliest times, people have been punished for crimes they didn't commit. Just as depicted in movies and television, evidence is sometimes "planted." Then the innocent goes to jail. That is, he or she is framed.

Clearly, Jesus also was framed. First, He was branded a troublemaker from the very beginning. Then there were so many eager false witnesses!

I think the songwriter poses a good question for us today. "Were you there?" I am right here, but I have to admit that I am part of the "crowd" that put Jesus on the cross. As Isaiah the prophet put it: "We all, like sheep, have gone astray, each of us has turned to our own way; and the Lord has laid on him the iniquity of us all" (Isaiah 53:6).

There is always a falseness about sin—it pretends to be something beautiful, ultimately satisfying. But it is a fake; it bears false witness to any potential for lasting joy. It is also purely self-destructive. Yet thankfully, God offers to save us— we, the practised false witnesses—from ourselves.

Lord, thank You for the opportunity to boldly approach Your throne, seeking forgiveness for my part in Your continual betrayal and crucifixion. I am so glad for the second chance that comes through justification by faith. In Christ's name I pray. Amen.

Heed These Words

"Do not be afraid, Daughter Zion; see, your king is coming, seated on a donkey's colt." At first his disciples did not understand all this. Only after Jesus was glorified did they realize that these things had been written about him (John 12:15, 16).

Scripture: John 12:14-19
Song: "The King Is Coming"

Have you ever thought something was just too good to be true? I certainly have. We all need to be on the alert to "good deals" that come too easily or too inexpensively.

Did this happen with the disciples? They'd been with Jesus all along, watching Him perform awesome miracles. Yet now, on the donkey, He demonstrated His humility. It should have been simple to see—or did they consider it too good to be true? A real, humble king, set on conquering hearts for a kingdom of peace!

There is so much of the faith that we don't understand, so much of our infinite Lord that we can't see. And our response to this? A simple willingness to do our Lord's bidding, just as the disciples carried out His instructions. I like how the great devotional writer Oswald Chambers said it: "The golden rule for understanding spiritually is not intellect, but obedience. If a man wants scientific knowledge, intellectual curiosity is his guide; but if he wants insight into what Jesus Christ teaches, he can only get it by obedience."

Dear Lord, You are all good, all the time—but never too good to be true! So, even when I don't quite understand, help me immediately to obey. Through Christ, amen.

In the Spotlight

As they approached Jerusalem and came to Bethphage and Bethany at the Mount of Olives, Jesus sent two of his disciples, saying to them, "Go to the village ahead of you, and just as you enter it, you will find a colt tied there, which no one has ever ridden. Untie it and bring it here" (Mark 11:1, 2).

Scripture: Mark 11:1-11
Song: "To Be Used of God"

If a donkey can receive 15 minutes of fame, so can we. Therefore, always be prepared to be used by God.

And how awesome to be used by the Lord of all! Lyrics from a particular gospel song go like this: "I want to live so God can use me anytime and anywhere."

I do want to be used by God, and I think the first requirement is obedience, as I stressed yesterday. When the disciples were given instructions about the colt, certain things were already in place. All they had to do was follow their Lord's instructions.

In a Bible study one night, we received several instructions from our teacher—the first being to *read all the instructions* before doing anything else.

Some did so, and some didn't. And in the end, we all had a good laugh. I recall that particular Bible study as one of the more enjoyable ones I've attended at my church. Why? I followed the instructions!

Father God, help me to follow Your instructions and be prepared for Your kingdom's use. Open my heart and mind to Your good commands. Help me to do, say, and go where You want me to go with a willing spirit. In the name of Jesus, amen.

Abandoned

"My God, My God, why have You forsaken Me?"
(Matthew 27:46, *New King James Version*).

Scripture: Matthew 27:45-50
Song: "Bind Us Together"

In the book, *Angel in the Rubble,* Genelle McMillan tells that when a plane hit the World Trade Center in September 2001, she was buried alive. She called out, "Help, somebody help!" over and over again. But she was truly abandoned—until rescued by two firefighters, 27 hours later.

The Lord Jesus was abandoned for our sakes with a purpose clearly predicted and powerfully proclaimed. He was abandoned by the Father so that He could pay the price of all our sin. Why? There's mystery involved in our rescue, but we know for sure that Jesus came to deliver us because He loves us so much. Sin would destroy us, after all. Therefore, we can view Jesus as God's angel, rescuing us from the rubble of sin. Yet, because all the sin of the world was upon Him in those hours, the Father— a perfectly good and just judge—must turn His back.

To those who are aware of the *life* of Jesus—the *death* of Jesus—must surely strike a chord. There was a three-hour span of darkness, and then He gave up His spirit. It was a horrible death, but what supreme love!

Dear Father, I am so thankful that Jesus Your Son was willing to leave behind all the glories of His eternal dwelling place to become a human being. I bow my heart to You, great Trinity—Father, Son, and Holy Spirit. Amen.

March 30, 31. David R. Nicholas is a minister and author who lives with his wife, Judith, in Australia. His interests are history and philately.

Alive!

Do not be afraid, for I know that you seek Jesus who was crucified. He is not here; for He is risen, as He said. Come, see the place where the Lord lay (Matthew 28:5, 6, *New King James Version*).

Scripture: Matthew 28:1-8
Song: "The Hope of the Ages"

Hope is vital. So much of life revolves around its presence. Even as I type these words, I hope the editor will approve of them. Our days, of course, depend on hope, and life without hope is like a broken-winged bird that cannot fly.

The angel of the Lord wasn't interested in the guards, but rather spoke to the women, who were evidently afraid. What assurance the angel provided when he made it clear that Jesus was alive—that Jesus had risen from the dead as He promised!

What amazing words, "He is not here." Truly Jesus had "gone with the wind" as we might say. But His absence from the grave proved clearly He is master controller, master commander of life and death. Our response? Be confident; Jesus is alive.

As if to add to the power of his message, the angel provided proof when he said, in effect, "Come see—look for yourselves—the grave is empty." There was no body where Jesus had been laid to rest. If only we could live as if Jesus is alive. Our faith sags. We need again to read the angel's words . . . and let them sink in.

Loving Father, thank You for raising Jesus from the dead. Help me to live my life in a way that shows I really believe He's alive. I pray this prayer in the name of Jesus, my merciful Savior and Lord. Amen.

DEVOTIONS®

APRIL

Since God so loved us,
we also ought to love one another.

—1 John 4:11

Gary Allen, Editor | **Margaret Williams,** Project Editor | Photo iStockphoto | Thinkstock®

DEVOTIONS® is published quarterly by Standard Publishing, Cincinnati, Ohio, www.standardpub.com.
© 2014 by Standard Publishing. All rights reserved. Topics based on the Home Daily Bible Readings,
International Sunday School Lessons. © 2012 by the Committee on the Uniform Series. Printed in
the U.S.A. All Scripture quotations, unless otherwise indicated, are taken from the *HOLY BIBLE,
NEW INTERNATIONAL VERSION*®. *NIV*®. Copyright © 1973, 1978, 1984, 2011 by Biblica, Inc.® Used
by permission of Zondervan. All rights reserved. The *New King James Version* (*NKJV*). Copyright
© 1982 by Thomas Nelson, Inc.

Assurance

Comfort one another with these words (1 Thessalonians 4:18, *New King James Version*).

Scripture: 1 Thessalonians 4:13-18
Song: "The Comforter Has Come"

When was the last time you arranged to meet someone—and they never turned up? Here's one from my life: My wife and I were to meet a friend at Singapore airport. He did not turn up. Strangely, we've never found out why!

This will not happen when it comes to our promised meeting with Jesus, for "there's going to be a meeting in the air." He will return. We will meet and greet Him. That's His promise.

But doubt had come upon young Christians at Thessalonica. So Paul spoke about their friends who had "fallen asleep" (v. 13, *NKJV*), assuring them that death is not the end for a believer.

Indeed, those who have believed in Jesus and gone to the grave are far from dead. They have simply passed from an earthly existence into a fuller life in the presence of Christ. They await, with us, the great day of the resurrection when bodies and souls will be reunited forever.

Paul had no doubts whatever and told his audience to comfort one another with these wonderful truths. So, are you impatient for it all to begin? I suppose we all need reminding at times: God's timing is not our timing.

Dear Father, how I look forward to the day when I see Jesus face-to-face! Help me to live this day in a way that will honor Him. In His name I pray. Amen.

April 1–5. **David R. Nicholas** is a minister and author who lives with his wife, Judith, in Australia. His interests are history and philately.

Do You Believe?

Jesus said to her, "I am the resurrection and the life. He who believes in Me, though he may die, he shall live" (John 11:25, *New King James Version*).

Scripture: John 11:20-27
Song: "Precious Promise"

When I was journeying toward Christ, I worked for a certain pharmaceutical company. My task was to find products on the shelves of stock so that they could be sent out to drugstores. One day, I couldn't find a particular item, so I asked a fellow worker for help. He said, "Seek, and ye shall find." I sought. I found the product. More importantly, I later found Christ after seeking Him. Not in a flash but slowly, like the rising of the sun. I also discovered that Jesus had been seeking me the whole time!

Belief is so hard for so many. First, because they are soaked in the things of this world; second, they put things in the wrong order. That is, they don't understand Hebrews 11:6, "Without faith it is impossible to please Him, for he who comes to God must believe that He is" (*NKJV*).

Jesus does not ask Martha "Who am I?" He asks her whether she believes that He dealt with her current crisis, that He had control over life and death. The question was—did Martha *believe*?

Gracious Lord, I believe. Help my unbelief. I know that belief is vital if I am to relate to You. And I also know that it is so easy to miss the most important facts of faith. I can get hung up and start sending my thoughts in the wrong direction. So, above all, let me first believe. In the name of Jesus, amen.

Changed

At one time we too were foolish, disobedient, deceived and enslaved by all kinds of passions and pleasures. We lived in malice and envy, being hated and hating one another (Titus 3:3).

Scripture: Titus 3:1-7
Song: "Humble Thyself in the Sight of the Lord"

There's a modern song, "Love Changes Everything." If only it were so! How many couples say they're in love, and then after a few short years, their love falls apart. What a difference with the love of Jesus!

When Jesus takes control of our lives, everything truly changes for the better. In his song "I Am His, and He Is Mine," George Robinson put it, "Heaven above is softer blue, Earth around is sweeter green. Something lives in every hue Christless eyes have never seen." The wonderful thing about becoming a Christian is that change becomes unlimited. We go on growing in Christ. Old things are finished. We grow from glory into glory.

The wonderful thing is that when Christ is in us, we continue changing into His likeness. So perhaps we need the reminder of Paul's words, "What no eye has seen, what no ear has heard, and what no human mind has conceived"—the things God has prepared for those who love him" (1 Corinthians 2:9). This is the difference between the Christian and the non-Christian. The non-Christian remains locked in sin. Christians know they have been unlocked, for Christ has set them free.

Print Your image, **O Lord of grace,** on my heart, and help me to go on growing in Christ. And when I stumble, may I find the courage to confess my sin and get back on the pathway with You. In the holy name of Jesus, my Lord and Savior, I pray. Amen.

The Facts

If Christ is not risen, your faith is futile; you are still in your sins! . . . If in this life only we have hope in Christ, we are of all men the most pitiable (1 Corinthians 15:17, 19 *New King James Version*).

Scripture: 1 Corinthians 15:12-19
Song: "Only Trust Him"

There's an old song that says, "You've got to accentuate the positive, eliminate the negative." But the Christian faith is more than positive thinking. In fact, it's mainly about a fact: Christ is risen!

If that fact is not a fact, then our faith is just a waste. This is Paul's basic argument. Without the resurrection we are without hope. After all, our salvation completely depends on the atoning work of Jesus being accepted before the heavenly throne of God the Father. Just as ancient sacrifices would need to be "offered" before gods, so the work of Christ must be presented. Thus, when Jesus ascended, His sacrifice was finally complete. And fully accepted.

The facts of Christ's death can easily be distorted. The deceiver of the brethren is ever active (see Revelation 12:9). He doesn't want us to have the facts; he'd rather we turn away from them. So today, let us remind ourselves, in the face of any direct or subtle invitation to doubt: "He who is in you is greater than he who is in the world" (1 John 4:4, *NKJV*).

O Father, the king of glory, when my emotions lead me astray, please help me to refocus on the facts of the faith. I trust You and all You have done for me in history. Praise to You, in the name of Jesus. Amen.

Achieved

As in Adam all die, even so in Christ shall all be made alive (1 Corinthians 15:22, *New King James Version*).

Scripture: 1 Corinthians 15:1-11, 20-22
Song: "How Great Thou Art"

Death comes to all and is mostly unwelcome (except in dire circumstances). We like life, and life *in abundance* is what Christ offer us. After all, He himself truly holds the key that opens the door marked *Death*. When He is in us and we are in Him, we have eternal life. What wonderful words the great Puritan pastor and writer Richard Baxter wrote, "Christ leads through no darker rooms than He has gone before."

Through the son of Adam, who was disobedient, the penalty was death. This penalty carried on through the generations. Why? Because humanity is less like single seeds in the ground than like a large tree with a single root. We are branches of a single human father, Adam. His sin is ours; it has infected our souls and damaged them horribly.

We need grafting on to a new root! That is Jesus, the "Root and the Offspring of David" (see Revelation 22:16). When we become branches of the true vine, His life cures our sin disease. We are made alive in Him.

All of this is the great good news of the gospel. Therefore, when Satan accuses, we are able to say, "I am just a branch, but look at my life-sustaining source! You no longer have any claim on me."

Gracious Heavenly Father, please help me to understand the wonderful truth of what Christ has achieved for me. In His precious name, amen.

Shining Light in a Dark Place

Whoever lives by the truth comes into the light, so that it may be seen plainly that what they have done has been done in the sight of God (John 3:21).

Scripture: John 3:16-21
Song: "I Will Rise"

Have you felt like a prisoner? Do you retreat to a dark place in the crevices of your heart on a daily basis?

So many of us have a memory in our lives that we cannot surrender—no matter what we do. It seems to creep back up on us. We go back to this scene and try to put the pieces of our lives back together. We sort through the woulda-shoulda-coulda's and try to rework the past.

This is impossible, but there is hope. Whatever the enemy is using to lure you back to that dark spot, the place you hide from the view of others, it is time to bring it out into the light and be free from it. After all, God gave us the gift of His Son, Jesus, to set us free.

Jesus has overcome, and the shadows must go away as we walk away from the darkness and into His light. From the dark place, listen for His voice. When He calls your name, rise, walk away once and for all, and know that He has saved you from the darkest corners. Lay it out before His bright gaze; He'll exchange your shame for His glorious light and hope.

Most merciful God, I need Your Son to pull me from this darkness. I long for the light that He gives, so I can be restored with hope. In Jesus' name, amen.

April 6–12. **Tammy Whitehurst** is a motivational Christian speaker and writer, who lives and works in White Oak, Texas.

Breakdown or Breakthrough?

See what great love the Father has lavished on us, that we should be called children of God! And that is what we are! The reason the world does not know us is that it did not know him (1 John 3:1).

Scripture: 1 John 3:1-5
Song: "Courageous"

There was a time when I swirled in a state of hopelessness—a time when I felt life was spinning around me in every direction, out of control. What helped? The truth of my true childhood, the remembrance of my true Father.

God often reminds me in His Word that I am His child, and that truth gives me hope. Sometimes I think of it this way: When we feel that we could have a *breakdown*, His Word holds the *breakthrough*.

When I stop and breathe my way through the situation instead of letting my chin go down, He will lift my head and restore my hope. That's when we move from so intensely focusing on our own preoccupations to an ability to tell others of our Father's goodness. If we share with others the promises found in His Word—rather than dwelling on the problems—we will be looking up more and not down.

One thing is for sure: Life rarely gets easier, but we can get better at it. Keep pushing, keep hoping, and keep believing!

Lord God of Heaven and earth, thank You for restoring my hope and showing me brighter days ahead. Thank You for making me Yours, a child of the king. Continue to help me see through the storm as I lean on the promises in Your Word. In the name of Jesus, Lord and Savior of all, I pray. Amen.

Feet and Faith

Now that I, your Lord and Teacher, have washed your feet, you also should wash one another's feet. I have set you an example that you should do as I have done for you (John 13:14, 15).

Scripture: John 13:1-15
Song: "Amazing Grace"

I have been an encourager all my life. I have taken it for granted. While I was in Romania doing mission work, a woman asked me to come to her home and encourage her. As we drove to her home, I thought this would be an easy visit.

Entering the house, I noticed the dirt floor and lack of running water. I began to give her Bible verses to encourage her, but I could tell she wasn't moved. Nevertheless, I continued to share words that I felt would lift her up.

I was failing miserably. I prayed to God for help and received a strange intuition. I suddenly knew I was to wash her feet. From an outside well we filled a large pan of water, and I washed her feet while singing "Amazing Grace" to her in English. She began to sing in Romanian as tears poured down her cheeks. She said, "Jesus has been here today." I was soon weeping too.

As I got back in the car, I prayed through tears and praised God for using me. I had thought my words would have some power. Instead, the silence, the listening, the song, and the water conveyed the love of Christ.

O God, thank You for Your mercy and grace. Please help me to convey that grace to others by whatever means You choose. In Jesus' name I pray. Amen.

Forgiveness Is Never Easy

I tell you, her many sins have been forgiven—as her great love has shown. But whoever has been forgiven little loves little (Luke 7:47).

Scripture: Luke 7:44-48
Song: "Forgiveness"

Ever been plagued by a spirit of unforgiveness in your heart? We can harbor that spirit for long periods of time, because forgiving doesn't come naturally. Yet it is the answer to a joy-filled life. When we hold on to unforgiveness, it gains a power over us, slowly creeping in and hardening our hearts. Thankfully, forgiveness can set us free.

In our Scripture today, we hear an amazing statement. Normally, when a person has been hurt by someone else, he or she is the only one who can say "I forgive you." That only makes sense. However, here in Simon's house, notice who says "I forgive." It is Jesus—*a third party!* This means, apparently, that when we sin against other human beings, we are just as surely sinning against our Lord.

Ultimately, this is a comforting truth. We are called to forgive others when they have hurt us. We may ponder our response, but Jesus is immediately offering his forgiveness to that one who's done us wrong. How can we, then, hold back? Bottom line: Let's give up trying to get even with those who have done us wrong and get even with those who have done us right.

Lord, only in Your strength can I forgive. Through forgiveness set me free from any root of bitterness in my heart today. Help me to be able to do for others what You did for me. I pray in the precious name of Jesus. Amen.

Stepping Across the Line

No one who is born of God will continue to sin, because God's seed remains in them; they cannot go on sinning, because they have been born of God (1 John 3:9).

Scripture: 1 John 3:6-10
Song: "How Blessed, from the Bonds of Sin"

I have been here before, and here I am again. I am a sinner, though my goal is to be without sin. In fact, I woke up this morning, looked in the mirror, and said something like this: "God, I am reporting for duty. Help me to walk in the light of Your path and not to step across the line."

I know it's important to pray such a prayer each day. Why? Because as I seek holiness in my daily routine, I am being prepared for the big tests of faith that will surely come. A nineteenth-century preacher, F. B. Meyer, said it so well: "The supreme test of goodness is not in the greater but in the smaller incidents of our character and practice; not what we are when standing in the searchlight of public scrutiny, but when we reach the firelight flicker of our homes; not what we are when some clarion-call rings through the air, summoning us to fight for life and liberty, but our attitude when we are called to sentry-duty in the grey morning, when the watch-fire is burning low."

Thankfully, as we make good decisions in the mundane choices of our day—moment by moment, attempting to avoid sinning—we're preparing ourselves for much larger victories in crucial kingdom battles.

Lord, open my eyes to the sin that hinders our fellowship together. Thank You for Your grace that instills in my heart the desire to do right. In Jesus, amen.

A Beautiful Tapestry of Love

A new command I give you: Love one another. As I have loved you, so you must love one another (John 13:34).

Scripture: John 13:31-35
Song: "Love Is Here"

I'm just going to talk about love in this devotional and try to weave a tapestry of heart-comfort for you with almost random statements about this marvelous word.

Love is a word that makes us smile.

There is power in love.

Love also can hurt, it can cause pain.

Love lost can be a burden on our shoulders, because we have been hurt by the ones we love.

There comes a time, though, when we let God's unfailing love and mercy shower us with hope again.

Love is not optional when we are Christians; love is a requirement.

It is why we exist—to glorify God through loving others.

Whatever we go through in life, love is always the answer.

Love doesn't enable. Love is tough, strong, and frees us to let go and live.

Love can melt our defenses and bring us back to our senses.

When we don't know where to go, we can always go toward love.

It is the answer. Trust it.

Lord, help me to focus on Your love that enables me to love others. Help me to see others as You see them and to use the power of love to bring others to You. In the name of my Lord Christ. Amen.

Let Jesus Reach Out!

Dear children, let us not love with words or speech but with actions and in truth (1 John 3:18).

Scripture: 1 John 3:11-24
Song: "Reach Out to Jesus"

Have you demonstrated your love for someone today? I say "demonstrated" because love is an action word. It holds, it kisses, it touches, it hugs. To love someone requires *doing* something in their best interest. It's not just something we say with our mouths; it is something we show with our hands.

Today, as I think back through my week, I'm blessed to see rivers of love flowing out. I've held the hand of a stranger, prayed for a friend, served food to the hungry, wiped tears from a friend's cheeks. All of this was simply the love of Christ flowing through me; I can hardly take any credit. But I am grateful.

In the same way, I can recall with great joy the times in my life when I have been powerfully and tangibly loved by others — times I will never forget. The time someone brought food to my house when I had no strength even to walk. When a friend mowed my lawn, and another friend just listened and listened and listened, as I poured out my heart's pain.

I want to pass along that kind of love in my days. In fact, how blessed the world would be if we Christians formed a chain of love that would heal every hurt. Through us, Jesus wants to reach out and do just that!

Gracious Father, keep showing me how to put love into action! Bring to my mind ways I can help others, and give me the boldness to step forward and offer Your loving kindness. Help me to love as You love! Through Christ I pray. Amen.

Coolerator Christianity

Of this salvation the prophets have inquired and searched carefully, who prophesied of the grace that would come to you (1 Peter 1:10, *New King James Version*).

Scripture: 1 Peter 1:8-12
Song: "We Give Thee But Thine Own"

In Sunday school we heard wisdom as 90-year-old JB testified: "Time was when farmers shared sides of beef with neighbors because all we had were coolerators, not freezers like today." How generous! And then some guilty feelings welled up in me as I recalled a time of personal selfishness as I sat in an airplane some years earlier.

"Practice English?" Two young Venezuelan engineers, who'd never flown before, gripped my wrist and refused to let go. Suddenly, at 32,000 feet a turbulent thunderstorm prompted the terrified pair to scream: "We fall! We fall!" Their panic made me repeat my standard airplane Scripture (paraphrased) aloud: "Hebrews 1:3, Lord. You are upholding this 747 with the word of Your power!"

God had changed my comfort zone into a field white unto harvest. But I wish I'd done a better job of doing what the prophets of old did, according to our verse today. What would it have meant for me to "preach" in that situation? How could I have been a "coolerator Christian" to those so needful and nearby?

Lord, "Silver or gold I do not have, but what I do have I give you" (Acts 3:6). Make me willing to share the riches of Your grace today! In Christ's name. Amen.

April 13–19. **Kay King** writes from Sky King Ranch in Eddy, Texas. A Baylor University graduate and retired English teacher, she has written 10 devotional books.

Folded Hands 101

For the eyes of the Lord are on the righteous and his ears are attentive to their prayer (1 Peter 3:12).

Scripture: 1 Peter 3:8-12
Song: "'Tis the Blessed Hour of Prayer"

The prayer of 3-year-old Nathan must have made God smile. After his morning shower, his allergies caused the little boy to fold his hands and utter one of the most honest prayers ever lifted to Heaven: "O God, please take away this stuff running out of my nose. . . . Well, thanks for tissues anyway. I sure love You, God!"

He didn't know he'd been overheard. But Nathan had nonetheless aligned himself with a "great cloud of witnesses"(see Hebrews 12:1) who worshipped their Lord no matter what. This queue of folks, who would have agreed with Robert Browning's adage—"The best is yet to be"—is a long one.

Abraham believed God but waited many years for the blessing to come forth. Hannah unashamedly poured out her heart's desire—but experienced long delay until her answer arrived. And the great apostle Paul was persuaded that even an imminent shipwreck couldn't wreck God's plans for him.

God heard their prayers, and He hears ours. And the best response? Our children can quickly teach us here: "I sure love You, God!"

O God, the king of glory, I love You. But I know that I can only express my love to You because You have first loved me. And I thank You, especially, for the way You hear my prayers. Give me the faith to trust that Your answers are always for my good and for the good of Your kingdom. I pray this prayer in the name of Jesus. Amen.

Ms. Kim's Counter

Rejoice with those who rejoice, and weep with those who weep (Romans 12:15, *New King James Version*).

Scripture: Romans 12:9-18
Song: "Tell It to Jesus"

Years ago our family's peaceful life was bombarded by continuous turmoil. Usually I collected my thoughts at home before venturing out into my world, but one day my sorrow spilled out as I stood in a small bookstore. It was awkward; I was embarrassed by my tears.

Quickly the owner placed her hands on my shoulders and smiled tenderly. "Your burden is way too heavy," she whispered. "Here, I'm taking it into my prayers."

The lady who prayed for me that day, Billie, has since moved into Heaven. But her perceptive "mantle" must have fallen on another lady, one named Kim, who works at a local discount store. When Kim asks "How are you?" she's mentally making her prayer list.

What a blessing she is to all who meet her! An amazing Christ-like compassion flows unstoppably from behind her counter: "I pray for my customers every day," she says.

Although I don't know Kim's family or birthday, her address or even her last name, I perceive she's been with Jesus. No barrier can separate God's comforting blessings from those who freely give them—and receive them.

Heavenly Father, give me Your wisdom to intercede for people in places where I've never walked. Love them through me, as I offer myself to You each day. In the name of my Savior, Jesus Christ, I pray. Amen.

The Good Fight of Faith

Yet in all these things we are more than conquerors through Him who loved us (Romans 8:37, *New King James Version*).

Scripture: Romans 8:31-39
Song: "He Just Put Himself in My Place"

Butch, a local minister, fought the good fight of faith all the way to the finish—Heaven. He was a consistent example of godliness, in word and deed. Before leaving, though, he delighted in telling a particularly inspiring story.

It seems that a courageous young wrestler faced the ruling world champion. Yet, with an overcoming power that only God could have supplied, he won! When his wife later received the prize into her own hands, she tearfully said, "Why, this means I am more than a conqueror. You fought—and won—the battle. But it brought me the benefits!"

Throughout the New Testament, we're assured of Christ's finished work on our behalf. The battle against eternal death was won for us when Christ rose from His grave. With His ascension to Heaven, the offering of His sacrifice has been eternally accepted before the throne of the Father's glory.

Yes, the war has been won, the outcome already settled by Christ's atoning work. Now, in our day-to-day world, the "mop-up" operation continues—life's little battles in a war that is already won. What confidence that should give us as we say "No" to each temptation today!

Yes, Father, I do glorify You for making me sure every battle is Yours to win. I praise You for being so personally involved in my troubling times. And I praise You for the victory of the cross! In Christ's name I pray. Amen.

That Same Big Book

You are of God, little children, and have overcome them, because He who is in you is greater than he who is in the world (1 John 4:4, *New King James Version*).

Scripture: 1 John 4:1-6
Song: "Every Day with Jesus"

A passenger in the backseat of the prison van yelled to the driver: "Hey, I know you! Do you always keep that same big book with you?" Dan, the third and rowdiest of our four sons, said yes he did.

Lots of people have known Dan over the years, because he tended to stand out. At 2, Dan roused from napping in church and, standing on the pew, blurted, "What? I've had two naps; let's go home!" After more preschool seasons, he impishly responded to an introduction by offering his left foot of fellowship, instead of a handshake, to the visiting minister. Swift and sure punishment followed the service.

As he grew, Dan became bolder. Outside the church one Sunday, all the worshippers looked upward. Holding onto the tall steeple was a jubilant boy waving good-bye to everyone!

This spring in a country church I heard a sermon about God's faithfulness toward believers, whom He calls and keeps, regardless of their ever-so-human failures. And I received communion from that adventurous son whose antics, mischief, and commitment to Christ are forever held by a nail-scarred hand, the Savior spoken of in Dan's big book.

O God, thank You for taking the most unlikely of vessels and making them useful in Your service. Thank You for using me and mine! In the name of Jesus, amen.

The Master Key Called Choice

Beloved, let us love one another, for love is of God (1 John 4:7, *New King James Version*).

Scripture: 1 John 4:7-12
Song: "My Jesus, I Love Thee"

Friends chuckled when Rufus rattled his keys after the small group meeting. Marilyn met her husband at the door, commenting on his consistent request of the guitarist: "Let's sing 'Beloved, let us love one another.'"

Lieutenant Colonel Rufus Scott, retired squadron commander and pilot of F-100s over Korea, had personal reasons for selecting choruses about loving God and loving others. This leather-skinned military man with bushy eyebrows and raspy voice had accepted the unconditional love of Christ in Vietnam and had lived for Him thereafter.

One big decision came after his plane had taken withering enemy fire over North Korea. Immediately, South Korea's tower radioed permission for him to quickly fly seaward and bail out. But Scott flew forward. He completed his mission before returning to base, where ground crews confirmed he'd landed on an empty fuel tank!

Colonel Scott had a difficult job to do—fighting tyranny with force. Sometimes, it seems, there is no choice but to do so, for the love of those who need defending. But along with him, may we pray for the kingdom to come, where finally, love will reign in every heart and in every corner of a redeemed creation.

Our Father, may Your will be done, on earth as it is in Heaven. And may Your will be done—by me, right now. In Christ's name I pray. Amen.

Displacement

There is no fear in love. But perfect love drives out fear (1 John 4:18).

Scripture: 1 John 4:13–5:5
Song: "A Mighty Fortress Is Our God"

Both joy and sorrow can coexist in a Christian's heart. But John's Gospel reminds us that darkness never dwells with light. Nor can fear keep company with perfect love.

Years ago I was caught in a fierce battle between fear and freedom. During one summer a sexual predator lurked in our neighborhood. While I wasn't always alone, I was always afraid. In devastating detail, local television reporters recounted the man's pattern. He secretly entered homes and moved a wall clock or turned chairs backward. Later, he would return.

My knowing the victims intensified my anxiety, until peace faded with each sunset. I even began to keep a loaded weapon by my bed as I prayed—and watched the door far into the night. Where was my sustaining faith?

One midnight I'd drifted into light sleep but awakened when a single-scene dream had flashed into my consciousness. I saw a solid alignment of towering military beings surrounding our ranch.

And then three words came to me: "Shoulder to shoulder!" No place remained for fear's assault after that, for perfect love had come to cast away the intrusive enemy.

Father, You are that "bulwark never failing" in my life. Thank You for protecting me so many years ago—and giving me the assurance of Your presence. My heart overflows with joy because Your truth triumphs where I live. In Jesus' name, amen.

I Want to Give Up!

Oh, that I had a place in the desert a lodging place for travelers, so that I might leave my people and go away from them (Jeremiah 9:2).

Scripture: Jeremiah 9:1-7
Song: "Trusting and Hoping"

I admit I get discouraged sometimes. I look around and see much evil in the world. And I realize there's not much I can do to change it. I have friends who have thrown away their marriages and ignored their children, neighbors who've turned against me, and friends who seem to be in total "self-destruct mode." I do what I can . . . sometimes. But often I feel as if there's really nothing I can do, and I just want to get away from it all.

Does God feel that way sometimes? Jeremiah said he'd rather run a motel in the desert than preach. As a prophet, was he speaking for himself or for God? (After all, it's God who should be discouraged, right?)

After everything He's done for me, the Lord watches as I focus on petty things, as I feel inadequate and give up, rather than keeping on doing what He has called me to do. But if He doesn't give up, why should I? Others' failings can't hurt me more than they hurt Him. My part is simply to be a light in the darkness—not to curse that darkness—but to shine within it as brightly as I can.

Lord, remind me today that the whole world is in Your hands. Sustain me with the assurance of Your promised presence, and give me peace. Through Christ, amen.

April 20–26. Janet Mountjoy and her husband are now retired after working with churches in Wisconsin, Nebraska, North Dakota, Florida, and Missouri for 35 years.

Sharing Freedom—with Everyone

The people read it and were glad for its encouraging message (Acts 15:31).

Scripture: Acts 15:22-35
Song: "Whosoever Will May Come"

I was in love with Jesus! As a new Christian, I saw beauty in everything around me. I quickly forgave and prayed for any who offended me—even those who cut me off in traffic! I sang hymns throughout the day. I rejoiced that I was forgiven, freed from the sins that had held me. And I felt so free to share His message with others.

But after a while, I started noticing other Christians who didn't live up to what I thought they should be doing. Sadly, I started secretly judging them.

I was a lot like the early Jewish Christians. They judged the Gentile Christians because of their pagan backgrounds and the "baggage" they apparently brought into the church. But reading our Scripture today, I was struck by how the people were "glad" for this encouraging message: all are accepted in Christ.

These same people had once believed they needed to keep all the Commandments in order to be saved. When they realized that God had given them freedom and had made it available for the Gentiles as well, it was so encouraging to them!

Like them, we are to share Christ joyfully with all people, regardless of their backgrounds. Let us keep hearing within our hearts the words of the old hymn: "Whosoever will may come."

O Lord, You loved me when I was unlovable and brought me into Your family long before I could claim to be living as a child of the king. Thank You! In Christ, amen.

Deceivers Offering False Hope

At that time . . . many false prophets will appear and deceive many people (Matthew 24:10, 11).

Scripture: Matthew 24:3-14
Song: "My life Is in You, Lord"

"Get me out of here, Joe." My mother-in-law had asthma, and whenever they were riding and got around smoke or diesel fumes, that's what she'd say to him. It became an endearing, sweet memory to our family and something we all say when we're around something unpleasant.

I've felt that way recently, as so many difficulties arose. My mother passed away four months ago; a good friend was diagnosed with stage 4 melanoma; and the cable news each night had been overwhelming, replete with horrific violence and economic collapse worldwide.

But have you noticed that, along with the bad news come countless deceivers who promise to give us hope? Arm yourself! Eat right! Vote right! Buy right! But none of these can give true and lasting hope.

Jesus warned that tough times will come, but promised that those who stand firm in the faith, to the end, will be saved. So, during those times when I want to cry out, "Get me out of here, Jesus!" I try to remain quiet in His peace. I focus on my real life in Him. And I remind myself that I am not yet living in the best of possible worlds. I am not home yet.

Dear Lord, today I realize that only by focusing on things that aren't of this world can I find peace. Only by looking toward Heaven can I find the strength to live through these trying times. So keep my eyes focused on You! In Christ's name, amen.

Keep Away from Them

Note those who cause divisions and offenses, contrary to the doctrine which you learned, and avoid them. . . . and by smooth words and flattering speech deceive the hearts of the simple (Romans 16:17, 18 *New King James Version*).

Scripture: Romans 16:16-20
Song: "O Be Careful Little Eyes"

When our children ranged from ages 4 to 15, our oldest boy suggested we not watch TV all summer. We'd already decided we were watching too much television, but every evening, it would draw us back into shows that just did not edify us. We were proud of him. So we put the television set in the closet.

It was such a major change in our routine that we floundered for a couple of nights. Then we began playing games, taking walks, reading, sitting on the swing, and talking rather than mindlessly sitting and facing the small, but powerful box in our living room.

We read our Bibles more and discussed what we were reading. We studied Proverbs together and found that no matter what age our children were, they could apply what we were reading to what they saw around them.

Needless to say, it was a summer to remember! Sadly, a school assignment that fall brought the TV back out of the closet. And we realized even more how much we had to be on guard.

O Lord my God, lead me not into temptation, but deliver me from evil! Help me to consciously put away the mindless things that influence me. Guide me by Your Spirit into the real and God-pleasing life. I pray this prayer in the name of Jesus, my merciful Savior and Lord. Amen.

Wishing or Knowing?

He who has the Son has life; he who does not have the Son of God does not have life. These things I have written to you who believe in the name of the Son of God, that you may know that you have eternal life, and that you may continue to believe in the name of the Son of God (1 John 5:12, 13, *New King James Version*).

Scripture: 1 John 5:6-15
Song: "Thy Mercy and Thy Truth, O Lord"

"I hope I get an 'A' in that class." "I hope my mom will let me go swimming on Saturday." "I hope my dad gets a raise so we don't have to move." All my crossing-my-fingers hoping as a girl was much different than the hope I hold onto now as a Christian. As a girl, my hoping was really just *wishing*.

Today, my hope is sure. After all, I've experienced so much evidence of His loving care and sustaining presence. Does that mean everything goes the way I want it to? Absolutely not! But no matter what happens in my life on earth, I have a peaceful knowledge that God exists and is with me as He promised.

Can I prove it? By scientific standards—Yes! For both science and faith must depend on the same assumptions about the nature of reality. If nothing is self-evident, nothing can be proved. Every human being, the brainiest scientist and the lowliest preacher, must bow to that simple, profound truth.

Dear Father in Heaven, my hope is based on Your promises, not on anything I have done for You. But thank You, just the same, for the privilege of serving You with gratitude in my heart! In the name of Jesus, my Savior and Lord. Amen.

Idol Worship

We are in him who is true by being in his Son Jesus Christ. He is the true God and eternal life. Dear children, keep yourselves from idols (1 John 5:20, 21).

Scripture: 1 John 5:16-21
Song: "In Christ Alone"

"He worships idols! He worships idols!" The boys at a Christian school laughed and pointed at the young child from China during recess. Their taunts, however true, were insensitive and cruel. But on Sunday, these same boys were unable to be at worship because they had a baseball game to play. What's wrong with this picture?

In truth, anything that takes the place of God is an idol. And we certainly live in a society overwhelmed with material and emotional temptations that take His place. Every magazine cover tells what currently is the biggest, best, most delicious or fashionable. For many Christians more time is spent in recreation than in God's Word.

A missionary friend of ours told of prayer wheels used in China. They are small rattling boxes that people twirl almost constantly so their prayers will be heard by the gods. I shook my head. *How ridiculous!*

But don't I often seek some truly suspect solution for my problems? Or try to manipulate others for what I need or want? Ridiculous, too! Surely of no more value than a prayer wheel.

Dear Father, I thank You for revealing yourself to me through Your Son and by Your Spirit. Please keep reminding me of who You are and that You are sovereign over all things. Please forgive me when I rely on anything else! Through Christ, amen.

Rejoicing In a Child's Faith

It has given me great joy to find some of your children walking in the truth, just as the Father commanded us (2 John 4).

Scripture: 2 John
Song: "What a Friend We Have in Jesus"

Ray was a wayward son. His parents, like us, had become Christians later in life and had embraced Jesus' call to seek and save the lost. They devoted their lives to ministry and started attending a Bible school. While there, they grew spiritually. But Ray grew aloof. He'd experienced the life of this world and wasn't about to give it up. When they entered a full-time ministry, Ray's parents struggled to keep a good relationship with their son.

When Ray was old enough to leave home, he did. He would occasionally drop by, but his visits were short and usually ended badly. His parents grieved, and they continued to pray.

One night when Ray was in his late 30's, he called his folks. "I want to tell you something important," he said. Worrying about what it could be, they were elated as he told them he had entered the waters of baptism. And he wanted to attend Bible school—the same school they had attended. Upon graduation, he went to a foreign mission field and is still there.

Ray rejoiced. His parents rejoiced. And we rejoiced, knowing that our friends' son now walked in the truth.

Father, You have been so faithful to me and to those I love. I thank You for working in Ray's heart and for hearing the prayers of all parents whose children have said "No" to Your call so far. Help me never to give up praying for them. In Christ, amen.

The One Forever Kingdom

I praised the Most High; I honored and glorified him who lives forever. His dominion is an eternal dominion; his kingdom endures from generation to generation (Daniel 4:34).

Scripture: Daniel 4:34-37
Song: "We Bless the Triune God of Might"

Admiration and hope flow deep on American inauguration days. For a few days it seems as if a new era of cooperation and goodwill has finally arrived. But disappointment follows close behind. Before the ink is even dry on the new administration's letterhead, it becomes obvious that we're in for more of the same old politics.

Even the great King Nebuchadnezzar realized how fragile was his hold on power. One military overreach, one political conspiracy, or one mental breakdown could result in the total loss of an empire. History shows this to be true. The Babylonian, Persian, Greek, Roman, and British Empires each dominated the world for a time. But now their times have passed.

Human governments, both great and small, are short-lived and unsteady. So how comforting to know that God's kingdom is different. We never have to wonder about His character. He is without fault. His power is unmatched. His judgment is perfect, and no army can threaten Him. Earth's rulers come and go. God's great kingdom is here to stay.

Eternal King, how thankful I am to be Your servant in this life. Guide me in Your work and my witness to will and to do of Your good pleasure. Through Christ our Lord. Amen.

April 27–30. **Matthew Boardwell** is an avid reader and enthusiastic musician. More importantly, he is husband to Pam, father of nine, and a church-planting missionary in the west of Ireland.

King of Kings

Observe what the LORD your God requires: Walk in obedience to him, and keep his decrees and commands, his laws and regulations, as written in the Law of Moses (1 Kings 2:3).

Scripture: 1 Kings 2:1-4
Song: "Jesus Shall Reign"

Recently, I stood before a judge for a traffic violation. Before any cases were heard or any judgments were passed down, the judge listed at length the limits on his power. I didn't know what would happen in my case, but I knew what could *not* happen. In other words, the authority in the courtroom was under the authority of the law.

In contrast, an ancient monarch was an absolute authority. His word was law, his rulings final. For example, when Solomon revealed the true mother in his renowned "splitting the baby" decision, no one questioned his right to carry out the judgment. He was the king, and the king was the highest authority.

But before he ascended to the throne of Israel, before he asked for his famed wisdom, Solomon was counseled by his father, David. Solomon would be sovereign over citizens but still subject to the sovereign God. Others would do the king's bidding, but he must follow the Lord's commands. David wanted his successor to know that even lords must obey the Lord.

Knowing that our authorities have a higher authority should give us confidence. The King of kings will be just, even when lesser rulers are not.

Sovereign Lord, I know You rule over the earth and its rulers. Remind them You are real and sovereign in my own life today! Through Christ I pray. Amen.

The Deadliest Heart Disease

They are darkened in their understanding and separated from the life of God because of the ignorance that is in them due to the hardening of their hearts (Ephesians 4:18).

Scripture: Ephesians 4:17-25
Song: "Change My Heart, O God"

For 30 years he had lived with heart disease, resulting in one heart attack, two surgeries, a daily exercise regime, and a restrictive diet. He turned in early one night feeling weak, pausing only to tell Grandma, "I love you. Whatever happens, don't call the ambulance." Then Grandpa went to bed for the last time. Finally, after all those years, his heart simply gave out.

Although his physical heart was weak, Grandpa's spiritual heart was healthy and whole. Many years before his death, he made his peace with God through Jesus and in doing so, he was given a tender new heart. Reborn of the Spirit, he was always open to spiritual truth and responsive to spiritual conviction.

Just the opposite was true of the Gentiles in Paul's day. Their physical hearts pumped away, but their spiritual hearts were hard. This led to a variety of serious symptoms. They were afflicted with dead-end thinking, separated from God, and numb to the prompting of their own consciences.

The only cure for spiritual heart disease like that is to receive a new heart from God. That heart comes with new attitudes, a new identity, and a new character.

Father, I praise You for new life in Christ. My old life, with its habits and attitudes, is being replaced by this new life. Please give me a tender, responsive heart that is eager to adjust to Your Spirit living within me. In Christ's name, amen.

Mutual Inspiration

Let us consider how we may spur one another on toward love and good deeds, not giving up meeting together, as some are in the habit of doing, but encouraging one another (Hebrews 10:24, 25).

Scripture: Hebrews 10:23-27
Song: "Children of God"

Jimmy did baseball drills every day. He swung the bat. He rounded the bases. He practiced his slides into home plate. He studied signals and scenarios. He lifted his weights and ran his sprints. He was prepared for any game situation.

If only he had joined a team!

Gaining proficiency in baseball rules and technique will never make an actual baseball player. That requires playing on a team. You have to face the challenge of hitting and fielding in actual game situations. You have to learn your position in the context of a whole team. Best of all, as the other players make you a better player, they benefit from your improvement as well.

Many Christians think they can follow Jesus without the church. But Jesus never intended discipleship to be a solo sport. From the calling of His first disciples, He has been calling Christians into relationships with one another. We each need the church to stretch us, encourage us, confront us, and support us. And as surely as we grow from the interaction with the people of God, they benefit from our increasing spiritual maturity.

Lord God, how You love Your church—Your flock, Your own body, Your bride! I am so grateful that You called me out of my isolation and into Your church. Thank You for a place to belong. In the name of Jesus I pray. Amen.

My Prayer Notes

_____

_____

_____

_____

_____

_____

_____

_____

_____

_____

_____

_____

_____

_____

_____

_____

_____

_____

_____

_____

_____

_____

_____

DEVOTIONS®

May

Now you are the body of Christ,
and each one of you is a part of it.

—*1 Corinthians 12:27*

Gary Allen, Editor   **Margaret Williams,** Project Editor   Photo Creatas Images | Thinkstock®

DEVOTIONS® is published quarterly by Standard Publishing, Cincinnati, Ohio, www.standardpub.com. © 2014 by Standard Publishing. All rights reserved. Topics based on the Home Daily Bible Readings, International Sunday School Lessons. © 2012 by the Committee on the Uniform Series. Printed in the U.S.A. All Scripture quotations, unless otherwise indicated, are taken from the *HOLY BIBLE, NEW INTERNATIONAL VERSION®. NIV®.* Copyright © 1973, 1978, 1984, 2011 by Biblica, Inc.® Used by permission of Zondervan. All rights reserved worldwide. *New American Standard Bible (NASB),* © The Lockman Foundation, 1960, 1962, 1963, 1968, 1971, 1972, 1973, 1975, 1977, 1995. *King James Version (KJV),* public domain.

Learn to Use the Tools

Do your best to present yourself to God as one approved, a worker who does not need to be ashamed and who correctly handles the word of truth (2 Timothy 2:15).

Scripture: 2 Timothy 2:14-19
Song: "Standing on the Promises"

My father was a tool-and-die maker by trade, so he had all kinds of fascinating, mysterious tools in his workshop. He learned to use each one with skill during his seven-year apprenticeship. When faced with a particular tooling challenge, he knew exactly which device from which drawer to use.

As a kid I failed to appreciate the proper use of these tools. To me an expensive precision instrument seemed like a complicated doorstop or a tie tack. More than once I watched dismay spread across my dad's face when he found a tool being used as a third base, for instance.

Every new Christian needs an apprenticeship in Scripture. Applying the Bible in a fitting, skillful way is a must-have ability for every disciple. For there will be times when religious people argue over religious words. Occasions occur when silly prattle will masquerade as profound spirituality. We must watch out for dubious predictions and blatant false teaching.

How will the Christian know what to think, what to say, or what to do? We'll know, if we know how to use the tools.

Master, Your Word refreshes my soul, makes me wise, gives me joy, and enlightens me. Keep me ever hungry to study and meditate on Scripture. In Jesus' name, amen.

May 1–3. **Matthew Boardwell** is an avid reader and enthusiastic musician. More importantly, he is husband to Pam, father of nine, and a church-planting missionary in the west of Ireland.

Praying for Authorities

I urge, then, first of all, that petitions, prayers, intercession and thanksgiving be made for all people—for kings and all those in authority, that we may live peaceful and quiet lives in all godliness and holiness (1 Timothy 2:1, 2).

Scripture: 1 Timothy 2:1-7
Song: "Revive Us, O Lord"

The ministers of our city have often gathered to pray for our civic leaders. We have also invited those leaders to speak about community needs. Over the years, mayors, university presidents, police chiefs, school administrators, and commissioners have been the guests of these gatherings. And we have always concluded these meetings with public, personal prayers for the officials themselves.

I will never forget the time when an outspoken atheist educator broke down in tears at the kindness of prayer on her behalf. It was never more obvious that prayer is powerful in creating an atmosphere conducive to sharing the gospel.

If we long for a spiritual awakening, we can pray for those in authority. Let us pray for those who are warm toward the Lord, that they would stay strong in the face of opposition. And we can pray for, not against, those who are hostile toward the Lord—that they experience His boundless love toward them. The apostle Paul tells us that such prayers aid in spreading the message that Jesus came to make peace between God and His enemies. Our prayers demonstrate that good news.

Lord of All, forgive me for praying against leaders I don't admire or support. Remind me to offer prayers and petitions for their good. Through Jesus, amen.

Famous Love

You are faithful in what you are doing for the brothers and sisters, even though they are strangers to you. They have told the church about your love (3 John 5, 6).

Scripture: 3 John
Song: "They'll Know We Are Christians by Our Love"

For many years, our church has opened its doors to the annual town fair in the streets surrounding our building. When we do this, we don't have a booth. We don't have a promotional campaign. We don't have an activity. We have . . . restrooms!

All day fairgoers stream through the building to use the clean restrooms and enjoy the air-conditioned space. This simple ministry has had a profound effect. And it has made us famous. Welcoming hundreds of strangers to use "the facilities" is such an unusual service that vendors look forward to coming to this town with this local church. They are often appreciative and curious, asking, "Why do you do this?"

We always answer the same way: To show God's love in practical, unexpected ways.

Gaius was famous too. The apostle John commended him for his generous love toward strangers. In fact, his love had become the talk of the church. When Christian ministers came to town, Gaius welcomed them in and provided for their needs. Because they held faith in Jesus in common, he joined them in their labor through hospitality. He was famous for it. And by the way: What would you like to be famous for?

Father, make me famous for the extravagant love of Your Son flowing through me! You loved me even when I was estranged from You. Thank You, in Christ. Amen.

Gifts: Bows or Strings?

When you enter the land which the LORD your God gives you, and you possess it and live in it . . . (Deuteronomy 17:14, *New American Standard Bible*).

Scripture: Deuteronomy 17:14-20
Song: "He Giveth More Grace"

We usually think of gifts as being wrapped in beautiful paper and tied up with colorful bows. And we don't expect a gift to bring with it any restrictions. But sometimes gifts do come with strings attached.

Think about a 16-year-old who has worked part-time jobs and saved his money to buy a car. Now, his parents have agreed to give him half the purchase price. Wise parents will put some requirements in place to help the teen learn responsibility. "You'll have to buy your own gasoline and help pay for insurance and the license tag. And we expect you to take good care of it."

Likewise, it is not unreasonable when God gifts us that He might include some requirements that will reflect our commitment to Him—and give us a chance to show our gratitude. In today's Scripture, God's people were pleading to have a king appointed over them. God granted their wish and gave them a king, but He also spelled out what He expected of them in return.

What about the gifts God has given you—how does He expect you to live as a result of the goodness you've received?

Lord, may I have the grace to accept the gifts You give me, knowing that they are always for my own good. In Jesus' name, amen.

May 4–10. **Randall Murphree,** of Tupelo, Mississippi, works as an editor and writer with the American Family Association.

Both Sides of the Coin

The gifts and the calling of God are irrevocable (Romans 11:29, *New American Standard Bible*).

Scripture: Romans 11:25-32
Song: "Freely, Freely"

Tyrus and Casey Morgan have three children, one of them adopted, so they know something about God's gifts. They encountered some unexpected bonus blessings when Casey began to research the meaning of the name of their Ethiopian adopted daughter, Mahelet. Casey told Tyrus, "Mahelet means 'gift to God.'"

"That's great," Tyrus said. "Gift of God."

"No," she corrected him. "Gift *to* God."

Digging deeper, the Morgans found more descriptions of their daughter's name. For one thing, it also suggests a deep state of worship in the Ethiopian Orthodox Church, and it is the name of a musical instrument often used in praise and worship.

All three definitions have a special significance for the Morgans. You see, Tyrus is a Nashville, Tennessee, music artist who writes songs and leads worship in his local church.

According to our Scripture today, a license may be revoked, an agreement may be forgotten, a contract may be broken. But a gift from God is irrevocable. What a remarkable, musical gift God gave the Morgans in the person of Mahelet, a little Ethiopian child who embodies both sides of the "gift coin"—God's gifts to them and their worship and gifts back to Him.

Dear Father of all, You have freely given to me. Help me freely to give back to You the things of my life. In Jesus' name, amen.

The Gift That Keeps on Giving

It was confirmed to us by those who heard, God also testifying with them, both by signs and wonders and by various miracles and by gifts of the Holy Spirit according to His own will (Hebrews 2:3, 4, *New American Standard Bible*).

Scripture: Hebrews 2:1-9
Song: "God, Whose Giving Knows No Ending"

Tina Barber one day began wondering what happens to all the beautiful flowers when a wedding is over. So the Tupelo, Mississippi, mother began asking brides in the city if she could have flowers left over from their weddings. Barber called her project "Blooms of Grace." Before long, she and her children were using their talents to rearrange wedding flowers into smaller vases and deliver them to hospice patients.

Some call that recycling. But we might draw a valid parallel between that and the practice known as "regifting." Have you ever received a shirt that just didn't fit or a vase that didn't match anything in your house?

So what do you do with it? Most of us have probably faced that dilemma . . . and some of us have passed the gift along. Maybe we gave it to a charity or contributed it to a friend's yard sale. Our generous gesture might be accompanied by a twinge of guilt, but we do it anyway. However, it doesn't seem too much of a stretch to compare regifting to recycling. Do you have a talent or an interest that you might use to recycle—or regift—in order to bring blessing to others?

Lord, thank You for the many gifts and abilities You pour into my life. May I always use them to show Your love for others around me. Through Christ I pray. Amen.

Serving Is Giving

Since we have gifts that differ according to the grace given to us, each of us is to exercise them accordingly . . . if service in his serving (Romans 12:6, 7, *New American Standard Bible*).

Scripture: Romans 12:1-8
Song: "Go, Labor On: Spend, and Be Spent"

Steve Tybor was stunned in 2005 when Hurricane Katrina ravaged the Gulf Coast south of his Mississippi home. The swath of devastation in the area still bears scars. He wondered what little thing he could do in relief efforts. Meanwhile, Tybor's father called from New York and wanted to help too. They decided to recruit a few friends in the construction industry and go to work on repairing a home or two. It was going to be a one-time mission called Eight Days of Hope.

No one who knows Tybor was surprised that he would put his serving gifts to good use. But he's also a great organizer. He and his dad wound up with 693 volunteers. They worked on 35 homes, installing 610 squares of roofing shingles, 2,210 sheets of drywall and 320 rolls of insulation. Eight years later, Eight Days of Hope #10 drew 2,500 volunteers who did more than four million dollars worth of work in LaPlace, Louisiana, one of the cities hit hard by Hurricane Isaac.

We can't all produce the numbers of a well-oiled mission organization. But we can be *one* of the numbers by joining such an effort.

Dear Father, when I think I have nothing to offer You, please help my mind to see and my heart to accept that You have given me gifts to serve others and thus honor You. In the precious name of Jesus I pray. Amen.

Whose Plans Take Priority?

Now we have received, not the spirit of the world, but the Spirit who is from God, so that we may know the things freely given to us by God (1 Corinthians 2:12, *New American Standard Bible*).

Scripture: 1 Corinthians 2:11-16
Song: "I Am Thine, O Lord"

Australian photographer Ken Duncan is earning a reputation as one of the premiere landscape photographers of our time. In his book *America Wide*, he tells of how he was once among a crowd of photographers trying to capture the beauty of some Colorado mountains in early morning light. He grew annoyed with the selfish behavior of others and left the site in frustration.

Later that day, as he calmed down, he asked God to lead him. Duncan soon became convinced that God wanted him to return to the mountainside site of his morning frustration. He was the only photographer there, and he captured a moving, phenomenal photo of a rainbow stretching over the valley below.

At the 2013 World Congress of Families in Sydney, Australia, Duncan addressed a sold-out dinner of pro-family leaders from many nations. Despite the fact that not all groups represented there were faith-based, he spoke freely of his faith and the role it plays in his life.

Duncan's primary advice? Let us refrain from trying to control our own lives. We must not plead with God to follow our plans, but seek earnestly for God's plan—and follow it.

Lord, You know how hard it is for me to try to control my life and plan all the things I want to do for You. Help me seek first Your plan! In Jesus' name, amen.

Not a Prophet—Gifted Nonetheless

Pursue love, yet desire earnestly spiritual gifts, but especially that you may prophesy (1 Corinthians 14:1, *New American Standard Bible*).

Scripture: 1 Corinthians 14:1-5
Song: "The Little Drummer Boy"

"I'm not a prophet, or the son of a prophet," Ed Stetzer declared. "But I work for a *nonprofit!*" He drew the anticipated chuckle as he joked to make a point with his audience at a conference for Christian journalists in 2013.

He went on to talk to his media audience about the fact that everyone has gifts given by God, and God expects us to be good stewards of those gifts. We are all called to ministry upon our conversion. The only questions are where, when, and to whom. God intends us to use our gifts—and it isn't a big deal if our abilities aren't listed among the "official" gifts of the Spirit.

In other words, no follower of Christ should say, "I have no gift to give." The little drummer boy in the familiar Christmas carol played his drum for the Christ child. Ask your minister or your friends where they think you can serve. What abilities do you have? woodworking? sewing? baking? auto maintenance? keyboarding? organizing? reading? driving? singing? playing checkers? There's a place for you to use your abilities as an expression of your love for Christ and His love for others.

Almighty and everlasting God, help me to be a good steward of the talents and abilities You have given. In every way, I want to reflect Your love to those around me. Remind me again and again that You alone are the life within any fruits produced. In the name of Jesus, Lord and Savior of all, I pray. Amen.

Faith—the Greatest Gift?

To one is given the word of wisdom through the Spirit, and to another the word of knowledge according to the same Spirit; to another faith by the same Spirit (1 Corinthians 12:8, 9, *New American Standard Bible*).

Scripture: 1 Corinthians 12:1-11
Song: "Faith of Our Fathers"

On August 29, 2005, Hurricane Katrina assaulted the Gulf Coast, one of the deadliest natural disasters in U.S. history. Among the victims were Fred Luter and his congregation at New Orleans' Franklin Avenue Baptist Church. The church facilities took on more than eight feet of water, and many of its members met with even more devastation at their homes. Many members had to leave, scattering across the country.

Luter himself lost his house and his vehicles—everything but the clothes on his back. In effect, he lost his job, for his congregation was scattered far and wide, disconnected and in disarray.

Evangelist Phil Waldrep watched Luter's response to that tragic season. Waldrep said, "Fred Luter had the closest-to-Job experience of anyone I know, and he never lost his faith." Any follower of Christ has a measure of faith, but faith is mentioned numerous times in the Scriptures as a spiritual gift. So it is reasonable to think that some have an extraordinary level of faith.

It's almost certain that you and I will never face the calamities Job faced—or even those of Fred Luter. But we can let their examples encourage us amidst our own trials today.

Father, I want to be a follower of Christ who demonstrates great faith. Help me strengthen my faith by following examples You have provided. In Jesus' name, amen.

Poor Petey!

So Moses went back and summoned the elders of the people and set before them all the words the LORD had commanded him to speak. The people all responded together, "We will do everything the LORD has said" (Exodus 19:7, 8).

Scripture: Exodus 19:1-8
Song: "O Jesus, I Have Promised"

My siblings and I may have been some of the first latchkey children in the early 1960s. Before going to work, Mom left us strict instructions for when we came home midday: (1) eat your lunch, (2) clean up, (3) put the cat out, and (4) lock the door when you leave. We "responded together" that we would. And we did—except once.

"It's so cold out! Let's leave Nikita in." So Nikita the cat stayed in with Petey the parakeet. When we got home, there was Nikita—warm and looking quite content. It didn't take but seconds to figure out Petey's whereabouts. The cage was empty, but green and yellow feathers littered the entire dining room. We hadn't done everything we said we would do, and Petey paid the price.

The Israelites of Moses' day made grand promises, but they didn't make good on them. The consequences would prove much more devastating than the loss of a parakeet.

Heavenly Father, help me to walk humbly in Your way, according to Your Word. I want to obey You in all things. Give me the grace to live in consistent obedience to You. I pray through Christ my Lord. Amen.

May 11–17. Ohioans **Katherine Douglas** and her husband had no success with their first attempt at reaping beans from heirloom "beanlings." This year they're trying heirloom tomatoes.

Singled Out

You are to worship at a distance, but Moses alone is to approach the LORD; . . . the people may not come up with him (Exodus 24:1, 2).

Scripture: Exodus 24:1-7
Song: "We Worship Thee, Almighty Lord"

Today was Christy's big day. She didn't know yet just how big it would turn out to be. In spite of being born with Down's syndrome, Christy had her favorites—in sports, in music, and in politics. At 27 years of age, she had a favorite U.S. president. And today he was coming to her city.

Christy and her mom were among the hundreds to hear the president's campaign speech for reelection that day in Toledo, Ohio. After his speech, the president moved through the crowd signing autographs and shaking hands.

But Christy? The president singled her out. The leader of the free world engulfed Christy in a Texas-sized bear hug. Her mom snapped a picture. The president's smile in the picture is every bit as genuine and spontaneous as Christy's in that treasured photograph.

Like Christy, Moses had been singled out. He didn't buckle under the responsibility put on his shoulders. When Moses died, we're told no prophet was like him. Whenever the Lord singles us out for a job or for some encouragement, He again makes clear that He is the infinite, personal God. Not even a hug from the president brings more joy or blessing than that.

Thank You, **Lord,** that You are both the great and mighty God and yet the one who knows me intimately. Thank You for Your loving mercy to me. In Christ's name, amen.

Led Astray

I am afraid that just as Eve was deceived by the serpent's cunning, your minds may somehow be led astray from your sincere and pure devotion to Christ (2 Corinthians 11:3).

Scripture: 2 Corinthians 11:1-5
Song: "Where He Leads Me"

Over a generation later, people in northwest Ohio still talk about the blizzard of '78. After hours of pouring rain, the thermometer dropped, and the raindrops became snowflakes. Under a foot of snow were several inches of ice. Nobody went anywhere for days, though some made the attempt.

Ron decided it wasn't all that bad out. Though the snow continued to fall, he was an experienced driver. He threw his snow shovel into the trunk—just in case—and started out. He had a big car, and it wasn't all that far to work.

He crept along and realized the landscape looked decidedly different under a foot of snow, in the dark, and with snow still falling. He was glad he knew the route well. A few drivers followed in their cars, convinced the driver in the lead car knew the way. When Ron drove into the ditch, they followed along right behind him.

On that snowy day, Ron wasn't out to deceive anyone. Yet he still led them astray. Neither "a Jesus other than the Jesus" Paul preached, nor "a different gospel" will keep me on the right path (see v. 4). Only the true gospel of the Scriptures will keep me from deception.

Lord, I pray to have discernment in all of life's challenges. Let my devotion to You be pure, sincere, and rooted in the truth of Your Word. In Jesus' name, amen.

In the Long Run

Each of us should please our neighbors for their good, to build them up. For even Christ did not please himself (Romans 15:2, 3).

Scripture: Romans 15:1-7
Song: "If We Are the Body"

In January of 2013, long distance runner Iván Fernández Anaya of Spain pursued, but could not catch, the race leader. Olympic bronze medalist Abel Mutai was way out front. Then Iván saw the African stop a full 10 meters short of the finish line at the international race in Burlada, Navarra.

What was he doing?

Iván realized Abel didn't know he hadn't reached the finish line. When Iván came alongside his competitor, he gestured dramatically. He didn't speak Abel's language, and Abel didn't understand Spanish. Iván made gestures indicating the goal lay ahead. The Spaniard let Abel cross the finish line first.

Fans applauded Abel for his finish; they applauded Iván for his sportsmanship. Iván said later, "He was the rightful winner. He created a gap that I couldn't have closed if he hadn't made a mistake."

As a follower of Jesus, I need to be ready to close the gap for a weaker brother. Maybe he still thinks speeding is acceptable behavior. Maybe she doesn't realize gossip—even if it is true—is disobedience. Humbly helping others in their faith walk is a most important way to work for their good.

God, I thank You for those in my life who mentor and encourage me. I pray for Your anointing to encourage those who come to me for help too. In Jesus' name, amen.

Sidelined, but Not Sidetracked

If I am to go on living in the body, this will mean fruitful labor for me (Philippians 1:22).

Scripture: Philippians 1:21-30
Song: "I Am Thine, O Lord"

For 28 years Vicki served in Africa as a single missionary, teaching school in four different African countries. When she became extremely ill in early 2010, she was sent home to the U.S. for a barrage of tests.

That March Vicki was diagnosed with aplastic anemia, a rare, but serious blood disorder. Two months later she had a successful bone-marrow transplant and eventually made a wonderful recovery. But she couldn't return to Africa. What could she do?

Today Vicki ministers to foreign students who attend one of the universities in her hometown. When she isn't busy shuttling students from place to place or teaching them their way around an American kitchen, Vicki teaches English as a second language to the growing numbers of Arabic women and children in her city. Vicki, like the apostle Paul, was ready to "depart and be with Christ, which is better by far" (v. 23). But God had other plans, and she continues in godly, fruitful labor.

I want to be like Vicki and the apostle Paul. If I can no longer do the "first thing," whatever it is, I want to continue to serve Him however and wherever I can. I may not understand everything God allows, but I can bloom wherever He plants me.

Heavenly Father, when difficult times pour into my life, I pray that I won't despair. Help me choose to serve others in action, or at least in fervent prayer. In Christ who gives me strength I pray. Amen.

Hybrid and Heirloom Seeds

If you belong to Christ, then you are Abraham's seed, and heirs according to the promise (Galatians 3:29).

Scripture: Galatians 3:23-29
Song: "Father Abraham"

Our friends, Nick and Robin, have grown and harvested heirloom vegetables for years. Heirloom seeds enable the grower to have plants for the future. The harvester saves some of the seeds from his tomatoes (or whatever heirloom produce he's raising), and he never has to buy seeds or plants again. Once purchased, the seeds of each generation become the parent plant for the next generation of seeds.

Hybrid seeds have no such "staying power." If a farmer wants to have the same tomatoes next year as this year, any harvested hybrid seeds will yield very little, if any, produce. Hybrids produce once. They may be more resilient and require less tender loving care, but they are only good for one growing season. When the next year rolls around, it's back to the store and into the wallet to purchase more seeds.

As Abraham's seed, we have the same reproducibility as heirloom seeds. Because Christ is Abraham's seed (see Galatians 3:16), and we are in Him, we're "heirlooms." Adam's hybrid seed ends in death—one season of life, for "in Adam all die" (1 Corinthians 15:22), But in Christ "all will be made alive." I'm so glad that in Christ I'm not a hybrid, but an heirloom variety.

O Eternal Lord God, make me fruitful for Your kingdom today. I pray that the fruits of the Spirit will show themselves in all I do and say. And as that happens, to You be all the glory and honor! In Jesus' name, amen.

An Alarming Diagnosis

Just as a body, though one, has many parts, but all its many parts form one body, so it is with Christ (1 Corinthians 12:12).

Scripture: 1 Corinthians 12:12-31
Song: "One of Us"

One of the most ominous diagnoses in medicine is that of sepsis, or "blood poisoning." Every local infection, whether a wound or something like a respiratory infection, has the potential to develop into sepsis—a spreading of the infection throughout the body. Sepsis kills over 215,000 Americans every year.

I worked in an intensive care unit for years, and I witnessed the dangers of sepsis firsthand. For example, a newborn baby had a scratch on his head from the forceps used in his delivery. When the grandmother held her new grandson, she kissed his "boo-boo." She didn't realize that the cold sore she had on her lip could be deadly. She unwittingly transferred the cold sore virus to her grandson. He became septic. Only with aggressive life support, powerful anti-viral medications, and much prayer did her little grandson live.

Scripture tells us the body of Christ is a unit. "If one part suffers, every part suffers with it" (v. 26). As a Christian, I don't live in isolation. I'm part of the body of Christ. I don't want to do anything as a member of Christ's body—even in ignorance—that can fester and poison the body.

Lord God, thank You for the unity in the body of Christ. Help me to guard against saying or doing anything that could bring harm or hurt to my fellow Christians. I pray this prayer in the name of Jesus, my merciful Savior and Lord. Amen.

How Soon We Forget!

Or has a god tried to go to take for himself a nation from within another nation by trials, by signs and wonders and by war and by a mighty hand and by an outstretched arm and by great terrors, as the LORD your God did for you in Egypt before your eyes? (Deuteronomy 4:34, *New American Standard Bible*).

Scripture: Deuteronomy 4:32-40
Song: "Remember Christ, Our Savior"

This is so human, so common to our experience that it almost seems pointless to bring it up. But especially when a crisis suddenly arises, don't we usually forget what God has done for us in the past? We get overwhelmed by the latest problem and forget that He has been with us for years, guiding us and rescuing us from dangers innumerable. Nevertheless, we worry and fret.

And what about the things that God surely prevents? So often we have a "close call" in traffic or almost fall off the roof. If we could for a moment see our lives as God sees them, we might be amazed at His constant intervention and care.

In our Scripture for today, God was making a point about who He is, how He loves us, and what He has done that demonstrates all of this. In other words, our fearful questions have already been answered by His actions.

Dear heavenly Father, I am thankful today that Jesus has risen for me, gone to Heaven to prepare a place for me, and will soon return to receive me to himself. Help me to remember—and rest in Him. Bring to my life today all that Your great heart has purposed for me. Through Christ I pray. Amen.

May 18–24. **Brian Doud** is a retired minister working as the resident violin maker at a well-known violin shop in Cleveland, Ohio. For a time he hosted his own radio program, *Man to Man*.

Am I a Fire Starter?

So also the tongue is a small part of the body, and yet it boasts of great things. See how great a forest is set aflame by such a small fire! (James 3:5, *New American Standard Bible*).

Scripture: James 3:1-5
Song: "Channels Only"

We are all horrified and greatly concerned about the fires that sometimes rage through California and other areas. People lose their lives, their homes, and their businesses to the flames. We seem to be so helpless in the face of such conflagrations. We often don't know what caused it all. But sometimes we do know — and it can be the smallest of unintended sparks.

A similar thing can happen in a church. A tiny assumption, an implication, or a question raised can start a forest fire of outrage, criticism, and bitter attitudes. It starts with a small, uncontrolled part of the body: the tongue! Once the tongue is "let loose," much destruction can follow, and damage control can be almost impossible.

Of course, the tongue reports to the mind and heart. If we don't think it, we won't say it. Later on, in the fourth chapter of James, we're told that our behavior can be controlled by a gentleness of wisdom — wisdom that comes from the Lord. Then the contribution of the tongue results not in a fire but in peace, mercy, and "good fruits." So the question is, am I a fire-starter or a peace-starter?

Lord God, make me a fire extinguisher rather than a fire-starter! Help me to be a peace starter, through the Prince of Peace, the Lord Jesus. I pray in His precious name. Amen.

The Language of Worship

"Amen, blessing and glory and wisdom and thanksgiving and honor and power and might, be to our God forever and ever. Amen" (Revelation 7:12, *New American Standard Bible*).

Scripture: Revelation 7:9-12
Song: "O Sacred Head, Now Wounded"

What happens in your church when you are in a "worship service"? I was once in a Japanese worship service, and I had no clue at all what was being said to God. The hymn tunes were familiar, but I couldn't read the words. Knowing the testimony of the people, I am sure they were praising God. And, of course, *He* knew what they were saying.

In our Scripture today, the great multitude was worshipping, saying "Salvation to our God" (v. 10). One of the things for which He is to be praised is the salvation He has worked for us through His Son, the Lord Jesus Christ.

The biblical text doesn't say what language they were speaking, although they came from all peoples and tongues—and they were all saying the same thing. Then the angels, who know God much better than we do, worshipped God. And in their worship they repeated some of the praiseworthy attributes of God.

He is the originator of all that is good. He is the author of blessing, glory, wisdom, thanksgiving, honor, power, and might. And since God is infinite, there are probably an infinite number of wonderful attributes about which He may be praised. Let us begin with at least one this day.

Holy and beautiful God, thank You for showing me at least some of Your great personhood. I bless You for Your mercy and kindness toward me. In Jesus' name, amen.

He Speaks My Language

How is it that we each hear them in our own language to which we were born? (Acts 2:8, *New American Standard Bible*).

Scripture: Acts 2:8-13
Song: "Lord, Speak to Me"

I was born in Pennsylvania, and although I have lived in 15 different states, you could tell (if you were a student of these things) that I talk like a Pennsylvanian. You can tell from their speech when people come from the deep south or the far northeast. And don't you just love a clipped British accent? We all nominally speak English, but we were born to a certain accent, learning it at home from a young age.

That's what our verse is about. Unless you are very good at accents, you can't fake the mother tongue of someone else. And far beyond that, on this Day of Pentecost, the marvel was actually a miracle. One person speaking was heard in the different mother tongues of several people listening to the same words!

The hearers wanted to know how this could be possible. The answer was short and to the point: God's Holy Spirit was at work. The message of Jesus Christ, crucified and risen again, was being sent to their very hearts for perfect understanding.

The hearers knew that the speakers were Galilean and that they should have been hearing a Galilean dialect. When we speak to people of their need for the Lord Jesus, let's pray the same Holy Spirit will let them hear it in their heart language.

Lord, may Your Holy Spirit so work in my heart that I hear You in my heart language and speak to others in theirs. And may they see nothing in me that clouds the message, but rather that which enhances it. For Jesus' sake, amen.

Calling on the Name of the Lord

The sun shall be turned into darkness, and the moon into blood, before the great and notable day of the Lord come: And it shall come to pass, that whosoever shall call on the name of the Lord shall be saved (Acts 2:20, 21, *King James Version*).

Scripture: Acts 2:14-21
Song: "Join All the Glorious Names"

It never ceases to shock and unsettle me when people so easily say, "Oh, my God!" They aren't really calling upon God, of course, but simply using His name vainly. Similarly, when people lightly say, "God damn it!" do they really want God to condemn something and send it to Hell forever? Again, this is a vain usage; that is, an "empty" use of the fullness of God's name.

According to our Scripture today, there is a good way to use God's name—call upon it with a sincere heart. It's the heart-cry of the person who squarely faces the issues of life and death and sees he or she needs some help. And help will come, for God's name represents all that He is: Creator, Sustainer, Judge of all the earth, and Savior.

Have you called on His name for salvation through the Lord Jesus Christ? Do you call on Him daily for guidance and protection? Are you honoring His name by calling upon it the way He has invited you to do?

Father in Heaven, I bow my knee to Your Son in gratitude and surrender, lest I am compelled to bow to it later in anguish and fear. That You are my Savior is all I plead before Your throne of glory. Your name is great, and I seek to honor it with a true heart, today and always. In the holy name of my Lord, Jesus. Amen.

Others!

So also you, since you are zealous of spiritual gifts, seek to abound for the edification of the church (1 Corinthians 14:12, *New American Standard Bible*).

Scripture: 1 Corinthians 14:6-12
Song: "I Would Be True"

The founder of the Salvation Army, General William Booth, although in ill health, went to speak to the annual assembly of his denomination. His entire sermon was a shouted "Others! Others! Others!" It was the theme of his entire life.

What a great example for all of us! And, of course, our Lord Jesus himself is the fount and source of the general's sermon theme: "Just as the Son of Man did not come to be served, but to serve, and to give His life a ransom for many" (Matthew 20:28, *NASB*).

As our Scripture today reminds us, we are to abound spiritually, but it is mainly for the others in the congregation. Even our expressions of praise are not just for our pleasure. First of all, they are for the Lord, for He delights to hear us rehearsing back to Him what may be known of Him. However, one of the main benefits of praise is that others in the church may be taught, encouraged, uplifted, and drawn out in worship themselves by our expressions.

That is the essence of the word *edification*, which comes in verse 12. It means to "build up" or to fortify others. We do it not just by our words, but through our example.

Lord Jesus, You are Lord of the church and of each saint, no matter how great or small. May my thought be for others in the church today. Bless them, build them up in faith, give them great joy. In Jesus' name, amen.

Speak It Clearly for the Other Guy

Otherwise, if you bless in the spirit only, how will the one who fills the place of the ungifted say the "Amen" at your giving of thanks, since he does not know what you are saying? (1 Corinthians 14:16, *New American Standard Bible*).

Scripture: Acts 2:1-7, 12; 1 Corinthians 14:13-19
Song: "In Christ There Is No East or West"

No-num sayin? (That's "do you know what I am saying?" on the streets of New York City.) Isn't it amazing how many different thoughts the same words can convey, depending on how they are said? And how they are interpreted?

It's like an accident, described from within the speeding car, then by an observer by the roadside, or by the police officer who comes along to pick up the pieces.

In chapters 12 through 14 of First Corinthians, Paul seeks to make sense of the "take" different people had on what happened in Acts 2. The bottom line turns out to be, "We're all in this together, so let's agree on what we're doing."

If I give thanks to the Lord and you say "Amen!" we are worshipping Him together. Neither is better or more spiritual than the other. We are each supposed to be contributing to the spiritual experience of the other.

Let's not try to "one up" the other guy, as they seem to have been doing in Corinth. Let's make sure everyone else knows what we are saying, and why. Let's all get in on the prayers, the praise, and the teaching in the church.

Lord of Your great church across the world and down through the centuries, make my words to You and to others simple and clear. Through Christ I pray. Amen.

Unmerited Consequence

What can I do with you, Ephraim? What can I do with you, Judah? (Hosea 6:4).

Scripture: Hosea 6:1-6
Song: "Nothing but the Blood"

"What am I going to do with you?" I've heard it from parents, teachers and, yes, even from my wife. Experience has taught me to focus not on the words but on how they're spoken. Sometimes, the hint of a grin accompanies them. (Whew!) Then there are those times when exasperation drips from each word. (Uh oh.) The worst is when I'm not sure what I'm dealing with.

The people of Ephraim and Judah likely wondered how much trouble they were in with the Lord. I can relate. We all have things in common with Ephraim and Judah—and with one another. We're human. As such we are, by nature, sinners. Who better to irk someone, God included, than us? Thankfully, we Christian believers have one huge advantage over those living in Old Testament times. Let me explain.

Those whom I've occasionally perplexed have, in truth, always been more understanding than I likely deserved. Never, however, have I received such an unmerited consequence for my actions than when Christ, while being crucified, petitioned God on my behalf, "Father, forgive them, for they do not know what they are doing" (Luke 23:34).

Merciful God, we both know it. Even my best efforts will inevitably fall short of what You deserve. Thank You for loving me while yet a sinner. Through Christ I pray. Amen.

May 25–31. **Robert L. Stephens,** a retiree, enjoys spending time with family, freelance writing, and faith-based speaking. He and his wife, Linda, live in Glen Allen, Virginia.

Anger Management

Is it right for you to be angry? (Jonah 4:4).

Scripture: Jonah 3:10–4:11
Song: "Great Is Thy Faithfulness"

As a youngster, my opinion on things often differed with that of my mother. And my take on things was often expressed with a "Why not?" Such encounters had other recurring features. She prevailed. I got mad.

Jonah was no stranger to anger. Scripture suggests he was mad a lot. At odds with one of high authority, he made no attempt to hide his rage. Sounds familiar. Jonah's antagonist, like mine, was a parent unwilling to stray from doing what was best for the child. In Jonah's case, the parent happened to be God.

Thankfully for me, my mother steadfastly refused to be swayed by my childish reactions. She always did what she knew was best — even for her quick-to-anger little boy. Once I calmed down, she was sure to reaffirm her love for me. Her behavior was patterned after that of the Lord she worshipped.

As for Jonah, he did OK too. God responded to Jonah's anger as my mother had to mine — compassionately. It was the same compassion with which He had saved Jonah from drowning. It's the same compassion shown toward the Ninevites. Eternally faithful, God's compassion remains available to all His children. Glory be to God!

Most patient, **Lord,** thank You for tolerating my misplaced wish for control and my anger upon realizing I can't have it. Stay with me, Father, as I strive to surrender my wants, my needs, all that I have, and all that I am into Your loving arms. Through Christ I pray. Amen.

It's All About the Pattern

I warn you, as I did before, that those who live like this will not inherit the kingdom of God (Galatians 5:21).

Scripture: Galatians 5:19-26
Song: "Lord, I Want to Be a Christian"

It's quiet now, but there was a time when the chatter of that sewing machine filled the house. Though quite a seamstress, my mother knew that before sewing even a single stitch she had a decision to make. She had to choose just the right pattern from store shelves filled with alternatives.

Paul also knew the importance of the right pattern, a pattern for living. He wrote to the churches of Galatia about two life patterns. The first was guided by "acts of the flesh"(Galatians 5:19) or human nature. Many of its characteristics were harmful to individual and community. The alternative, though, would promote personal and communal harmony. Such a life is given over to the Spirit and produces its fruits. As with the Galatians, each of us ultimately faces a similar choice.

My mother knew that failure to adhere to a pre-designed pattern when sewing would result in an ill-fitting garment. Paul knew that fashioning a life based upon human tendencies alone would have a far more dire consequence. On the other hand, living by the Spirit results in walking with fellow believers in the footsteps of Jesus Christ.

Patterns for living are limitless. The choice remains ours.

Lord of provision, I ask that You give me the strength and courage to abandon a life fashioned after the world around me. Let me follow the life exemplified by my Savior, Jesus Christ—the one true, eternal pattern for living. Through Him I pray. Amen.

Perseverance with Purpose

All this is evidence that God's judgment is right, and as a result you will be counted worthy of the kingdom of God, for which you are suffering (2 Thessalonians 1:5).

Scripture: 2 Thessalonians 1:1-5
Song: "Thy Way, Not Mine, O Lord"

My son-in-law is a career Marine. His job, like most, requires he and his family be prepared to accept many things, not all of which are to their liking. Military personnel have little say as to where they will live and serve. Long periods of separation are commonplace. Sadly, over the ages countless soldiers have made the ultimate sacrifice. For those who survive and persevere, however, the rewards can be significant.

Those who chose to be members of the early churches of Thessalonica also endured much. Many former friends shunned them. Threats of persecution and death, though predictable, could not be taken lightly.

Paul, no stranger to persecution himself, was so impressed by their steadfast devotion that he even bragged about them to other churches. He also proclaimed that a reward—far exceeding anything this world could offer—awaited each believer.

My son-in-law can retire while still a young man. Important benefits remain available to him and his wife throughout their lifetimes. The reward Paul wrote of to the Thessalonians, however, has no such human limitation. Incredibly, through God's unmerited grace, it remains available to each of us.

Heavenly Father, You have promised that I will never be alone when facing the trials and tribulations of life upon this earth. Thank You, Lord, in Jesus' name. Amen.

In Need of Protection

The Lord is faithful, and he will strengthen you and protect you from the evil one (2 Thessalonians 3:3).

Scripture: 2 Thessalonians 3:1-5
Song: "We Rest on Thee"

A bride at 18, she was now alone for the first time in over 40 years. The trip to the doctor's office came just months after the couple moved some 500 miles into their newly built post-retirement dream home. The stomach cancer diagnosed that day was unrelenting in its progression; her beloved husband was soon gone. Within days another unexpected reality intruded upon her—an acute need for protection.

The believers of Thessalonica were feeling particularly vulnerable as well. Many nonbelievers within their midst wished them harm. Perhaps even more alarming, such individuals were not always easy to spot.

The promised return of their Savior, Jesus Christ, offered some comfort. They feared, however, that He would not reappear soon enough to save them. Paul wrote to offer reassurance, a need that endures.

Our longing for safety and security, both individual and collective, grows with each new trial in life. And Christ has yet to return. Evil thrives. Yet our one true refuge continues to be that to which Paul alluded—God's love and our patient waiting for Jesus.

Assailed by worldliness, **Lord**, I continue to look in all the wrong places for the sense of peace and security I so desperately seek. Guide my footsteps, Father, until I reach the one safe haven of Your loving arms. Through Christ, amen.

Big Enough for Everyone

I pray that you, being rooted and established in love, may have power, together with all the Lord's holy people, to grasp how wide and long and high and deep is the love of Christ (Ephesians 3:17, 18).

Scripture: Ephesians 3:14-21
Song: "The Love of God"

I can't say how many we have. Were we to count them, the results would likely be surprising. We've got wooden, metal, and even cloth ones. We've got straight, coiled, wide, or skinny ones. Suffice to say, there's not much around our house we can't measure. We've got rulers and measuring tapes galore.

The church members in Ephesus were among the more prominent of early believers. Paul wrote in hopes of even further strengthening their faith. He challenged them to consider the dimensions of God's love for them. He believed it to be a love encompassing all of life, lasting from first breath to last and beyond, always present in the best of times and the worst. To Paul, God's love was immeasurable.

My earliest memory involving measurements? I watched my father unfolding length after length of that shopworn yellow ruler, laying it along the length of a piece of lumber, and much to my delight, asking me to mark off the desired spot. Were we, God's children, to attempt to measure our heavenly Father's love for us, I suspect we would soon be unanimous in our conclusion. It's more than big enough for everyone.

Father, in the midst of a world claiming to offer the biggest of everything, I fall to my knees in adoration of Your immensity. I praise You through Christ my Lord. Amen.

A Matter of Focus

The greatest of these is love (1 Corinthians 13:13).

Scripture: 1 Corinthians 13
Song: "Jesus Loves You"

It happened while sitting with my best buddy at a drugstore luncheon counter. I reached for the small menu wedged between the napkin holder and the jukebox. He ordered, instead, from a menu positioned just above the counter-length mirror in front of us. It was obvious. He saw things I couldn't. A subsequent visit to the eye doctor revealed just how distorted my focus had become.

Paul was concerned about the spiritual focus of believers in Corinth. Blessed by God with a full range of spiritual gifts, they were equipped to bring much honor and glory to their generous Father. Paul sensed, however, a disturbing shift of focus. Time previously spent in praise and response to God's unceasing love was now given to creating a "hierarchy" of His gifts. Matters of the world had indeed blurred their vision.

Options for adjusting, even restoring, human eyesight continue to evolve. The sole remedy for a loss of spiritual focus, however, was and always will be the unmerited love of God.

Perhaps nothing better exemplifies that love than God's willingness to sacrifice His only Son as a final payment for our sins. When striving to sharpen our spiritual vision, where better to focus than upon the cross?

While on this earth, **Father,** Your Son caused the blind to see. In faith and thanksgiving, I ask that You remove the scales from my eyes. I want to gaze upon the cross and experience Your eternal love. I pray in Jesus' holy name. Amen.

DEVOTIONS®

JUNE

Seek good, not evil, that you may live.
Then the LORD God Almighty will be with you.

—*Amos 5:14*

Gary Allen Wilde, Editor   **Margaret Williams,** Project Editor   Photo iStockphoto | Thinkstock®

DEVOTIONS® is published quarterly by Standard Publishing, Cincinnati, Ohio, www.standardpub.com. © 2014 by Standard Publishing. All rights reserved. Topics based on the Home Daily Bible Readings, International Sunday School Lessons. © 2012 by the Committee on the Uniform Series. Printed in the U.S.A. All Scripture quotations, unless otherwise indicated, are taken from the *HOLY BIBLE, NEW INTERNATIONAL VERSION®. NIV®.* Copyright © 1973, 1978, 1984, 2011 by Biblica, Inc.® Used by permission of Zondervan. All rights reserved. *New American Standard Bible®,* (NASB) Copyright © 1960, 1962, 1963, 1968, 1971, 1972, 1973, 1975, 1977, 1995 by The Lockman Foundation. Used by permission. (www.Lockman.org). The *Revised Standard Version of the Bible (RSV),* copyright 1946, 1952 [2nd edition, 1971] by the National Council of the Churches of Christ in the United States of America. Used by permission. All rights reserved. The *Holy Bible, New Living Translation (NLT).* Copyright © 1996, 2004, 2007. Used by permission of Tyndale House Publishers, Inc., Wheaton, Illinois 60189. All rights reserved. The *Revised Standard Version* of the Bible *(RSV),* copyrighted 1946, 1952, © 1971, 1973. *Contemporary English Version (CEV),* © 1991, 1992, 1995 American Bible Society.   Volume 58 No. 3

Share His Love

As for me, I will declare it forever; I will sing praises to the God of Jacob (Psalm 75:9, *New American Standard Bible*).

Scripture: Psalm 75
Song: "Come, Christians, Join to Sing"

Yesterday was our children's day of worship at church. They conducted the entire service, from showing people to their seats and taking up the offering to singing special songs and playing handbells. What a thrill it is to witness how much the children are learning from our dedicated teachers and mentors. Older ushers were standing by to help with the offering collection. Song leaders were there to sing with their young charges and to aid the handbell ringers. But it was their service.

The kindergartner's teacher explained how the children love knowing what to expect. They get use to the order of the service and expect it always to be the same. She explained that on one occasion we did not sing the doxology after the offering was collected; instead we sang a different song. One of her students was quite upset. All the next week he kept pestering his father, who is our minister of music, about the failure to sing "Praise God, from whom all blessings flow."

We know our children are always watching us. We know, also, there are good habits as well as bad. Church and school attendance are among the good ones.

Lord, I repeat the child's benediction, "Go now to tell the story, to spread the kingdom, to welcome the children." In Jesus' name, amen.

June 1–7. **Cos Barnes** is a freelance writer from Southern Pines, North Carolina. One of her favorite hobbies is playing handbells in her church.

Justice and Righteousness

It was I who brought you up from the land of Egypt, and I led you in the wilderness forty years that you might take possession of the land of the Amorite (Amos 2:10, *New American Standard Bible*).

Scripture: Amos 2:9-16
Song: "Stand Up, Stand Up for Jesus"

It was Mother's Day, and I had talked to each of my three children. We had shared laughter, memories, and future plans. It dawned on me later that I didn't speak to my son-in-law, whose mother had died during the past year. Alarmed at my insensitivity, I called him and apologized. It took an effort on my part to make the call after my forgetfulness. But his appreciation made me thankful that I had done so. Sometimes we get so wrapped up in our own lives that we forget to think of the hurts of others.

I was taught to respect my elders. I taught my children to stand when older people left or entered a room and to hold doors for them. I am well aware that times have changed; however, I still use my grandmother's words, "Have your hat off and stay a while," when a man neglects to remove his hat in my house.

From what I have read, Amos was a man of moral decency who urged unity and integrity among the Israelites—a right relationship to God and loyalty to neighbors. He reminded them of God's goodness to them. He wanted their response to be kindness to fellow citizens.

Thank You, **God,** for parents who taught me to be kind to others. Bless those, dear God, who did not have that privilege. Make me ever grateful. In Jesus' name, amen.

Follow This Example

Surely the Sovereign LORD does nothing without revealing his plan to his servants the prophets (Amos 3:7).

Scripture: Amos 3:1-8
Song: "I Love to Tell the Story"

My old friend's letter arrived today. We were in high school together, and our friendship spans many years. She and her husband separated years ago; he lives on the west coast, she lives on the east. The ex-husband suffers from Alzheimer's, and one of her sons is there with him.

She wrote, "Joseph contacted us, saying his dad had fallen and broken his hip. But yesterday's surgery went well, and pins were inserted. With his dad's confusion, it's been difficult to keep him in bed, as he doesn't remember what happened. I think Joseph probably spent last night at the hospital, since his dad responds better to him than to the nurses. Joseph has learned how to deal with his dad in a way that calms him."

Amid my tears I thought of this young man and his love for his father. So many children are caring for their parents in their incapacitated states. We look after those we love.

I think Amos loved his charges in Israel, and they were a chosen people. But as a prophet called by the Lord, his job was to make the people understand who they were, what God had done for them, and how they were expected to live. He endured opposition, but he was God's servant and did not run from his duty. May we follow his fine example.

Lord, many of us have seen our parents reduced to childlike actions because of Alzheimer's. Helps us to respond with hearts of love. In the name of Christ, amen.

Don't You Know How to Do Right?

"They do not know how to do what is right," declares the LORD, **"these who hoard up violence and devastation in their citadels"** (Amos 3:10, *New American Standard Bible*).

Scripture: Amos 3:9-15
Song: "If You Will Only Let God Guide You"

Many years ago we toured the battlefield at Gettysburg, Pennsylvania. It was during a time in our history when young men were killing others for their designer running shoes. So, the irony churned deep emotions in me. I wept throughout the whole tour as I thought of the young boys who died on that battlefield, selflessly giving their lives for a grand cause.

I read an article recently in which the writer decried the American people's love of things. She focused on the poorly built factories and child labor in other countries, which permit us to amass cheap goods. She urged consumers to buy at home, to look for materials that were made in regulated factories that paid a living wage. And not to fight over running shoes.

Amos admonished his people, telling them they just didn't know how to do right. He warned them that they had lost their sense of direction. The rich had amassed wealth through violence against the poor . . . and only destruction would follow.

Though Amos spoke to a specific, historical situation—and that is its first application—we too can learn from this prophet. Let us take a second look today at our buying habits and consider the justice or injustice they promote.

O God, I am guilty of storing up assets for my own use, oftentimes at the expense of others. Help me to discern right from wrong in this! Through Christ, amen.

True Worship: More Than Show

Burn leavened bread as a thank offering and brag about your freewill offerings — boast about them, you Israelites, for this is what you love to do (Amos 4:5).

Scripture: Amos 4:1-6
Song: "Worthy of Worship"

"You know, you make Daddy and me nervous." I knew what my youngest daughter was talking about. I'm one of those people who's always doing something. I was a "multitasker" before there was such a thing! My daughter and my husband, though they work hard, know how to relax at the end of the day.

Was my constant "busyness" a little obnoxious to those around me? As I read our Scripture for today, I recalled something my mother told me years ago. She was a florist, and when garden clubs made their advent, she said, "All women thought they needed to be master flower arrangers."

Women who before then had gladly gathered blossoms from their gardens to decorate the church altar, now became hesitant. New "rules" arose about how many flowers should be used and how they should be placed in containers. Women backed off because they were afraid of criticism.

Possibly with tongue in cheek, Amos admonished his people for worshipping for self-satisfaction, to be seen and noticed by people in the community. They were busy rebelling — while the poor were being forgotten amidst a mockery of religion.

Heavenly Father, I can't fake a genuine faith. You've declared me righteous in Your sight by grace. Now make me truly good in my efforts to live for You. I pray this prayer in the name of Christ the Lord. Amen.

Discipline or Punishment?

This is what I will do to you, Israel, and because I will do this to you, Israel, prepare to meet your God (Amos 4:12).

Scripture: Amos 4:7-13
Song: "Moment by Moment"

I belong to a generation who spanked their children. Our first daughter was stubborn, and she once told her daddy, "It didn't hurt a bit through my blue jeans!" She ended up having second thoughts about the wisdom of that pronouncement.

In my day, the common parental line was: "This will hurt me more than it does you." Of course, most of us children seriously questioned the factual basis of that statement! (Then there are still those adults today who will tell you they'd rather have been physically punished—better than having had Dad look them in the eye and have a heart-to-heart talk with them.) Still, I wonder if "time out" would've been more effective in those days in our culture?

As we look at the words of Amos, who warned his people of the dark days of impending judgment to come, it seems he was more concerned with discipline than punishment. There is a big difference. Discipline has a goal: reform, improvement, renewal. So, with fire and fervor, the prophet exposed the extravagant ways of sophisticated Samaria, urging them to establish a right relationship with God and their fellow man. Spiritually, they needed to grow up.

Lord, so many of my fellow believers are hurting through broken relationships, financial loss, or weather-related destruction. Help me to help them! And may they find a way to see it as "discipline" that brings growth. Through Christ, amen.

In the Context of Bad: Good!

So I will send fire upon Judah and I will consume the citadels of Jerusalem (Amos 2:5, *New American Standard Bible*).

Scripture: Amos 2:4-8
Song: "Rescue the Perishing"

We all need help for the journey, and I am excited when I read of practical ways that people in our society have learned to assist those in need. For example, some people are installing grab bars in the homes of the elderly, knitting "chemo hats" for cancer patients, and crocheting lap robes for the ill. Others travel to tornado-and earthquake-destroyed communities to give assistance and build houses for suddenly homeless families.

Yes, we read of murders and mistreatment, and robberies and desertion, we hear of atrocities upon children and acts of injustice toward the "powerless" in our communities. It was like that in the days of Amos too. But we pray we'll remember the lessons we were taught by God: to be quick to forgive, to be an instrument of God's peace, and to be a light in the darkness for others. Much good can be done, even in the midst of much surrounding evil.

Amos calls attention to the people's rejection of God's laws. He calls them to remember all that's been done for them and respond with acts of love. Their ruthless oppression of the poor is also a sin against God. But may they turn back and do good once again.

I want to do Your will, **O Lord!** But I need the help of Your grace to follow through. Help me to put others first and offer Your light of truth to them—not just in words, but through my compassionate actions. In Jesus' name, amen.

Godly Understanding

The LORD looks down from heaven on the entire human race; he looks to see if anyone is truly wise, if anyone seeks God. (Psalm 14:2, *New Living Translation*).

Scripture: Psalm 14
Song: "God Is So Good"

So often, when faced with imminent death, people call out to God. During the American Civil War, both Union and Confederate chaplains tell of soldiers reading their Bibles and attending prayer meetings before battles. Young men, who had rarely attended church at home, crowded into camp revival meetings until there was standing room only.

This was especially true after a soldier's first experience in heavy fighting. The men understood the next battle could be their last, and they wanted to prepare for eternity.

Whether we live in peaceful or dangerous situations, God is actively searching for people who understand something very important about human existence. He wants us to know our lives will one day end (see Hebrews 9:27). He also wants us to know He loves us and has provided a way for us to spend all eternity with Him. When Jesus died on the cross, He purchased a glorious eternity for every person who believes the good news. Seek God in prayer — not just in danger, but always.

Lord, thanks for Your great plan of salvation through Jesus. It's awesome to realize: You have planned a glorious future for me beyond the grave. Through Christ, amen.

June 8–14. **Jewell Johnson** lives in Arizona with her husband, LeRoy. They have six children and nine grandchildren. Besides writing, Jewell spends her time reading, walking, and quilting.

A Judge or a Friend?

Would it turn out well if he examined you? Could you deceive him as you might deceive a mortal? (Job 13:9).

Scripture: Job 13:7-12
Song: "I Want to Be Like Jesus"

When Liz, a 15-year-old girl in our church, became pregnant, we planned a baby shower for her. Not everyone approved. Some felt it wasn't right, since Liz was single. But as Liz's friends, we agreed it wasn't our place to judge her. She knew our moral perspective, and we hoped she'd grow in Christ — along with us! — over the years ahead. We figured the best way we could help Liz now was to show love for her and her baby.

As Job's life swirled with tragedy, his friends rushed to judge. Surely he had sinned! And, true, God sometimes uses trials to call attention to areas in our lives that need changing. But this was not the case with Job: he was perfect in all his ways.

As the friends saw Job sitting on a pile of ashes, scraping painful boils, why didn't their hearts melt with pity? Did they forget that "there, but for the grace of God, go I"? Rather than judgment, Job needed encouragement from his friends.

I know I'm called to stand for what is morally upright. But most of the time, when I'm tempted to condemn a friend's actions, I need to remember to look for what they really need from me. What will help them soften their heart toward God or take the next step toward His love? Would it be a hug, an encouraging word, a whispered prayer?

O God, grant me a heart of love for people, no matter their actions. May I see them as You see them—needy, often afraid, and seeking acceptance. Through Christ, amen.

A Sincere Heart

Outwardly you look like righteous people, but inwardly your hearts are filled with hypocrisy and lawlessness (Matthew 23:28, *New Living Translation*).

Scripture: Matthew 23:23-28
Song: "Sunshine in My Soul"

As the family sat together in church—mother, father, three sons, and a daughter—they seemed like the perfect family. But at home, the situation was not good. The husband abused his wife, and often the children had to flee to their grandmother's until their dad's anger subsided.

Outward appearances can be deceiving. That's why Jesus used strong words to describe the *hearts* of the religious people of His day. The Pharisees looked good as they prayed on street corners and gave money to the poor. How righteous they felt as they paid tithes on insignificant items like spices.

Jesus commended them for what they did, but as He looked into their hearts, what he saw was not pretty. "You are like whitewashed tombs—beautiful on the outside but filled on the inside with dead people's bones and all sorts of impurity" (v. 27, *NLT*). They had lost sight of the importance of right motives and inner holiness.

If there's any trait God wants in His people, it's sincerity. Therefore, may our motives match our good deeds. May a clean heart complement our fine exterior.

Almighty and most holy God, I admit my motives are not always pure. Cleanse me from all devious ways so I will serve You in sincerity and truth. Today I take inventory in Your presence, and I ask You to "Search me, O God, and know my heart; test me and know my anxious thoughts" (Psalm 139:23, *NLT*). In the name of Jesus, amen.

Play by the Rules

Obedience is better than sacrifice, and submission is better than offering the fat of rams (1 Samuel 15:22, *New Living Translation*).

Scripture: 1 Samuel 15:17-23
Song: "We Are Able"

When I play board games with my 4-year-old grandson, the rules don't always suit him; we bend them a bit so he wins. I don't worry about it too much. I know when he gets older and plays with his friends, *they'll* hold him to the rules of the game.

God told Saul to completely destroy the Amalekites, but as the battle progressed, Saul made up new rules. When he saw the Amalekites' sleek cattle, he thought it was a waste to destroy them. So he took some cattle to sacrifice to God. When Samuel questioned Saul's obedience, Saul blamed the soldiers who accompanied him; they also took cattle to sacrifice.

Saul thought he had won a great victory, but God saw it for what it was—a failure, because Saul had disobeyed and lied to Samuel. Did Saul understand God's command? Yes. But he reasoned away the words of God as unimportant.

Obeying God from the heart is much better than dry and Spirit-less "religious observance." Even attending church, giving to the poor, or visiting a sick friend can have little heart.

Today I plan to "listen" to God by reading Scripture with a meditative attitude. I want to soak up the Word, not just understand the words. Thus I'll have a better chance of living by it.

God, I sometimes lack a depth of sincerity as I approach You and Your will for me. Today I make a new commitment to live by Your grace. Through Christ, amen.

Turn . . . and What Will Follow?

Come back to the LORD and live! Otherwise, he will roar through Israel like a fire, devouring you completely. Your gods in Bethel won't be able to quench the flames (Amos 5:6, *New Living Translation*).

Scripture: Amos 5:1-6
Song: "Turn Your Eyes upon Jesus"

One afternoon we got a call from a nearby hospital. They told us our daughter had a car accident and was in the emergency room. When we got to the hospital, we heard some good news — our daughter was alive. The bad news — her arm had smashed through a window and was horribly mangled, full of glass. Long days of therapy and healing must follow.

God gave Amos, a rancher living in Judah, a vision of what was to happen to the people of Israel, the northern kingdom. When this prophet proclaimed God's message to the Israelites, he had good news and bad news for them. Because they worshipped idols and treated the poor badly, an enemy nation, Assyria, would soon overrun their land and take them as slaves.

While the outlook was grim, Amos also had good news for the wayward nation. He pled with them to "Come back to the Lord and live!" (v. 6).

How merciful is our God! In love, He discloses our sin and possible punishment. But God doesn't stop there; He always provides a way out. If He shows you areas of spiritual neglect, confess them to Him. Mercy and forgiveness will follow.

Father, thank You for forgiving my sins through Your Son. Today I celebrate the joy of the Lord that comes through the good news! Through Christ I pray. Amen.

The Lord Is in Control

It is the Lord who created the stars, the Pleiades and Orion. He turns darkness into morning and day into night. He draws up water from the oceans and pours it down as rain on the land. The LORD is his name! (Amos 5:8, *New Living Translation*).

Scripture: Amos 5:7-13
Song: "This Is My Father's World"

This spring I planted vincas and petunias in pots on our patio. The plants soon sported magnificent white flowers. In the mornings as I sit outside, I am aware that God is in my garden; He is at work on my patio, creating beauty. In fact, if we look, we can see God's works all around us in the earth and sky.

When Amos called the Israelites' attention to their national sins, he also reminded them of God's control of the elements: day and night and the rain. His hand in nature was predictable. So was His attitude toward their sin. Just as night follows day, so punishment would follow injustice.

Times were good for the northern kingdom of Israel, yet sin lurked under the surface. Honest people were oppressed. People often slipped money to officials to gain favor. The poor didn't get justice in court. For these sins, Amos said, just as sure as God turns day into night, disaster was coming.

God controls the seasons. And just as His hand in nature can be depended upon, so He has principles of grace and mercy. "Choose Christ and live" is just as sure as night following day.

Father, open my eyes to see You in my world and to worship You for Your great mercy, as shown in the life and death of Jesus. In His name I pray. Amen.

Let Justice Prevail

I want to see a mighty flood of justice, an endless river of righteous living (Amos 5:24, *New Living Translation*).

Scripture: Amos 5:14, 15, 18-27
Song: "Holy God, We Praise Thy Name"

My mother was raised in an extremely poor family. So, as an adult, she felt great empathy for the needy of our community. Widows received Mom's rye bread and jams. Bachelors in our town came to eat dinner with our family. At Christmas, it was my job to distribute boxes of homemade goodies to poor families. In other words, Mom did her part to assure the needy people of our community that they were important and cared for.

The prophet Amos proclaimed a new way for the northern kingdom of Israel. They must attend to the plight of the poor. Their law courts should dispense justice, regardless of economic status. They must transcend the false accusations, bribery, and corruption that had been the rule of the day. As each Israelite took a firm stand to help those in need, justice would prevail.

God still calls us to help the needy. Often the poor have no defenses, so how we respond means much to their security. But our attitude and actions have specific application to us too: the disclosing of our true character. Let us join with Amos in praying for justice to roll on like a mighty river, flooding our land, our courts, our homes, and our hearts with right living.

Lord God Almighty, I want to do my part to ensure that needy people of my community are treated kindly, respectfully, and justly. Give me a sincere and heartfelt compassion. I pray this prayer in the name of Jesus. Amen.

Who Needs It Now?

Rather give alms of such things as you have; then indeed all things are clean to you (Luke 11:41, *New King James Version*).

Scripture: Luke 11:37-42
Song: "Pass It On"

We all love surprise gifts. I was no exception when a coworker presented me with a beautifully framed art piece that included my favorite Scripture delicately scrolled across the bottom. I thanked her sincerely, already eyeing a special place on my desk to show it off. And it didn't take long before someone noticed.

A visiting client came back to counsel with me on an accounting matter. We barely knew each other, but as she talked, I could sense a sorrow in her countenance. When she saw the serene beach scene combined with the Scripture, her eyes lit up. "That's so gorgeous!" she exclaimed. "I would love to be walking on that sand right now."

That's when I could feel the prompting in my spirit to give her the picture. I had owned it a whole 20 minutes. While my spirit tugged me toward giving, my head was saying something else: "That's *your* special present. It's not like she's asking you for it."

I struggled a few seconds more before reaching down for the artwork. In that moment, I realized again that all of our possessions are merely loaned to us by God. Sometimes we "own" them just long enough to pass them to someone else.

Father, I thank You for supplying all my riches. Help me to hear You when it's time to pass things along for Your glory. You are my provider. In Jesus' name, amen.

June 15–21. **Melanie Stiles**, of Spring, Texas, is an author and a mentor to younger women. She loves coaching, writing, and playing with her granddaughter.

For the Sixth Time!

Commit your works to the LORD and your plans will be established (Proverbs 16:3, *New American Standard Bible*).

Scripture: Proverbs 16:1-11
Song: "Oh, to Be Kept for Jesus"

I have the pleasure of working for two very detail-oriented bosses. Allow me to share a bit of my day. I never type a letter for either of them less than six times, as they make numerous alterations and changes. They both need their correspondence to be perfect. Each has his own version of what letterheads and formats should look like. Each requires mail to be processed differently. Even phone messages have to be delivered in two ways. They are so entirely opposite, I have lovingly nicknamed them "Staples" and "Paper Clips."

Many people have asked me how I've maintained the patience to work at our company for the past 16 years, doing and redoing so many documents. I always admit it was a bit frustrating in the beginning. Eventually, I came to understand a simple truth: I don't really work for these two bosses; I work for the Lord.

The Lord knows each of us is unique and that we have differing gifts, abilities, and habits. After all, He created us and calls us to be the hands and feet of Jesus everywhere to everyone. Recognizing my work as kingdom work changes my focus. As I retype a letter for the fourth or fifth time, I remind myself that my Creator (and real boss) sees the work of a servant ministering to His beloved creatures.

Lord, in times of frustration, let me see people as You see them—beloved creatures whom You are calling to become Your beloved children. In Jesus' name, amen.

Which One?

Some indeed preach Christ even of envy and strife; and some also of good will (Philippians 1:15, *King James Version*).

Scripture: Philippians 1:12-20
Song: "Immortal, Invisible, God Only Wise"

Driving down the road, I punched randomly through the buttons on my car radio in search of a sermon. It only took me a couple of minutes to figure out there'd be no lack of voices ready to share the Word of God. As I bounced from one voice to another, listening for something to resonate within me, a question arose in my mind. Were all of these ministers *appropriate* to hear? How could I discern which had God's "seal of approval"?

When I wanted to buy a new television, I did my research. I web-searched and read everything I could. I went to the library to survey consumer report publications. After a couple of weeks, I felt confident enough to make my purchase. But what about imbibing anonymous, on-the-spot preaching?

Continuing to drive, I realized God was way ahead of me. He'd supplied me with my own spiritual consumer report. By investing in the daily habit of reading, studying, and meditating on Scripture, I had been doing my spiritual research. In a spirit of prayer, I am able to hear what the Lord wants to impart. I am able to discern which voices may stray from the "treasury of faith"—that body of doctrine delivered from the apostles. In the end, He gives me the knowledge I need to make good choices.

Thanks, **Lord,** for giving me everything I need, including faithful teachers to interpret Your Word. Help me to be disciplined and spend time daily in Your Word and in prayer. I want to live in the choices You make for my life. In Jesus' name, amen.

Spring-Cleaning

He said to them, "Take heed, and beware of all covetousness; for a man's life does not consist in the abundance of his possessions" (Luke 12:15, *Revised Standard Version*).

Scripture: Luke 12:15-21
Song: "God Will Take Care of You"

It was time to tackle my clothes closet. I decided to take the advice of the experts. First, I emptied everything out and began trying on garments. I discovered shoes and blouses I hadn't worn in a very long while. I was also a little surprised to find several articles of clothing with the price tags still attached! They'd been lost in the abundance.

Strangely, I really wanted to hang on to what I'd set aside for the shelter's thrift shop—even though I'd probably never wear any of it. I took a moment to explore why the urge was so strong. I considered myself to have a giving nature. Why would these items with a price tag be any different from the hundreds I'd donated to the shelter before?

As I sorted out my thoughts, I began to wonder whether coveting is primarily about possessions. Rather, isn't it ultimately a condition of the heart that essentially says, "God, I don't *trust* You to meet my needs"? To covet is to lack faith in God's ability to care for us.

I stared at the overflow of apparel still left in my newly organized closet. My spiritual blessings surpassed every material thing hanging there.

Lord God, thank You for showing me the true blessings of my life. You want to give to me in abundance—and You do! Through Christ my Lord, amen.

Wake Up!

Turn my eyes from worthless things, and give me life through your word (Psalm 119:37, *New Living Translation*).

Scripture: Psalms 119:31-38
Song: "Awake, Awake! O Heart of Mine!"

It's so easy for me to hit the snooze button on my alarm clock each morning. My brain quickly starts trying to justify how I can grab more sleep and still make up missed time. "C'mon, you can skip having breakfast and making your lunch just once." A breakfast bar in the car on the way to work and a quick trip to the deli would suffice. Ten minutes later, I start over when I hit the snooze button again.

Before too long, I've lost 30 minutes or more. And I now have to live through if-you-snooze-you-lose consequences. Gone is my healthy eating regimen as I munch on the raspberry bar I've found buried in the back of the pantry. My budget will get stretched by eating lunch out rather than bagging it.

But more importantly, I've started the day without acknowledging who gave the day to me. I've slept through the moments when I receive my peace and purpose from Him, when I prayerfully place my day in His loving hands.

God never snoozes when I am ready to connect with Him. He never has to explain being late or justify why He "didn't show up" when I face sorrows, hardships, or trials. He is always there in my life. Will I turn to Him—or just roll over?

Lord, help me stay disciplined and seek You first every morning. I want to live my day knowing I've spent time with You before any other thing. I know You have my best plan in Your heart. I pray in Jesus' holy name. Amen.

A Healthy Temple?

Those who obey the LORD are daily in his care, and what he has given them will be theirs forever (Psalm 37:18, *Contemporary English Version*).

Scripture: Psalms 37:14-22
Song: "Come, Mighty Spirit, Penetrate"

In the midst of working and raising a family, I'd found it easy to ignore my long-term health needs by focusing on what seemed more immediate. Therefore, year upon year, I added the pounds. I heard an inner voice warning me to eat better and to exercise. But I thought my agenda—with all its family needs—was more important. I simply ignored the internal messages.

Eventually, I showed up in my doctor's office 18 months late for a check up and 50 pounds overweight. My justifications to my doctor sounded like gibberish—even to me. I left reeling with the blunt truth of my current physical condition.

In 1 Corinthians 6:19, Paul says our bodies are not our own, but temples of the Holy Spirit. Somehow, along the way, I chose to ignore that. I would never treat my own church the way I had treated my body!

I soon learned that correcting disobedience was a lot harder to accomplish than being obedient in the first place. Yet, I found unexpected perks, such as the loss of joint aches and pains, a growing self-esteem, and an absence of guilt at day's end. I'm not there yet, but I certainly am looking forward to a whole and healthy temple in the near future.

Father, In my witness for You, my appearance says something important. Help me stay in Your will today and care for Your temple, my body. Through Christ, amen.

It's Not My Place

Do horses run on rocks? Or does one plow them with oxen? Yet you have turned justice into poison and the fruit of righteousness into wormwood (Amos 6:12, *New American Standard Bible*).

Scripture: Amos 6:6-8, 11-14
Song: "The Bond of Love"

I grew up in the south. For me, that meant a silent code of behavior existed that I secretly believed everyone should follow. I could see someone dressed a bit differently or notice a lack of what I perceived to be "good manners," and my first impulse was to judge them harshly.

As a believer, I've adjusted my southern ways in light of Jesus' example. I can now see that judging is a form of arrogance, that it turns "justice into poison," as the prophet Amos said. For example, in school, if I thought I was doing better than the girl with black nail polish, then I was higher on the plain of social acceptance. That's not a just attitude in the least!

I see things differently now. And growing in my spiritual perception has blessed me with friends I wouldn't have gone near in the past. My friend Danielle is teaching me distance bike riding. My friend John taught me what loving someone unconditionally actually looks like. I suspect these same people might have rejected me in their past, as well. Now we are one in the body of Christ, and we know it.

Heavenly Father, only You know the human heart, and therefore all judgment belongs to You. Thank You for giving me new spiritual eyes that overcome my past prejudices. I praise Your holy name, through Christ my Lord. Amen.

Famine of Truth

"The days are coming," declares the Sovereign LORD, **"when I will send a famine through the land — not a famine of food or a thirst for water, but a famine of hearing the words of the LORD"** (Amos 8:11).

Scripture: Amos 8:11-14
Song: "Lord, We Hear Your Word with Gladness"

In the days of Amos the prophet, Israel was in deep spiritual trouble. Their covenant with God was long forgotten. The people mixed Baal worship with their devotion to the one true Jehovah. And they copied religious activities from pagan systems, incorporating them into their daily lives. Thus, for instance, the sin of Samaria (see v. 14) referred to the worship of Ashima, a Canaanite goddess.

Bottom line: Israel had borrowed gods and accepted counterfeit worship. In fact, their entire culture, their ideals, their standards, and their morality were riddled with sin. What a "famine" of truth! And now the kingdom was in danger of takeover by Assyria and Egypt.

As the book of Amos closes, the destruction of Israel is complete. But "I will bring my people Israel back from exile," God promises in Amos 9:14. In this there is hope: even when Israel was unfaithful, God remained faithful. He is a keeper of promises, and He will restore His people.

Father, thank You for being my faithful, trustworthy Lord. Keep me safe in Your Word today, as You feed me with Your truth. I pray in Jesus' holy name. Amen.

June 22–28. **Jan Pierce** is a retired teacher who lives in Vancouver, Washington, with her husband of 46 years. She travels to India working with churches, orphanages, and schools.

Empty Shells

They sow the wind and reap the whirlwind. The stalk has no head; it will produce no flour. Were it to yield grain, foreigners would swallow it up. Israel is swallowed up; now she is among the nations like something no one wants (Hosea 8:7, 8).

Scripture: Hosea 8:7-14
Song: "Restore Us, O God"

Have you ever cracked open a beautiful, brown walnut only to find a withered, black piece of refuse inside? The perfectly formed and tasty nut meat you anticipated had long since turned to dust. Or worse, it was eaten away by the worm left wiggling inside.

The nation of Israel, now divided into two kingdoms, was a bit like that rotten, empty shell. Israel abandoned God in favor of serving the nations around them. In trying to appease both Egypt and Assyria, they lost the respect of both and became mere shadows of the once-mighty nation they'd been. According to the prophet Hosea, even the meager fruit they might produce would be taken away by their enemies.

It would seem God's people were doomed. But, no! In Hosea 11 we see that God's plan is always to redeem and renew. He says, "'How can I give you up, Ephraim! . . . I will settle them in their homes,' declares the Lord" (vv. 8, 11).

Only the Lord can restore that which was once useless. He takes empty, wasted lives and fills them with vibrant life.

Merciful God, draw me near to Your heart that I might find life in You. Restore me when I stray from Your side. May I bear fruit in Your kingdom. In Christ's name, amen.

A Risk Worth Taking

Because your sins are so many and your hostility so great, the prophet is considered a fool, the inspired person a maniac (Hosea 9:7)

Scripture: Hosea 9:5-9
Song: "We Limit Not the Truth of God"

A missionary friend just spent seven weeks in a prison cell in northern India. He was falsely accused of entering the country illegally. His real "crime" was the fact that he and his wife—and the team of evangelists they've trained—became highly successful at publicly sharing Bible stories. Hindu people were hearing about Jesus. Teams were baptizing scores of new believers, and the Hindu political and religious authorities began to feel threatened. Yet all this man did was . . . speak the truth.

The Old Testament prophets had a difficult assignment. God himself had called them to speak harsh judgments upon Israel. *Beware! Stop! Repent!* they shouted. But the people didn't receive the words, even though they were the truth. And just as the prophets warned, calamity befell Israel.

There is a price to pay for speaking God's truth. Most people don't want to hear words of warning, don't want to believe those words are for them. Sometimes the consequences of speaking truth can be quite serious, as with our missionary friend. But for most of us the risk is much lower. Will we be considered foolish or a bit maniacal? Isn't that a risk worth taking in obedience to almighty God?

Father, grant me courage to speak truth today, to friends and neighbors, with all wisdom and kindness. May my words draw them to Your Son. In His name, amen.

The Danger of Prosperity

Israel was a spreading vine; he brought forth fruit for himself. As his fruit increased, he built more altars . . . The LORD will demolish their altars (Hosea 10:1, 2).

Scripture: Hosea 10:1-8
Song: "Simple Gifts"

During my years as a teacher, I often read a story to my first graders called "The Fisherman and His Wife." The children loved the characters—a poor fisherman and his scheming wife—and they loved the repetitive lines, "Oh fish in the sea, come listen to me, my wife begs a wish, from the magic fish."

The wife was extremely selfish and never satisfied. The fish granted her one wish after another, and the old couple moved from a hut, to a modest home, to a mansion. However, the wife's last request to become Queen of the land cost her everything. She found herself back in the miserable hut, just as she'd begun.

The people of Israel had been prosperous. They'd enjoyed a land of plenty and the favor of their God. Furthermore, they had His protection as long as they worshipped Him only. But as Israel prospered the people moved further and further away from obedience and godliness. The result? They lost everything, were overthrown, and were taken captive by their enemies.

First Timothy 6:6 says, "Godliness with contentment is great gain." Let's focus on loving God—and being content with the good things He gives us.

Loving Father, help me today to take my eyes off of my possessions. I am grateful to You alone for all I have, and I humble myself before You to worship only You. In the name of the Father and of the Son and of the Holy Spirit, I pray. Amen.

Maturity or Folly

It was I who taught Ephraim to walk, taking them by the arms; but they did not realize it was I who healed them. I led them with cords of human kindness, with ties of love. To them I was like one who lifts a little child to the cheek, and I bent down to feed them (Hosea 11:3, 4).

Scripture: Hosea 11:1-7
Song: "Where Cross the Crowded Ways of Life"

Our congregation has a whole raft of new babies — 10 of them born in the past year. We love their chubby cheeks and innocent smiles. And it's a joy to see young parents nurturing these little ones, day by day.

The parents eagerly anticipate the milestone events of baby life — turning over, first words, first steps. But before they know it, those babies will become willful toddlers, then independent elementary students and — horrors — teenagers. Even with the most diligent parenting, some children stray from God's safe pathway. They make poor choices, and parents' hearts break.

God loved Israel as a treasured child, nurturing, training, protecting her. But the people broke His heart. You see, they wanted independence, and their folly was costly. They suffered the loss of God's favor and were overcome by their enemies.

The Bible says, "The fear of Lord is the beginning of wisdom" (Proverbs 9:10). Wisdom and maturity are gained through obedience to God, the one who sees the beginning and the end. It's a lesson worth learning.

Father God, teach me to honor You, worship You, and love You. May I grow up strong in Your love, until the day I stand before You. Through Christ, amen.

Streams in the Desert

Although our sins testify against us, do something, LORD, for the sake of your name. For we have often rebelled; we have sinned against you (Jeremiah 14:7).

Scripture: Jeremiah 14:1-10
Song: "O Healing River"

In the 1930s the heartland of America suffered a devastating drought. Year after year there was no rain, and the people endured dust storms known as black blizzards. Thousands of farm families had to abandon their land during this time of great despair and suffering. The people scattered, searching for a new way to make a living.

God's covenant people suffered a different kind of drought—a drought of the spirit. They too were about to be scattered because they chose to turn away from God. Their lives became more and more barren, their enemies threatening on every side.

Only in their defeated state did they begin to cry out to God for mercy. "Do something," they begged, "not for our sake, but for your own glory." But only streams of living water would restore them. "Rescue us," they called out as they finally saw the result of their sin.

When you and I recognize our sin and surrender to God, only then can He begin to heal our spiritual dryness. Isaiah 35:6 says, "Water will gush forth in the wilderness and streams in the desert." That is beautiful imagery for a simple truth: God surely will rescue His people when they surrender to Him.

Lord, refresh me with Your life-giving waters throughout this day. Restore me to spiritual health, and empower me to serve You all of my life. Through Christ, amen.

Summer Fruit

This is what the Sovereign LORD showed me: a basket of ripe fruit. "What do you see, Amos?" he asked. "A basket of ripe fruit," I answered. Then the LORD said to me, "The time is ripe for my people Israel; I will spare them no longer" (Amos 8:1, 2).

Scripture: Amos 8:1-6, 9, 10
Song: "For the Healing of the Nations"

I live in a beautiful part of the Pacific Northwest, the Willamette Valley. It's home to some of the richest farmland in America. Although urban growth has claimed much of the land, family farms still dot the valley. Many of these are berry farms — blueberries, blackberries, marion berries, and strawberries.

A strawberry farmer's greatest nightmare occurs when our usually temperate climate warms up a bit but stays damp and rainy. Then acres and acres of plump, perfect fruit can turn in just one day to moldy, inedible mush.

Amos envisions a basket of summer fruit. The fruit still looked colorful and good to eat, but it was overripe, past the time of goodness and fit only for destruction. It's a hard word that Amos brought to the people. But they had continued in their sin. And though grace would yet return to the people (see Jeremiah 15:19, "If you repent, I will restore you"), Israel would now experience the shame of exile.

King of glory, give me eyes to see Your truth and a heart of courage to follow it. I want to be a useful servant in Your kingdom. And I lift up my country to You as well. Restore righteousness and justice among us, and bring us back to the honoring of our Creator. Through Christ the Lord. Amen.

It's the Response That Matters

Whoever heard me spoke well of me, and those who saw me commended me (Job 29:11).

Scripture: Job 29:7-17
Song: "Leave It There"

People spoke well of me. The future looked bright. I loved my job and worked hard at it. Then tension developed at my workplace, and I was dismissed. Like Job—who abruptly lost his possessions, his children, and his health—I felt as though all my righteous living had been for nothing. Feeling my reputation was ruined, I wanted to run and hide. *How could God allow such a bad thing to happen to a good person who had done so much for Him?*

A wise old minister suggested I let God protect my reputation rather than trying to defend myself. And before long God blessed me with a new profession and a new direction that greatly enriched my life.

When adversity strikes, we may feel God is unfair. We've been reading our Bibles, praying, and serving. Surely God will reward rather than rob us! But as Job—and I—discovered, God's ways aren't our ways; His timing is not ours. But as our faith is tested, God becomes more real to us.

Circumstances don't ruin a good reputation. It is our *response* to those circumstances. It wasn't long until people once again spoke well of Job. (I hope that will be true of me, as well.)

Lord, guide me through this day, and please forgive my lack of faith when things go wrong. Remind me that You are sovereign in all situations. In Jesus' name, amen.

June 29, 30. **Shirley Brosius** is a writer and speaker living in Millersburg, Pennsylvania. She and her husband, Bill, have two married sons, five grandchildren, and a daughter waiting in Heaven.

Looking Back

If I have denied justice to any of my servants, whether male or female, when they had a grievance against me, what will I do when God confronts me? (Job 31:13, 14).

Scripture: Job 31:13-22
Song: "Peace Like a River"

When Job looked at his life in the rearview mirror, he saw he had lived with integrity and treated others justly. I cannot always make the same claim. In fact, I recall an incident that happened six years ago for which I needed to make amends.

On a snowy winter day, a teenage driver had parked so close to my car by a beauty salon that I scratched the paint on her car door when I tried to open mine. The salon owner said she would inform the driver, emphasizing that it was the driver's own fault for careless parking. But as I thought back on it, I knew I should have offered to pay to repair that scratch. So I wrote a check for $50 and mailed it to the girl's family with a note of apology. The family was kind enough to send me a Facebook message saying they tore up my check—and suggested I go shopping with that money!

It does our hearts good to look in the rearview mirror of life from time to time to see what our conscience reflects. While amends may cost us something, the cost of withholding amends may be a guilty conscience that hinders our relationship with God and others.

Lord, I know that my sins rob me of peace. Thank You for the grace of forgiveness that comes from You and others. Help me to pass on such mercy as opportunities arise. In Jesus' name I pray. Amen.

My Prayer Notes

_____
_____
_____
_____
_____
_____
_____
_____
_____
_____
_____
_____
_____
_____
_____
_____
_____
_____
_____
_____
_____
_____
_____
_____
_____
_____

DEVOTIONS®

July

For the LORD is righteous, he loves justice;
the upright will see his face.

—*Psalm 11:7*

Gary Allen Wilde, Editor   **Margaret Williams,** Project Editor   Photo iStockphoto | Thinkstock®

DEVOTIONS® is published quarterly by Standard Publishing, Cincinnati, Ohio, www.standardpub.com.
© 2014 by Standard Publishing. All rights reserved. Topics based on the Home Daily Bible Readings,
International Sunday School Lessons. © 2012 by the Committee on the Uniform Series. Printed in
the U.S.A. All Scripture quotations, unless otherwise indicated, are taken from the *HOLY BIBLE,
NEW INTERNATIONAL VERSION®. NIV®.* Copyright © 1973, 1978, 1984, 2011 by Biblica, Inc.®
Used by permission of Zondervan. All rights reserved. *New American Standard Bible (NASB),*
© The Lockman Foundation, 1960, 1962, 1963, 1968, 1971, 1972, 1973, 1975, 1977, 1995. *King
James Version (KJV),* public domain.

Snug as a Bug

LORD my God, I take refuge in you; save and deliver me from all who pursue me (Psalm 7:1).

Scripture: Psalm 7:1-8
Song: "In the Hollow of His Hand"

I vividly remember as a child running home from a neighbor's house during a thunderstorm. We lived in the country, and on the last leg of my sprint, a bolt of lightning struck an apple tree just as I ran by it. At least that is how it appeared to me. Terrified by the loud clap of thunder and gasping for breath, I raced up our lane.

Of course, the moment I slammed our screen door behind me, I felt safe. Even though lightning could strike our house as well, that never occurred to me. Once I reached my mother's arms, my heart stopped racing, and I felt safe and secure.

So it is when we run to God. Whether our pursuers are difficult people, past emotional hurts, or present challenges, they may cause us to panic and attempt escape. However, just as I felt secure once I reached the protection of my home, so we can feel secure when we recognize God as our refuge, waiting to protect us, to shelter us from storm. No matter how difficult circumstances appear to be, He is in control and He is with us. Rather than bolt, we can boast of the safety we find in God's embrace.

Lord, as I see Your hand in nature, remind me that You hold control over all things—and over my circumstances as well. You are my refuge. In Jesus' name, amen.

July 1–5. **Shirley Brosius** is a writer and speaker living in Millersburg, Pennsylvania. She and her husband, Bill, have two married sons, five grandchildren, and a daughter waiting in Heaven.

You Reap What You Sow

Whoever digs a hole and scoops it out falls into the pit they have made (Psalm 7:15).

Scripture: Psalm 7:9-17
Song: "Bringing in the Sheaves"

Whether they receive a paddling, such as we may have received as children, or a "time out," children of every generation quickly learn that their behavior carries consequences. If siblings cooperate, they may be rewarded with a cone of ice cream. If they don't play nicely together, they may find themselves alone in their rooms. Their actions result in consequences.

So do ours. Our consequences may not be as immediate, but they are as certain. If we harbor unforgiveness in our hearts, we may develop insomnia. If we fail to be friendly toward others, we may become lonely. If we treat loved ones unkindly, they may fail to show us compassion as our own needs arise. On the other hand, if we extend grace and forgiveness, we usually receive the same in return.

Therefore, as Christians, we need never seek revenge on someone who has hurt us. As Psalm 7 reminds us, those who do evil often find themselves tangled in its deadly web. In fact, they may bring upon themselves a far worse consequence than we might wish for them. For our part, we can leave things in God's very capable hands. We can simply do the right thing rather than attempting to get even.

Lord, when someone hurts me, help me to extend the forgiveness that You have extended to me in Christ. Rather than seek revenge, help me to leave the consequences of past hurts where they belong—on Your doorstep. Through Christ, amen.

No Bullying Allowed

Arise, LORD, do not let mortals triumph; let the nations be judged in your presence. Strike them with terror, LORD; let the nations know they are only mortal (Psalm 9:19, 20).

Scripture: Psalm 9:15-20
Song: "God of Our Fathers"

The leaders of powerful nations may feel they rule the world. They may think no other nation can thwart their wishes, stand in the way of their advancements, or stop them from doing as they please. But there is a ruler even more powerful: God. He allows nations to rise, but He also permits their decline, if they do not respect His principles.

Therefore, we are called to pray for our nations' leaders: that they may be wise and discerning, that they will take into account what is best for all peoples, that they fear God and seek to know Him while withstanding any temptation to flaunt their power. We can pray that we ourselves may lead quiet, peaceable lives in our homes, our communities, and the world.

No nation is immune from the justice of God. We do well to thank God for the blessings He has granted us in spite of our imperfections. We do well to seek His forgiveness and mercy for past sins that are dark blots on our collective conscience. And we do well to pray that righteousness may reign supreme in our nation and in the world.

Lord, Your Word reminds me that "righteousness exalts a nation" (Proverbs 14:34). I pray that Your Spirit might inspire me to live with honesty and integrity. Work through our leaders to bring world peace, and work through Christians to bring the peace of Christ to the hearts of all people. In His name I pray. Amen.

Needs, Wants, and Me

Wealth is worthless in the day of wrath, but righteousness delivers from death (Proverbs 11:4).

Scripture: Proverbs 11:1-10
Song: "I'd Rather Have Jesus"

I need only watch television commercials to become dissatisfied with my life: Am I driving a classy car? Do I have the latest gadgets for cooking? Am I using beauty products to keep me looking younger? Then there's the content of the programs themselves: Am I enjoying the luxuries of sitcom characters? the sensual pleasures portrayed on the screen? the runway fashions? Perhaps my faith restricts my enjoyment of life.

If God is mentioned at all on television, it's often flippantly. Judging by the content of many programs, one would hardly guess we are a nation founded under God. So I simply ask: During the hours we spend in front of our television sets, might we be listening to the wrong voices? Do they suggest we should trust in possessions for satisfaction instead of trusting in God?

The message of the Bible is that satisfaction comes to us as our hearts rest in Christ. As I spend time in Scripture, I am molded by faith-building words that counter the "gimme, gimme, gimme" messages of television. As I spend time in nature, I am filled with praise for God's creation. And as I respond to a needy world, I become content and grateful for the blessings I already have.

Lord, help me to see that following You doesn't limit me but rather frees me to become all You call me to be. Lead me not into temptation, but deliver me from a world system where wealth and power might lure me away. In Jesus' name, amen.

Rocky Paths and Muddy Trails

Does the LORD become impatient? Does he do such things? Do not my words do good to the one whose ways are upright? (Micah 2:7).

Scripture: Micah 2:4-11
Song: "I Must Tell Jesus"

As my husband and I climbed over tree roots and rocks, I realized the park attendant's idea of an "easy" trail must be quite different from mine. Our path ran beside a sparkling brook that splashed and gurgled its way through shallow falls, but I certainly hoped the trail's condition would improve. It didn't. In fact, we soon found ourselves tiptoeing across black mud, gingerly stepping on mossy rocks left slick by morning mist.

At the trail's midpoint, where we needed to cross a creek, we found a bridge swept to the bank by a flood. We had to carefully jump from rock to rock to continue. Eventually, by faithfully following the blue-paint markings on trees, we arrived at our destination, safe and sound.

The people of Israel also expected conditions to be quite different from what they encountered. After all, they were God's chosen people. Why was their nation threatened? Why were the rocks of God's discipline and judgment obstructing their path? False prophets told them God would never let such things happen to them. But through their struggles, the people learned that God is faithful. And the true prophet Micah offered them hope for deliverance from their foes.

Lord, sometimes the pathways of my life turn rough and rocky. Yet You have set the course that will lead me to deeper trust. Thank You, in Jesus' name. Amen.

Whom Can I Follow?

Do not follow the crowd in doing wrong. When you give testimony in a lawsuit, do not pervert justice by siding with the crowd (Exodus 23:2).

Scripture: Exodus 23:1-8
Song: "Fully Surrendered"

Throughout nature we find valuable power structures. Elephant herds have dominant females to guide them to water and food. Geese take turns navigating the flock over hundreds of miles to their winter destinations. Ants march to the cadence of a commander to defend their domain. And lemmings follow their pack leaders without hesitation over cliffs of death.

Nonetheless, not all creatures share the instinct to "elect" a leader. Sheep, for example, seem to wander aimlessly over a pasture, gnawing at the grass until the ground lies bare. None take the initiative to climb the next hill to find a fresh meadow for grazing. Therefore, they need shepherds to guide them.

Although human beings understand the necessity of hierarchy, the Bible compares us to sheep. Unable to decipher the best way for ourselves, we often mindlessly follow questionable leadership. Therefore, wrong is strong, complacency rules, and justice is perverted.

Unlike sheep, however, we have a choice. We can turn from our "earthly shepherds" and follow the good shepherd.

O God, I am but a sheep—timid, unsure, hungry, and vulnerable. I need a shepherd to protect, feed, and guide me. Thank You for Your care. Through Christ, amen.

July 6–12. **Brenda K. Hendricks** enjoys writing and painting for children. She lives in Pennsylvania with her husband and ADHD Airedale, Hunter. Both give her an abundance of writing material.

Whom Can I Believe?

I am against your magic charms with which you ensnare people like birds and I will tear them from your arms (Ezekiel 13:20).

Scripture: Ezekiel 13:15-23
Song: "The Solid Rock"

As technology improves, knowledge flourishes and wondrous conveniences increase. But sadly, for every achievement of scientific understanding, a kind of deception follows.

Examples? A simple tweak of a photograph ruins a reputation. Electronic games consume our time and coarsen our language. Then there's the myriad worthless new products promising good health, financial gain, and the ultimate pleasures.

Like shoddy retailers, some religious leaders use modern technology to prey on unsuspecting individuals. These false prophets attract the seeker with profound speeches through Internet services. Some even go so far as to offer items of wood, stones, and precious metals that assure "miraculous" answers to prayer. These are dubious claims that still ensnare many.

Although technology has increased far beyond the imaginations of Ezekiel's day, wisdom has seemed to decrease. On that score we have no right to what some have called a "chronological snobbery." Let us never assume that a culture will inevitably evolve into something better than it was. Only God's leading can bring us to the best place personally and culturally.

Heavenly Father, when prayer cloths, fancy crosses, and other manufactured devices lure me from Your presence, bring me back to a humble heart, a bent knee, and an outstretched hand. In Jesus' name, amen.

Who Shall Judge?

Now let the fear of the LORD be on you. Judge carefully, for with the LORD our God there is no injustice or partiality or bribery (2 Chronicles 19:7).

Scripture: 2 Chronicles 19:4-10
Song: "Higher Ground"

The parking lot of a local restaurant is U-shaped with a one-way lane running from the entrance to the exit. Facing the building, you'll see the entrance sign in bold print on the right and the exit sign on the left. It makes no difference if you are traveling from the north or the south—the entrance is on the right and the exit is on the left. Occasionally, some people think the rules don't apply to them. So, naturally, they enter the exit lane.

One day while leaving the premises in my car, I encountered such a person and I wanted to refuse to budge from the center of the lane. I longed to become her judge, jury, and executioner!

I know and obey the rules of the road. I expect everyone else to do the same. So, naturally, I wanted to inch my way toward the exit, forcing her into a nearby parking space.

Believers make judgment calls daily in agreement with local regulations. Similarly, we must act according to the standard of God's character, revealed in Scripture, and extend love, mercy, and kindness to others. With that thought in mind, I pulled into an empty parking space and allowed the other driver to continue on her trip.

Lord, You are the judge of all mankind. Help me to always abide by Your precepts carefully, faithfully, and wholeheartedly. And at the same time, teach me to love, extend mercy, and to be kind to others. In Jesus' name, amen.

Who Can Enter?

LORD, who may dwell in your sacred tent? Who may live on your holy mountain? (Psalm 15:1).

Scripture: Psalm 15
Song: "Accepted in the Beloved"

During my school years, I never tried to join certain extra-curricular groups. Why? Well, softball coaches frowned upon ducking at fly balls. Cheerleading depended on the ability to do cartwheels and jump higher than two inches off the ground. Members of the chorus scowled at sour notes and monotone meanderings. The marching band director even insisted on a certain amount of innate rhythm. Imagine that!

Not everyone possesses the skills required to participate in such organizations, and I'm one of them. No matter how hard I would've tried or how patient and persistent the coaches and directors may have been, I would have failed. I simply had to accept my inability to perform as an athlete or a musician. Eventually, however, I found my place in the visual arts.

Finding our places in God's kingdom may seem daunting at first. But it's not; it's delightful, an invitation of pure graciousness. Although God has established a "prerequisite" for entering His presence, no skill is involved, and He promises to equip us with all He requires. It's called a willingness to trust Him. As we trust Him, He replaces our inadequacies with Jesus' righteousness. He dwells within us, teaching us how to walk blamelessly, to speak the truth, and to love, honor, and respect others.

Heavenly Father, thank You for providing entrance into Your kingdom through Jesus Christ. I have found my place, and I'm thriving! Through Christ, amen.

Whom Can I Trust?

Watch out for false prophets. They come to you in sheep's clothing, but inwardly they are ferocious wolves (Matthew 7:15).

Scripture: Matthew 7:15-20
Song: "My Soul, Be on Thy Guard"

I thought a lap desk in my living room would help increase my productivity while I enjoyed a little family time. I researched the market and ordered an item that promised to deliver.

The lap desk arrived in good condition. Nevertheless, the top of it was constructed of plastic-coated, wafer-thin chipboard. The material on the bottom looked like cheap felt that would wear through with minimal use. It didn't fit on my lap correctly, so I had to turn it backwards to keep my tablet from slipping off. This meant the cup holder was covered. And I had to twist the attached reading light to make it come close to hitting the tablet screen, which, in turn, caused the light to loosen. Inside, a Styrofoam block and a cushion of tiny Styrofoam balls offered unreliable support. Although I managed to make it work, I was more than a little displeased with this product.

"Buyer beware" when you purchase online. Serious disappointment may well follow. However, trusting the wrong people in other areas of life leads to a more serious devastation, especially in our Christian walk. The Lord cautions us about committing our spiritual well-being to just anyone. Through prayer and Bible study, we learn to make wise choices.

Father, grant me discernment when choosing leaders for the church and mentors for myself. Guard me from wolves in sheep's clothing. In Jesus' name, amen.

Who Created These Hands?

It is I who made the earth and created mankind on it. My own hands stretched out the heavens; I marshaled their starry hosts (Isaiah 45:12).

Scripture: Isaiah 45:5-13
Song: "My Times Are in Thy Hand"

Hands are fascinating. They perform intricate surgeries to save lives. They cradle newborn babies, caress the brows of the elderly, embrace the brokenhearted. They applaud the victor and wipe the loser's tears. Hands scrub floors, wash dishes, dust furniture, and fold laundry. They swing bats and catch fly balls. They build rockets to explore space and microscopes to examine electrons. Hands produce music, paintings, sculpture, tapestries, needlepoint, and the written word.

This seemingly endless creativity may be the most marvelous aspect of the human hand. However, its boundaries only stretch to the end of our finite minds.

Yet our creativity tells of our connection with the master creator. God used His own hands to shape us in His image. As He breathed the breath of life into us, He endowed us with imaginations and formed our hands with great potential.

Although this world confines us, God's creativity flows through eternity. His ideas abound, and His hands know no limitations. With these attributes, He tirelessly and continuously develops His most wondrous work—Christ's image in us.

Heavenly Father, what honor You've granted me in the gift of creativity! And then to think that Your hand is upon me, creating within me the image of Your Son. How great and wonderful You are! Through Christ my Savior, I pray. Amen.

Who Is Qualified?

As for me, I am filled with power, with the Spirit of the LORD, and with justice and might, to declare to Jacob his transgression, to Israel his sin (Micah 3:8).

Scripture: Micah 3:5-12
Song: "Spirit of the Living God"

Years ago, I watched a movie about two men who survived an airplane crash in the middle of nowhere. The pilot was critically wounded and needed an immediate tracheotomy. Desperate to save his friend's life, the passenger managed to connect with an experienced surgeon on the wreck's still-working radio system.

As the surgeon explained the procedure, the passenger used his pocketknife to slit his buddy's throat. The casing of a common ink pen substituted for a breathing tube. Naturally, the pilot survived the operation; a helicopter rescued them, and they all lived happily ever after.

I've found that speaking with people about my faith can be as scary as performing an emergency tracheotomy! Many of us feel we "lack the formal training" to lead others to Jesus. But are only seminary grads qualified to witness?

God simply calls us to tell what we know of His goodness, in our words and our deeds. As intimidating as our calling may be, we can proceed with confidence. Rarely would we ever point to peoples' sins, as Micah did. Rather, the Spirit of the living God will help us invite others to a gracious rescue.

Heavenly Father, may my confidence rest in Micah's statement—"I am filled with power, with the Spirit of the Lord, and with justice and might"—that I may fearlessly speak of Your grace in my life. I pray in the name of my Lord Jesus Christ. Amen.

Showing Mercy

He defends the cause of the fatherless and the widow, and loves the foreigner residing among you, giving them food and clothing. (Deuteronomy 10:18).

Scripture: Deuteronomy 10:12-22
Song: "I'm a Pilgrim"

Bill's childhood nanny in Ada, Oklahoma, not only took care of him while his mother worked, but she also took him with her on her daily missions of mercy. "Kathryn Taylor, or K.K., as I called her," he says, "went to the church every day to sort and fold clothes given for those in need. She took home garments to launder and iron if needed. On Mondays, she collected the altar flowers, put them in vases, and delivered them to shut-ins."

"Doctors and dentists in town saved out-of-date magazines for her, and I went with her to gather them. We made up little boxes, each with several magazines, a Bible, and fruit donated by her husband's produce company."

"She'd go to the jail," Bill continues, "and the guards simply unlocked every door so she could wander freely from cell to cell. She gave each new inmate a gift box. The men behaved themselves because they so appreciated K.K.'s kindness and care."

Kathryn was still making her rounds, with assistance, at age 92. "God put her in my life," says Bill, "not just to care for me as a kid, but to help me understand the meaning of generosity."

Lord, my own mother moved in the gift of mercy much like Kathryn. Thank You for her influence on my life. May I too demonstrate Your love today. In Your name, amen.

July 13–19. **Patty Duncan** stays busy during the school year teaching fifth graders at Eugene Christian school. She also leads a weekly after-school art class and summertime art camp.

Until the Day . . . Help!

Who makes them deaf or mute? Who gives them sight or makes them blind? Is it not I, the LORD? (Exodus 4:11).

Scripture: Exodus 4:10-17
Song: "Open My Eyes, That I May See"

Helen Keller suffered a severe illness and lost her sight and hearing when she was about 2 years old. She couldn't speak, except to giggle if pleased or scream in a choked voice if unhappy. But just before Helen turned 7, her father took her to Alexander Graham Bell. He directed them to an institute for the blind, and they sent Anne Sullivan to help them.

The partially blind Sullivan firmly and patiently worked with the young girl, spelling out letters into her hand and refusing to give in to her temper tantrums. Miraculously, her method worked and finally taught Helen how to communicate.

At age 10, Helen took lessons and learned to speak. With Sullivan interpreting for her, she later went to college and graduated with honors. That's when Helen began working to improve the lives of others who were blind and deaf. She spent the rest of her life advocating for them, writing books, and lecturing around the world.

Though God has it in His power to give or withhold sight and hearing, He allows these difficulties into the world until the great day of resurrection. Until then, let us work, like Helen Keller, to help those around us who need our eyes, our ears, and, so often, just a helping hand.

O God, when tragedy leaves someone with a great loss of sense or movement, please come alongside them. Give them new purpose and ministry. In Christ, amen.

Environmental Impact

Now this horde will lick up all that is around us, as the ox licks up the grass of the field (Numbers 22:4, *New American Standard Bible*).

Scripture: Numbers 22:1-14
Song: "As We Gather"

What is a church? In the Middle Ages, splendid cathedrals rose to the sky with elaborate spires and stunning stained glass windows. They stand today, and tourists marvel at their majesty.

Yet while buildings provide the setting for people to worship, fellowship, and learn, the church, at its most basic level, is not the structure. It's the people who gather there.

In fact, some congregations don't even own a building. For instance, New Hope Church in Honolulu, Hawaii, meets on a high school campus. The minister, Wayne Cordeiro, explains that land is so expensive and scarce on Oahu, he considers it better stewardship to rent the school.

Ekklesia, my home church, gathers for services in a middle-school gymnasium, with children's classes held in the cafeteria. Five-years old, the church has grown from a handful meeting for Bible study to nearly 2,000 people. Dozens of volunteers, serving with cheerful hearts, set up and tear down a stage and sound equipment and rearrange schoolrooms to make it all work. In a town that emphasizes "living green," all of this demonstrates careful stewardship of spiritual resources too.

Lord, I thank You for *Ekklesia's* focus on reaching people rather than building an edifice. Thank You for the intense friendliness shown at our gatherings and the energy and kindness of all who serve every week. In Jesus' name, amen.

Sacred Solitude

Only the word which I speak to you shall you do
(Numbers 22:20, *New American Standard Bible*).

Scripture: Numbers 22:15-21
Song: "You May Have the Joy-Bells"

Ice coated the steps of my porch one morning as I hurried to
load my suitcase into the car. I slipped on the ice and fell, hard.
By now I'd be half an hour late for the overnight women's retreat. Should I just stay home? Unable to contact the leader to
cancel, I drove nearly an hour to the destination.

To my surprise, a dozen ladies had waited for me in the
lodge of the camp, unwilling to begin without me. The leader
explained that our 24 hours of solitude with the Lord would begin with group worship and sharing. Then we would maintain
silence, speaking only if absolutely necessary.

I asked for prayer for my neck and back, which were hurting.
The women prayed, then a physical therapist taught me gentle
exercises to help the muscles relax and ease the pain.

For several hours that afternoon I sat at a table in the lodge
poring over a concordance for every reference to "unfailing
love." I looked up each Scripture and wrote it on one note card
until I had a set of 30, enough for a month.

In the days that followed, I read one card each morning,
reminding myself of hearing from the Lord tenderly at that
blessed rustic camp.

Loving Lord, You are so willing to spend time with me if I take time with You. Thank
You for communicating with me through Your Word, which comforts and confronts,
strengthens and sustains. In Your precious name, amen.

Divine Opposition? Good!

I have come here to oppose you because your path is a reckless one before me (Numbers 22:32).

Scripture: Numbers 22:31-38
Song: "He Leadeth Me"

On the 4th of July, our family got up early for the big parade. We'd drive our 1950 Buick in the Classic Cars division, and my mother would show off her olive green 1971 Plymouth Scamp.

Waiting for Mama to arrive, we were eating breakfast when the phone rang. A man explained that he'd seen a little old lady driving a car the wrong way on the expressway! Drivers passed her, blasting horns. Seeing her perilous situation, he drove alongside her, across the concrete median, honking and hollering out the window. "Pull over!" he yelled. Eventually she heard him and complied. Parking his car safely on the shoulder, he ran across to her car. "Scoot over, Sweetie" he gently told Mama. "I'm driving."

She slid over on the bench seat, and he drove her car to safety before phoning us. Construction signs had apparently confused her, and she'd taken the wrong exit, heading eastbound. Knowing our house was to the west, she had turned left, directly into oncoming traffic, and then just kept driving until the kind man intercepted her. Although she was a bit shaken, she still enjoyed the parade . . . but riding in our car. (Note: Sometimes, when we're reckless, it's good to have somebody oppose us!)

Lord, I'm so thankful You rescued my mother on that 4th of July. I'm sure I have no idea how many times You have rescued me from danger! In Jesus' name, amen.

Carrying God's Message

Must I not speak what the LORD puts in my mouth? (Numbers 23:12).

Scripture: Numbers 23:1-12
Song: "Send the Light"

As I neared the bike path near my home, I noticed a woman sitting on the pavement with her dog. I hurried over to see if she was hurt. She was fine and just resting in the sunshine.

I admired her Corgi. "She's gotten a little pudgy," she said pleasantly as she stood, "so the vet has prescribed walks—and I need them too."

We chatted awhile, her blue eyes sparkling. Then I said good-bye and began my brisk walk. I was drawn to her openness and, as I walked, thought of asking her to church. Catching up to her in the parking lot, I invited her to our services. "What kind of church is it?" she asked.

"It's a simple, Bible-believing church," I explained. "Our minister teaches through books of the Bible. It's all about Jesus."

"I used to go to church until I moved here eight years ago. I have a 2-year-old son, and he's very active. It would be hard for him to sit through a service."

"We do have children's classes—and energetic people who care for them." We visited a bit more, exchanged names, and hugged each other before parting. I'm praying for my new friend and thankful to have met this lovely young woman.

Lord, I love Your divine appointments! You said to lift our eyes to the harvest fields, for they are ripe, and You are calling people to yourself. Bless my new friend and bring her back into fellowship with You. In Your name, amen.

Not by My Hand

Shall I offer my firstborn for my transgression, the fruit of my body for the sin of my soul? (Micah 6:7).

Scripture: Micah 6:3-8
Song: "He Who Began a Good Work in You"

Lynette had a miscarriage before giving birth to a healthy, full-term baby girl. Three miscarriages followed, including a stillborn son, then a difficult pregnancy with months of bed rest and a premature daughter. She was definitely done with having children. A year later, a doctor diagnosed her with CMV, cytomegalovirus. It only causes serious problems during pregnancy. "No problem," she said, "I'm on the pill."

Two weeks later, a blood test revealed she was pregnant. Suspecting a life-threatening tubal pregnancy, her doctor performed tests, explaining the potential birth defects CMV could cause. He showed her pictures of babies with anencephaly (no brain) and hydrocephalus (fluid on the brain). Then he offered the option of abortion.

Sitting in his office in shock, Lynette nevertheless gathered her composure. "I understand why you have to tell me this," she said, "but if this child is going to die, it will not be by my hand."

Visits to a perinatologist later showed the brain developing normally. Lynette went into pre-term labor and endured some bed rest but delivered a 9-pound girl two weeks past her due date. Hallelujah!

Lord, thank You for letting me hear this amazing story. Thank You for the courage of this young mother in carrying her child, in spite of incredible odds against her. Praise You for sustaining mother and child. Through Christ the Lord, amen.

How Long, O Lord?

I trust in your unfailing love; my heart rejoices in your salvation (Psalm 13:5).

Scripture: Psalm 13
Song: "Softly and Tenderly"

My dad's health had been failing for over a year. My sisters, brother, and I always hoped he'd get better. And so did he.

He entered the nursing home figuring that three square meals, proper administration of his meds, and regular physical therapy would speed his recovery. But those things didn't help. Finally, his doctor told him he would die soon.

Dad was relieved. He'd been fighting a losing battle for a long time. He was ready to go home to Heaven.

But we were not ready to see him go. The round-the-clock hours we spent with him during the days before he died made us long for more time with him.

The most difficult part of grief has been dealing with the regrets, as I considered the things I would have done differently had I known what I know now.

Perhaps you are experiencing similar waves of heartache and regret. During times like these, it's good to remember that God cares. Yet it's OK to cry out, as the psalmist did, "How long. . . How long . . . How long, O Lord?" Eventually, as we trust in His steadfast love, our hearts will begin to rejoice once again.

Dear Lord God, please help me through this time of sadness. Remind me, Lord, of the joy I can have in You, both now and for all eternity, thanks to Jesus. Amen.

July 20–26. **Kathy Hardee** writes from her home in rural Mendota, Illinois. She likes to fish, ride her motorcycle with her husband, work in the yard, and spend time with her family.

Our Forgiving God

You have not strengthened the weak or healed the sick or bound up the injured. You have not brought back the strays or searched for the lost. You have ruled them harshly and brutally (Ezekiel 34:4).

Scripture: Ezekiel 34:1-6
Song: "Gentle Shepherd"

My aunt and uncle thought they were doing the best thing possible for their children when they enrolled them in a parochial grade school. The school's rules were strict, but their kids were obedient, so they figured there wouldn't be a problem.

They were wrong. One day two little girls, my cousin and her friend, decided to try smoking. When I was young, just about everyone tried at least one cigarette. The horrible taste was punishment enough for those who didn't get caught. For those who did get caught, a strong reprimand usually sufficed.

But when the school officials found out that my cousin had taken a puff, she was expelled. Even though this happened over 40 years ago, it came rushing to my mind after reading today's Scripture.

Aren't you glad our God doesn't react to our sin with immediate force and harshness? He is nothing like those school officials or Judah's destructive leaders. He strengthens the weak, heals the sick, binds up the injured, and brings back those who have strayed. Our shepherd tends His sheep with patience.

Dear Lord God, thank You for being patient with me. Help me treat others with the same kindness You always show me. In Jesus' name, amen.

Dogs, Sheep, and People

I will search for the lost and bring back the strays. I will bind up the injured and strengthen the weak (Ezekiel 34:16).

Scripture: Ezekiel 34:7-16
Song: "The Way of the Cross Leads Home"

Our golden retriever, Waylon, was a wanderer. We were used to getting calls regarding our dog. One time, a family found him swimming in the Illinois River. Another time, he showed up at my dad's automobile dealership. And when we moved from the west side of town to the north, he took many jaunts back to our old neighborhood.

I once read about Bucky, a black Labrador, who traveled 500 miles to reunite with his owner. And I remember hearing a story about a dog who was sold to a family 2,000 miles away. The dog disappeared from his new owner, and six months later appeared at his old home.

Dogs can pretty much take care of themselves. And if they want to get back home, they're usually able to do so. But sheep are a different story. Once a sheep strays, it will never find its way back home. That's why one of the most important duties of a shepherd is to find lost sheep and bring them back to the fold.

Aren't you glad we have a shepherd who is committed to finding and restoring His wandering sheep? We can pray with confidence because we have a good shepherd who will not rest until He has brought all of His loved ones home.

Father, thank You for always being faithful to bring me back to Your side whenever I stray away from You. I praise Your holy name, through Christ my Lord. Amen.

God With Us

Then they will know that I, the LORD their God, am with them and that they, the Israelites, are my people, declares the Sovereign LORD (Ezekiel 34:30).

Scripture: Ezekiel 34:23-31
Song: "More Light Shall Break"

My dad loved it when I prayed with him. During the months before he died, I often ended our visits with a prayer. When the hospice nurse said Dad had less than two days to live, I asked God to let me be with him when he died. I wanted to say good-bye with a prayer, one last time.

All day Friday, Dad's condition stayed the same. On Saturday evening, we noticed his breathing had changed. My sisters, brother, and I gathered around him, and I knew it was time to pray.

I began my prayer with Psalm 23. As I said the words, "Yea, though I walk through the valley of the shadow of death" (v. 4, *KJV*), my dad was walking with God through that valley.

When I finished praying and opened my eyes, Dad was gone. He had quietly, peacefully, taken his last breath.

My brother said, "That was perfect."

God's presence with us made all the difference. He ushered my dad into Heaven and comforted us in that room.

We need not fear the future. God's presence will bring peace to Israel, and to you and me just when we need it most.

Almighty and most merciful God, please give me faith to rest in the promise of Your presence with me. Fill me today with Your peace. In the name of the Father and of the Son and of the Holy Spirit, I pray. Amen.

A Remedy for Trouble

What misery is mine! I am like one who gathers summer fruit at the gleaning of the vineyard; there is no cluster of grapes to eat, none of the early figs that I crave (Micah 7:1).

Scripture: Micah 7:1-6
Song: "Trust and Obey"

God gave me a very special friend. Her name is Karen. Karen probably prays for my children more than I do. Her prayer life amazes me.

If I have a problem or concern, I call Karen. I depend on her prayers and the God who answers them. I've called her often to thank her and tell her, "God answered your prayers for me!" And many times I've shared with her how God has blessed me, and she has exclaimed, "That's exactly what I was praying for you!"

But I must confess, her prayers sometimes seem too brave for me. For example, when her children stray from the Lord, she asks God to bring them nothing but trouble. She said, "I hope nothing goes right for them until they turn back to God."

The turmoil Micah speaks of in today's Scripture reminds me of Karen's prayers. God sometimes sends trials and troubles into individual lives and nations as a consequence of disobedience to His Word. Not always, of course. Most of the time our troubles are simply part and parcel of being human on earth until the kingdom fully comes.

Father in Heaven, I praise You for Your patience with me and the people I love. Please call our nation—and my loved ones—back into a right relationship with You. Let my love for them be a beacon of Your own love. In Jesus' name, amen.

For Sure!

But as for me, I watch in hope for the LORD, I wait for God my Savior; my God will hear me (Micah 7:7).

Scripture: Micah 7:7-11
Song: "In the Sweet By and By"

Ten hospice volunteers gathered around a conference room table. The speaker began her presentation with a simple question: *What do you know for sure?* She asked each of us to state our name and then share one thing that we knew to be true.

I thought the question was kind of silly; too easy to take seriously. Many things came to my mind, but to my surprise, the others were stumped. I'll never forget their dismay. Seven volunteers out of 10 said they couldn't think of anything that they knew to be true, for sure.

Aren't you glad God gave us His Word so that we could know many truths? We know God loves us and sent His only Son to take the punishment for our sins. We know God works all things together for the good of those who love Him. We know that God is preparing a place for us in Heaven, where we will live eternally with Him.

And Micah, the author of today's Scripture, knew something wonderful too. He knew for sure that God would hear him, and if God heard him, He would also act on his behalf. We can know that too!

Lord God, I praise You today for the confidence I can have in You. I praise You for the written Word that witnesses to Jesus—the living Word. Please give me the courage to live according to His truth today. In Jesus' name, amen.

Forgive and Forget

You will again have compassion on us; you will tread our sins underfoot and hurl all our iniquities into the depths of the sea (Micah 7:19).

Scripture: Micah 7:14-20
Song: "My Sins Are Gone"

My husband and I don't argue well. If I get upset with him, he becomes upset with me . . . for being upset with him. If it seems as though I'm blaming him, he quickly concedes by saying, "I know; it's always my fault."

Even though communication is key to having a good relationship, I thought it would be best for my marriage if I just "let things go." The problem? — I wasn't letting things go. I was letting them *simmer*. Before long, I had a list of unresolved disputes tucked deeply away in my memory.

Today's Scripture reminds me of the day I destroyed that list. I realized it had to be done away with if I wanted a happy marriage. First Corinthians 13:5 says, "[Love] keeps no record of wrongs." And that's the kind of love God showers down. He treads our iniquities under foot and remembers our sins no more.

God forgives us, over and over again, because Jesus paid the penalty for all our sin — past, present, and future. Perhaps the best way for us to demonstrate God's love is to forgive and forget. With God's help we can forgive the people we care about and praise Him for the many times He has forgiven us.

Merciful God, thank You for sending Your Son to bring me forgiveness and abundant life. Please give me courage to forgive others as You have forgiven me. In the precious name of Jesus I pray. Amen.

Sin Separates

Your iniquities have separated you from your God; your sins have hidden his face from you, so that he will not hear (Isaiah 59:2).

Scripture: Isaiah 59:1-14
Song: "Nothing but the Blood"

One of my favorite children's books is *Yummers!* by James Marshall. Emily Pig goes for a walk, all along the way passing by delicious-looking treats she just can't resist. Hot dogs, scones, milk shakes, candied apples . . . "Oh, yummers!" Emily has to have them all. Of course, after gorging on so much food, Emily feels sick. But the next morning, when she considers what caused her tummy ache, do you know what she says? (Spoiler alert!) "It must have been all that walking!" This lovable character, oblivious to the real cause of her troubles, makes us laugh.

Today's Scripture presents a more serious set of troubles, however: people walking in darkness, not being heard by God. Like Emily, they may not know the cause of their distress. But Isaiah explains clearly that their sins have separated them from God and have kept Him from hearing them (see John 9:31).

Thankfully, verse 1 reminds us that God can save, and He can hear, as long as the barrier of sin is removed. So, is there an area of your life where your own sins could be getting in the way of God's purposes? Confess them to the Lord.

O God, Your holiness causes You to turn Your back on sin. I confess my sins before You now, so that Your work in my life would not be hindered. Through Christ, amen.

July 27–29. **Karis Pratt** manages an office of biologists in Seattle. She is also a musician and world traveler who dabbles in graphic design. She loves mountain views and beautiful typography.

Instant Prayers or Real Guidance?

I am the LORD your God, who teaches you what is best for you, who directs you in the way you should go (Isaiah 48:17).

Scripture: Isaiah 48:12-19
Song: "The King Shall Come When Morning Dawns"

From a young age I've enjoyed acquiring information. I would read a book, go to a library, or ask people questions to gather new information. It took time; sometimes I had to wait to get the answers to my questions.

These days I have a new tool: the Internet. Instant information on every topic at my fingertips! But what seemed to be a gift has at times hindered my prayer life.

At one time, when I felt God's answers to my prayers didn't come quickly enough, I would actually look for answers on the Internet. I have even typed my own name in the search bar, along with a specific question I had asked the Lord, hoping that His answer would just pop up on the next screen! At that point, I was really out of touch with God's ways.

Thankfully, I saw the error of my ways. It's not that I wasn't praying — I was. But I wanted *instant* answers. I was impatient, not wanting to wait on His timing.

If you struggle with impatience, remember that the Lord is the one who teaches what is best for you, who leads you in the way you should go. There is no shortcut to receiving God's guidance. It will come in good time — His time.

Lord, You have promised to teach and lead me. Thank You. Help me to remember this when I need Your guidance. Help me to be patient and to wait for Your best answers, knowing that sometimes the best answers take time. In Christ's name, amen.

Monkey Mountain Mercies

In a surge of anger I hid my face from you for a moment, but with everlasting kindness I will have compassion on you says the LORD your Redeemer (Isaiah 54:8).

Scripture: Isaiah 54:1-8
Song: "Blessed Be Your Name"

Once I was chaperoning a group of junior high kids on a student exchange trip to Japan. When we had some unexpected free time on our tour day in Kyoto, the other two chaperones suggested we take a ride on the speeding bullet train. Sadly, only half of the students could afford this extra expense. I volunteered to stay behind with the disappointed group, hoping to find some kind of consolation activity. The answer came in the form of Monkey Mountain.

We took a short train ride, a 15-minute walk through a charming old town, and a small mountain hike up to an incredible sight: a hundred or more free-roaming monkeys! The kids couldn't stop talking about it, all thoughts of the missed bullet train forgotten. For a moment we were sad, but Monkey Mountain saved the day!

Have you faced a disappointment lately? Perhaps it feels as if God is hiding His face from you. But take a moment to reflect on God's promise that these "light and momentary troubles" (2 Corinthians 4:17) will be replaced by everlasting kindness.

Lord, I feel disappointed when things don't go according to my plan or when my hopes are unfulfilled. But You promise that Your mercies are everlasting. I thank You and praise You in faith for Your kindnesses I have yet to experience. In Christ, amen.

No Room for Pride

The arrogant one will stumble and fall (Jeremiah 50:32).

Scripture: Jeremiah 50:28-34
Song: "Let the People Praise"

The Babylonians had a pride problem, and they faced God's judgment for it. They had immersed themselves in idolatry, denied the true God, and wreaked havoc on His people.

Knowing the price of pride, I examine my own heart and ask the Lord to free me from it. After all, pride is not a pretty sight. Consider the words of the seventeenth-century poet Alexander Pope:

In pride, in reasoning pride, our error lies;
    All quit their sphere and rush into the skies.
Pride still is aiming at the bless'd abodes,
    Men would be angels, angels would be gods.

I think this means that, because of pride, we aspire to realms inappropriate to our particular callings. We "overextend" in our view of ourselves, always aiming at the next rung in the status and power ladder. Better to look in the mirror and see ourselves with pristine clarity. We are sinners. We are sinners saved by grace. We are beloved sinners, saved by a loving Lord. No room here for pride.

Thank You, **Lord,** for loving me unconditionally and calling me to depend on Your grace in my life. I return to You now, in all humility. Through Christ my Lord. Amen.

July 30. **Gary Wilde** is editor of *Devotions* and lives with his wife, Carol, in Venice, Florida. His twin boys, Tim and Dan, work as industrial engineers in Orlando and San Diego.

Walking in His Light!

Blessed is the people that know the joyful sound: they shall walk , O LORD, in the light of thy countenance (Psalm 89:15, *King James Version*).

Scripture: Psalm 89:11-18
Song: "In the Light"

One day a friend of mine suggested a hike—he had found the perfect spot on Mt. Rainier to watch the sunset. It turned out even better than we had imagined, and we wanted to soak up every last bit of those fantastic colors until they were completely blotted out by nightfall.

Suddenly—panic! We had overlooked a small but important detail: after the sun sets, it gets *dark*. Much to our relief, there happened to be clear skies and a near-full moon that was bright enough to light the two-mile trail back to the car. I have never been as thankful for the moon as I was that night!

Glorious metaphors of light and darkness dot the pages of Scripture. "God said, 'Let there be light'" (Genesis 1:3). "The people that walked in darkness have seen a great light" (Isaiah 9:2, *KJV*). "In him was life; and the life was the light of men" (John 1:4, *KJV*).

Do you ever become discouraged by the darkness you see in the world? What great comfort can be found in this verse, that we walk in the light of God's countenance!

Father, I see so much darkness in the world. Thank You that we, Your people, are given a path of light—the light of Your very face. Through Christ, amen.

July 31. **Karis Pratt** manages an office of biologists in Seattle. She is also a musician and world traveler who dabbles in graphic design. She loves mountain views and beautiful typography.

DEVOTIONS®

AUGUST

"This is my covenant with them" says the LORD.
"My Spirit, who is on you, will not depart from
you . . . from this time on and forever."

—*Isaiah 59:21*

Gary Allen Wilde, Editor   **Margaret Williams,** Project Editor   Photo Design Pics | Thinkstock®

DEVOTIONS® is published quarterly by Standard Publishing, Cincinnati, Ohio, www.standardpub.com.
© 2014 by Standard Publishing. All rights reserved. Topics based on the Home Daily Bible Readings,
International Sunday School Lessons. © 2012 by the Committee on the Uniform Series. Printed in
the U.S.A. All Scripture quotations, unless otherwise indicated, are taken from the *HOLY BIBLE,
NEW INTERNATIONAL VERSION®. NIV®.* Copyright © 1973, 1978, 1984, 2011 by Biblica, Inc.®
Used by permission of Zondervan. All rights reserved. *New American Standard Bible (NASB),*
© The Lockman Foundation, 1960, 1962, 1963, 1968, 1971, 1972, 1973, 1975, 1977, 1995. *Holy
Bible, New Living Translation (NLT),* © 1996, 2004, 2007. Tyndale House Publishers. Scripture
quotations marked *(NKJV)* are taken from the *New King James Version®.* Copyright © 1982 by
Thomas Nelson, Inc. Used by permission. *King James Version (KJV),* public
domain.

Displays of Power

I will bring you out from under the yoke of the Egyptians. I will free you from being slaves to them, and I will redeem you with an outstretched arm (Exodus 6:6).

Scripture: Exodus 6:2-8
Song: "Awesome God"

As a young child, I was terrified of tornadoes and thunderstorms. I'm still afraid of tornadoes, but I've come to love thunderstorms. Sure, lightening could strike a nearby tree or even the house, but can that be prevented from happening? No. Might as well sit back and enjoy the show.

I think what draws me to thunderstorms is the vivid, loud display of God's power. You can't miss the sound of the rumbling, crackling thunder and spectacular flashes of light.

In our text, God wants to reassure His people that He will rescue them. They were recently discouraged by a setback—when Moses asked Pharaoh to release God's people, the Egyptian ruler made their labor twice as difficult.

But God wants to remind Moses and His people that He will remember His promise; He will bring them out of bondage. Later we will see that He sends 10 plagues to display His great power and pronounce his judgment (see Exodus 7:14ff). All anyone could do was sit back and watch—whether with awe or with great fear depended on which side they were on.

Father, I'm in awe of Your power that I see in nature and in Your Word. Thank You for using Your power to rescue me and bring glory to Your name. Through Christ, amen.

August 1, 2. **Karis Pratt** manages an office of biologists in Seattle. She is also a musician and world traveler who dabbles in graphic design. She loves mountain views and beautiful typography.

Ultimate Hero

He was appalled that there was no one to intervene; so his own arm achieved salvation for him, and his own righteousness sustained him (Isaiah 59:16).

Scripture: Isaiah 59:15-21
Song: "Your Name"

What is a hero? Real life heroes are usually just regular people who happen to find themselves in a position to help someone in need. Their compassion moves them to help, even when their abilities may seem lacking.

In fictional tales, superheroes become heroes first because of their superpowers. Their special abilities give them an edge over the evil villains, so they can save people from oppression. However, the good superheroes are also characterized by compassion. In many cases the superhero tires of his "job" and just wants to live a normal life. But his compassion compels him to eventually go back to saving the day.

We have heard it said that the history of the world is His Story, an epic narration in which God is the ultimate hero. If we consider both power and compassion as the primary qualities of a hero, surely God tops the list in both areas.

Without God's heroic act of saving us when "there was no one" and there was no intercessor (v. 16), we would be lost. Praise God that He has saved us. And now consider how you, being made in His image, can also be a hero to someone in need.

O God, I praise You for Your great power and Your deep compassion. I am humbled to know You, and I pray that You will open my eyes to the needs around me and let me be a reflection of Your compassion, for Your glory. In Jesus' name, amen.

I Cry for Mercy

The LORD watches over the way of the righteous, but the way of the wicked leads to destruction (Psalm 1:6).

Scripture: Psalm 140:6-13
Song: "My Shepherd Is the Living God"

Believers are realists about the inequities in this life, but also faith-filled about eternity. Philip Yancey wrote, "The cross abolishes for all time the basic assumption that life will be fair." Yes, it is bad now. Often evil people are the wealthy and successful. Immorality is flaunted, righteousness scorned. And we all have to deal with corrupt politics, worldly marketplaces, and dysfunctional families. So as Christians we may feel vastly outnumbered. Life isn't fair!

But we can endure the injustices, distortions, bias, and persecution because we know how the story ends. We have this grand eternal perspective: We are tourists here, not residents. For now we pray with the psalmist against evil: "Do not grant the wicked their desires" (Psalm 140:8).

And Jesus offered peace, followed by these words: "In this world you will have trouble. But take heart! I have overcome the world" (John 16:33). We are fashioned in Christ for something better. We ache for it. The only sustaining worldview is that God will make all things right. Therefore, I will be faithful to Him, while continuing to pray, *Hear, Lord, my cry for mercy!*

Lord, "Defend the weak and the fatherless; uphold the cause of the poor and the oppressed. Rescue the weak and the needy" (Psalm 82:3, 4). In Jesus' name, amen.

August 3–9. **Bob Mize** is a minister, chaplain, and freelance writer living in Lubbock, Texas.

Self-Will Is a Choice

It's no use. We will continue with our own plans; we will all follow the stubbornness of our evil hearts (Jeremiah 18:12).

Scripture: Jeremiah 18:11-17
Song: "Following Christ"

God responds in kind to our response to Him. When we accept His grace, our will is transformed into His will. When we become living sacrifices, He honors us with every blessing in Christ. If He gives humans repeated opportunities for repentance but the response is, "We will all follow the stubbornness of our evil hearts," He honors that decision too. The Lord does not override our reluctance or quash our rebellion.

Nineteenth-century author George Eliot wrote, "No evil dooms us hopelessly except the evil we love, and desire to continue in, and make no effort to escape from." Yet evil is self-perpetuating, and always gets worse, not better, if left unhindered (see 2 Timothy 3:13). Purse-snatching devolves into identity theft and massive Ponzi schemes. Self-will becomes a hardened mob boss who continues his murder from behind prison bars. Con artists spend every waking minute planning the next scam.

My wife observed, "If people like that would invest the same amount of time and energy into honest endeavors, they would accomplish amazing good." Today I ask that you join me in praying against three Goliath evil industries: (1) the drug trade, (2) human trafficking, and (3) abortion. Let us pray that repentance will replace self-will.

Our Creator, I pray against evil, but especially pray for Your righteousness to prevail in the hearts of kingdom people. In Jesus' name, amen.

Courage from the Hand of the Lord

Because the hand of the LORD my God was on me, I took courage and gathered leaders from Israel to go up with me (Ezra 7:28).

Scripture: Ezra 7:21-28
Song: "All to Jesus I Surrender"

Where does courage originate? Only God can truly "encourage" (put courage into): "*Because* the hand of the Lord my God was on me." And genuine courage leads to meaningful action: "I took courage and gathered . . ."

Believers who are encouraged by the Lord are always activists. John Wesley said, "When you set yourself on fire, people love to come and see you burn." Our first Christian ancestors set the tone that reverberates today: "We cannot help speaking about what we have seen and heard" (Acts 4:20), and "We must obey God rather than human beings!" (Acts 5:29).

In other words, our convictions ought to lead to our witness and service. We fear God, not men. As present-day Scottish theologian Sinclair Ferguson writes, "The fear of the Lord tends to take away all other fears. This is the secret of Christian courage and boldness."

Like Ezra, we must personally repent, and then call a nation to repentance. Also like Ezra, we can then stand against the forces of Satan, rebuild the strongholds of righteousness, and spread God's favor to unbelievers. So, will you take the Romans 12:1, 2 pledge with me? (Yes, look it up!)

O God, I ask for the boldness of Your Holy Spirit, that I can both be encouraged and encourage others. In the name of our Lord Jesus Christ, amen.

If You Do Not Listen

He is patient with you, not wanting anyone to perish, but everyone to come to repentance (2 Peter 3:9).

Scripture: Jeremiah 26:1-7
Song: "Jesus, Lord of Our Salvation"

Had my wife and I been able to foretell the future, we would not have been in San Francisco on August 17, 1989, the day of the World Series earthquake. But we had arrived downtown that very day. We were looking for the Chamber of Commerce to ask about tourist attractions.

As we descended an outdoor stairway that leads to an open, sub-street park where the office was located, we passed an evangelist with an electric megaphone. He was leaning over the rail, blasting the milling crowd in the park below, "Repent!" Everyone ignored him.

After the earthquake began at 5:14 p.m., we dashed out of the trembling building for the safer environment of the open street above. There was the preacher in the same location shouting even more passionately, "You think that was bad? Wait until the *big* one hits! Repent *now!*"

The incident prodded me to reflect on my own unwillingness to repent. I consider how God's prophets of old were ignored, treated with contempt, persecuted, and even martyred. Certainly God's heart is broken when I do not respond to His messages, calling me to turn my attitudes and actions in a new direction.

Blessed Lord, I want to hear You in my heart. May I accept Your kindness, forbearance, and patience. And please reveal to me my need for repentance. In the holy name of Jesus, my Lord and Savior, I pray. Amen.

The Guilt of Innocent Blood

I have come that they may have life, and have it to the full (John 10:10).

Scripture: Jeremiah 26:8-15
Song: "Jesus Loves Me"

In what ways has the "guilt of innocent blood" spread in our lifetime? Jeremiah made it clear that if he were martyred, an entire city would suffer. And, indeed, there are historical examples of sin bringing down an entire city or nation. That is a core principle of the God-human relationship embedded in Jeremiah's story: *Evil has far-reaching consequences.* In the Scriptures, we find that the persecution and/or death of an innocent could bring punishment to more than the perpetrator.

But let's look at a present-day case. Murder is sin because life is sacred. Therefore, the legalization of abortion in the USA lays the charge of mass murder at the feet of our country's leaders.

How serious is the charge? How widespread is "the guilt of innocent blood" in our country alone? According to records kept by the US Center for Disease Control, there were almost 49 million legal abortions in the USA from 1970 to 2008. How desensitized we are when such infanticide receives scant national attention!

Let us pray that the message of the Lord will be heard. Please pray for our national leaders to embrace the sanctity of life. Pray for the perpetrators and practitioners of abortion.

O God, I especially pray for mothers who have given up the life in their wombs. May they seek and find God's forgiveness, as He invites them to himself. And, Lord, do bring our nation to repentance and greater reliance upon You. Through Christ, amen.

As Unreliable as a Faulty Bow

Like their ancestors they were disloyal and faithless, as unreliable as a faulty bow (Psalm 78:57).

Scripture: Psalm 78:56-62
Song: "Children of the Heavenly Father"

My hunter friend was elated when he received permission from a Colorado landowner to bow hunt for elk on his property. What an opportunity! The herd grazed regularly at the edge of his host's land bordering the National Forest. On the opening day, the largest of the bull elks – whom the locals called "Elvis" – was the closest to the hunter. Brad pulled the bow taut, held his breath, took aim, and snap! The bow string broke, and the herd trotted off. Brad's only trophy was a black eye from popping himself.

Having faithless, disloyal ancestors is worse than a faulty bow. By far. Israel's history proves that it takes only one faithless generation to bring about disastrous consequences. In this case, God "rejected Israel completely" (v. 59) and "abandoned the tabernacle" (v. 60). Israel was defeated and captured.

Can the same thing happen today? What will my spiritual heritage look like? Am I loyal and faithful to my family, school mates, coworkers, and friends? Does this generation look to me for spiritual loyalty and leadership?

"A good person leaves an inheritance for their children's children," says Proverbs 13:22. Let us pray that this will be true for parents of our day.

Dear God, help me to be faithful and loyal to You, serving my loved ones and friends as a spiritual example. In Jesus, Lord and Savior, I pray. Amen.

What's the Evidence?

This is what the LORD Almighty, the God of Israel, says: Reform your ways and your actions, and I will let you live in this place (Jeremiah 7:3).

Scripture: Jeremiah 7:1-15
Song: "True-Hearted, Whole-Hearted"

"Nominal Christianity" would be the title of the Bible passage in today's language. Has human nature changed since God scolded His people for being Israelites "in name only"? If we can have "Rino" and "Dino" (Republican/Democrat *in name only*), what about a "Cino" (Christian in name only)?

The religious leaders of Jeremiah's day claimed spiritual security because they were in the sanctuary chanting daily. Does God accept me because I "go to church," or have my name on a roster, or have Christian parents, or because I answered yes when asked, "Are you a Christian?"

Not so! In fact, Jesus spoke most harshly to those who were veneer followers (literally, painted tombstones full of deadness). It is one thing to say the words, "Lord, Lord," but another to do the Lord's will.

In other words: Am I serving a plastic Jesus or the God-man who defeated death? Do I have the mind of Christ? Do I follow in His steps? Am I willing to die for what I claim to live for? Or, as a bumper sticker asks, "If you were arrested for being a Christian, would there be enough evidence to convict you?"

O Lord, I have been saved by Your pure, unconditional grace. But now, out of gratitude, help me live as a loyal disciple. May I trust You completely and crown You as my king each day. In Your holy name I pray. Amen.

God Has the Final Say

Transgressors and sinners will be crushed together, and those who forsake the LORD will come to an end (Isaiah 1:28, *New American Standard Bible*).

Scripture: Isaiah 1:24-28
Song: "It Will Be Worth It All"

The newspaper headlines tell of a man accused of fraud. He's been stealing from the company for years, and lives have been ruined because of his larceny.

The trial is a whirlwind of media frenzy, and all of the evidence points to a guilty verdict. Then the high-priced defense lawyers start their legal dance. The trial drags on, a mistrial is declared, and the accused is set free.

However, the *final* verdict has not been issued.

God will have the final say and, have no doubt, justice will prevail. In today's world we wonder why evil persons often prosper, but we need to remember the words of Isaiah. Those who flaunt their evil ways and those who mock the Lord, will one day answer for their deeds. (And, thankfully, there will be reward for the faithful; see 1 Corinthians 3:14).

Bottom line: God is still in control, pouring out His blessings on us all of the time, even in the difficult times of our lives. His blessings now are a foretaste of the greater bliss in store for us. The evil ways of the world only remind us we are not yet home.

Father, great is Your faithfulness! Help me look beyond today's headlines and see what You have in store for me when Your Son returns. Through Him I pray. Amen.

August 10–16. **Danny Woodall,** of Port Neches, Texas, has written numerous articles and devotions for Christian publications. She also directs the Texas Christian Writer's Conference.

Speed Trap

The exercise of justice is joy for the righteous, but is terror to the workers of iniquity (Proverbs 21:15, *New American Standard Bible*).

Scripture: Proverbs 21:10-15
Song: "O Lord Most High"

The nice spring afternoon was perfect for driving. I was in a hurry to get home, zipping down Highway 190 through the piney woods of East Texas. Many of my fellow Texans were doing the same. So when I saw the flashing red lights in my mirror, I was convinced it must be the car on my bumper that the state trooper was after.

A few seconds later, I knew I was the target. The officer was polite as he wrote the ticket, explaining why he couldn't just give me a warning. My driving was being judged.

The remainder of the now three-hour drive gave me time to think. After reading about the number of deaths that occur on rural highways due to automobile wrecks, I understood why I got the ticket. If it could help save lives . . .

Sometimes God gives us a warning. He lets us know that we are going too fast—and off the track of spiritual growth. We get in trouble when we try to pass ahead of God or make a wrong turn and try to go on our own way.

If we heed the warnings, though, we can save ourselves trouble down the road. Now I'm a better driver, and that's good for me and other drivers on the road.

Lord, thank You for loving me enough to correct me when I stray. I pray You keep me on the straight and narrow road. Through Christ I pray. Amen.

Reward or Loss of Reward?

"Why should the son not bear the punishment for the father's iniquity?" When the son has practiced justice and righteousness and has observed all My statutes and done them, he shall surely live (Ezekiel 18:19, *New American Standard Bible*).

Scripture: Ezekiel 18:14-19
Song: "Blessed Assurance"

In Jewish tradition, the family is held in high regard. Furthermore, in Ezekiel's day the prevailing wisdom was that "the apple doesn't fall far from the tree." Bad parents equal bad children. That's not how God sees the family, however. We are each held accountable for our own actions. Children with good parents will be judged by what they do, and there are no free rides in God's economy.

Standards have not changed much today. If you are born on the wrong side of the track or do not have a college degree, you are often labeled with "limited potential." However, God judges us by what we *do*. In other words, He is more interested in how we finish than where we started.

In a world of snap judgments and labels, it is good to know that God judges us on actions. If we are already in His family by means of baptism, then the "judgment" is reward or loss of reward when we stand in Christ's presence. So, do what is right, and look forward to the greatest reward of all: hearing Jesus say, "Well done, good and faithful servant!" (Matthew 25:21, 23).

O Father, thank You for the eternal judgment that came at the cross on my behalf. Now, because of that atoning work, as Your child I want to please You in all I do. Pour Your grace into me for that very purpose today. In the name of Jesus, amen.

Will They See God Here?

"Do I have any pleasure in the death of the wicked," declares the Lord GOD, **"rather than that he should turn from his ways and live?"** (Ezekiel 18:23, *New American Standard Bible*).

Scripture: Ezekiel 18:21-28
Song: "We Shall See the King"

The world has given God a bum rap. The Bible declares that God is love, but how many times do we hear someone complain about God being mean and unfair? The world often sees God as if He were an angry man swatting us like bugs when we make mistakes. But Ezekiel portrays God as only wanting the wicked to repent and live.

In Genesis, God made a beautiful garden for Adam and Eve. He gave them one simple command, but they did not pass the test. Then, in order to restore our relationship with Him, He offered *himself*, in Christ, to die for our sins. Does that sound mean to you?

Maybe it's only the world's fault that God seems to get so much bad publicity these days. On the other hand, we as Christians can sometimes come across as rather vindictive saints. Having been saved by grace, let us treat others gracefully and graciously. That's crucial, really, because so many of the folks around us have the attitude of "out of sight, out of mind." In which case, they will only see God in us, if they are to see Him at all.

Creator of Heaven and earth, let me be the light unto the world that You want me to be—and may the world see Jesus in me. In the name of Jesus, who lives and reigns with You and the Holy Spirit, amen.

Doing What Counts

To do righteousness and justice is desired by the LORD more than sacrifice (Proverbs 21:3, *New American Standard Bible*).

Scripture: Proverbs 21:2-8
Song: "Joyful News to All Mankind"

A few months ago many Christians observed the season of Lent. It is a time to pause, reflect, and consider the path that Jesus trod on His way to the cross of Good Friday. Some people give up something important to them as a reminder of Jesus' own self-denial in sacrificing himself for us at Calvary. What to give up? It could be drinking coffee, watching TV, or any number of things.

However, there comes a time when sacrificing is over. The Lord honors His disciples' efforts when we observe Lent or spend time in fasting and prayer. And the key is to have a heart that stays prayerfully attuned to God's presence during the season. But—the Lord knows—it is much easier to drink a half-gallon of tea instead of two cups of coffee than to do what is right in resolving a conflict with a neighbor or helping a needful friend. Again, missing our favorite TV show is easier than standing up for justice.

When we go to the gym to work out and punish our bodies, we hear the words "No pain, no gain." But if we go from the gym and live an unhealthy lifestyle, our workouts will be in vain. Similarly, in our spiritual walk, we could live like a hermit in a cave, but if we don't help others, we have suffered in vain.

Father, I know that in the end it's not about denying my body, but how I serve others. Help me move beyond myself into others' needs. In Jesus' name, amen.

Smooth Path or Dead End?

Whoever is wise, let him understand these things; whoever is discerning, let him know them. For the ways of the LORD are right, and the righteous will walk in them, but transgressors will stumble in them (Hosea 14:9, *New American Standard Bible*).

Scripture: Hosea 14
Song: "Jesus, I'll Go Through with Thee"

In my younger days, I hiked a Revolutionary War trail in Morristown, New Jersey. Stay on the path, and everything's fine. Venture off on your own, and you run the risk of falling over rocks and tree roots or stepping into a hole. Having hiked there, I can see the Colonial army's challenge in moving men and supplies forward. Much grit and determination was needed!

Many teachers and books offer advice these days. And while these may help, reading our Bible is the best way to learn the ways of the Lord. It lays out a path for us to follow on this journey we call life. As the prophet Hosea said of God's ways: "The righteous will walk in them"—and not stumble.

The world offers alternatives to this godly trek, from success-driven hewn paths to tangled trails scattered with dubious temporary pleasures. Many will add a dose of religion, but they will leave you stranded on the road of life, nonetheless. For a while such roads will be smooth. But they only lead, inevitably, to a sad and lonely dead end.

Lord, I know that only Your wisdom and grace can lead me safely through this life and beyond. Help me to hide Your Word in my heart today, and keep me from stumbling amidst the poor choices that tempt me. In the name of Jesus, amen.

Enjoy That Fresh Aroma!

Cast away from you all your transgressions which you have committed and make yourselves a new heart and a new spirit! For why will you die, O house of Israel? (Ezekiel 18:31, *New American Standard Bible*).

Scripture: Ezekiel 18:1-13, 30-32
Song: "There's Room at the Cross for You"

There's nothing like the smell of a new car. You ease into the seat and look around; no signs of dirt, crumbs, or spilled soda. You turn the key; the engine starts instantly. The test drive is a breeze; no worn-out shocks or annoying rattles. After you sign the papers, you are the proud owner of a new, fine-smelling ride.

The Bible tells us that God gives us a new heart and a new spirit. He doesn't tinker with our old selves, He changes us completely. Nor are we a refurbished version of ourselves; we are thoroughly changed, complete with a new nature.

In other words, Christianity isn't merely a self-improvement course. The apostle Paul went from slave to sin to a slave for Christ. He also said that we were dead in our sins (see Colossians 2:13) before Christ made us alive. That's not a lifestyle "tune-up"; it's a brand new existence. The prophet Ezekiel, long before Paul, had the same idea, speaking of a new heart and spirit.

So, if ghosts of the past haunt you, stop driving that clunker of your old nature. Live your new life in Christ—and let the Lord enjoy that new-person smell: "For we are a fragrance of Christ to God" (2 Corinthians 2:15, *NASB*).

Lord, You've given me a new nature, Your Holy Spirit dwelling within. Now give me strength to live the way You want me to live. I praise You, through Christ. Amen.

All in the Same Boat

Your ancestors forsook me . . . and followed other gods and served and worshiped them (Jeremiah 16:11).

Scripture: Jeremiah 16:6-13
Song: "Give Us Clean Hands"

As the story goes: Two men were stranded at sea in a little boat. Moving ever closer to starvation, one of the men became insanely desperate. He grabbed a piece of metal and began to bore a hole through the bottom of the boat. Of course, the other man was horrified "What are you doing? We'll sink!" But his friend shot back, "Relax! I'm only boring the hole on my side."

With life in general, the old adage is true: *We're all in the same boat!* Each of us is responsible for our own actions, of course. But the reality is that our actions also have a positive or negative impact on others.

Jeremiah's audience wrestled with this basic truth. As they stared into the face of certain judgment, they asked God why His discipline was falling so heavily upon them. God's reply was simple: The unfaithfulness of their forefathers, along with personal disobedience, brought serious consequences.

We may have to overcome some "skeletons in the closet" based on our genealogy. Ultimately, though, the choice is ours, each day, whether or not to seek and do God's will.

Heavenly Father, I thank You for the forgiveness that comes through Your Son's atoning death, burial, and resurrection. Praise You for Your mercy to me! In the name of Christ my Lord, I pray. Amen.

August 17–23. **Pete Charpentier** is a husband, father, and professor of pastoral ministry. He enjoys spending time with his family, reading, and investing in others for God's purposes.

Providential Deliverance

In my distress I cried out to the LORD; yes, I cried to my God for help. He heard me from his sanctuary; my cry reached his ears (2 Samuel 22:7, *New Living Translation*).

Scripture: 2 Samuel 22:1-7
Song: "Sovereign over Us"

I'll never forget the birth of my firstborn son. I welcomed my first baby and nearly lost my wife. My wife, Wendy, had a "textbook" pregnancy until two weeks before her due date. At that time, she began experiencing severe pains. After waves of agony, she gave our doctor permission for an emergency C-section. Her hope of getting well meant our son had to be delivered.

Yet, just a short time after our baby's birth, Wendy experienced similar pains. Puzzled and panicked, we rushed to the hospital . . . to find her gall bladder was packed with stones.

We look back to our first son's birth as a sign of God's providential deliverance. We realize now that my wife's initial pains were likely a gall bladder attack, but the Lord knew we needed to be at the hospital because of the life-threatening illness lingering just around the corner.

David also knew God's providential deliverance. As a warrior, he often stood in the crosshairs of trouble. However, both David and all of us can rejoice in God's deliverance. Jesus said, "Here on earth you will have many trials and sorrows. But take heart, because I have overcome the world" (John 16:33, *NLT*).

Heavenly Father, I thank You for protecting and providing for me and my family. Apart from You, I have no hope. But because of Your sovereign power and perfect character, I can trust You in every season of life. In Christ's name I pray. Amen.

Just a Little Cajun Boy

He heals the brokenhearted and binds up their wounds (Psalm 147:3, *New King James Version*).

Scripture: Psalm 147:1-11
Song: "I Have Found a Friend in Jesus"

I wasn't raised in a Christian home, and there are no preachers in my family line that I know of. I grew up as a Cajun boy not far from a bayou in south Louisiana.

But when I came to know Christ as my Savior, my whole life changed dramatically. I wanted to serve Jesus with a relentless drive. It seemed that every time an altar call was given, I was the first to hit my knees there. This was so frequent that one older gentleman in our church shared with my minister that he thought something was perhaps wrong with me. Of course, my minister replied that he wished every person's heart was so sensitive to the Lord's touch.

And it's good to remain sensitive to the Lord's touch! After all, He is our salvation, healer, strength, refuge, and rock. Jesus is not a "means-to-an-end"; rather, He is *the* means and *the* end because He is our everything.

The psalmist voices marvelous words of praise in our Scripture today. All who receive God's salvation in Christ know His healing of their broken hearts and wounds. Only the Lord can truly transform the life of a little Cajun boy for all eternity.

O my Lord Christ, You have indeed done great things in my life, and I am eternally grateful! I want my life to be an offering of praise to You because only You came to seek and to save me. Thank You for adopting me into Your family. In Your precious name I pray. Amen.

Dear People of God, Pray!

The LORD . . . saved them out of the hands of their enemies as long as the judge lived; for the LORD relented because of their groaning under those who oppressed and afflicted them (Judges 2:18).

Scripture: Judges 2:16-23
Song: "Heal Us, Emmanuel, Hear Our Prayer"

This might be a true story: A little boy was misbehaving during a church service. At first, his father tried to get his attention by staring him down. But when that didn't work, the father reached over and nudged his son on the shoulder. While the boy made eye-contact and settled down for a moment, he soon resumed his misbehavior. Finally, Dad firmly grabbed his hand and began to escort him towards the backdoor.

Of course, everyone, along with the little boy, knew what was coming. So, in an effort to evoke sympathy from the congregation, the little boy lifted his voice, loud and clear, just before he and his father exited: "Dear people of God, pray! Pray! O, please pray, because if God doesn't do something, we're all in trouble!"

There's some truth here. The book of Judges reveals how Israel journeyed through several cycles of peace, disobedience, and deliverance. And its clear message is that although there are consequences for our sins, God is rich in mercy. He hears our cries and will "do something," albeit in His way and time. Our job is to keep trusting, keep behaving, keep praying.

Father, Your mercy for me as Your child is new and fresh every morning. I'm thankful for Your perfect, patient, and persistent love. You sustain me through all things with Your promise to complete the good work You began in me. In Jesus' name, amen.

It's Part of the Gift

Every man shall give as he is able, according to the blessing of the LORD thy God which he hath given thee (Deuteronomy 16:17, *King James Version*).

Scripture: Deuteronomy 16:16-20
Song: "Sweeter As the Years Go By"

There was once a missionary who lived on a remote island. While the island wasn't large, it was quite a rocky trek from one end to the other.

On the missionary's birthday one year, she heard a knock on her door. Standing there was a poor native child without shoes, grinning from ear to ear and lifting his hands, which were filled with seashells.

The missionary was surprised by his gift. She knew these shells could only be found on the opposite end of the island. And when she asked the boy about his gift and the long, hard journey he must have travelled without shoes, he said with a smile, "The journey is part of the gift!"

It's been well-said that the Lord doesn't desire equal gifts but equal sacrifice. Although the amounts of our gifts will doubtlessly vary because of the different ways God has blessed each of us, the same heart of love motivates us to give to the Lord from the overflow of His blessings in our lives. This kind of giving is what the people of Israel were called to do in our Scripture. And it is what God also wants us to do joyfully each day.

O Lord, Your blessings are so amazing! I could never recount all the ways You've blessed me, and I desire to faithfully give offerings to You which overflow from my heart of gratitude. Thank You for allowing me that privilege! In Christ's name, amen.

Take a Million Dollars?

The light of the moon will be as the light of the sun, and the light of the sun will be seven times brighter . . . on the day the LORD binds up the fracture of His people and heals the bruise He has inflicted (Isaiah 30:26, *New American Standard Bible*).

Scripture: Isaiah 30:18-26
Song: "In His Time"

Very early in my marriage I made some extremely selfish mistakes. My failures hurt my new bride deeply, and our marriage really took a blow right out of the gate.

While things gradually healed, I'd cut a deep wound. Then at least once a year, we'd have a huge meltdown (as though our heavenly Father was reopening our wound in order to clean it a little bit deeper). Finally, the Lord brought us through a major point of restoration after 13 years together.

I've often told people that I would not want to relive those dark days for a million dollars. But nor would I take a million dollars to *not* have lived them. You see, I've realized that God often teaches us the most profound truths of victory in the wake of our deepest moments of defeat. In fact, our failures are usually the most fertile patches of soil for spiritual growth.

God's people have always struggled, failed, and experienced His restoration. This was true in Isaiah's time, as he declared God's promise of restoration to his people. We too can rest in the fact that God is at work, even in our most desperate times.

Father, I know that You will never leave me nor forsake me. And You are at work even during the darkest hours of my life. So I trust You always, and I thank You for working everything together for good. In Christ's name I pray. Amen.

Learning the Hard Way

They made their hearts as hard as flint and would not listen to the law or to the words that the LORD Almighty had sent by his Spirit through the earlier prophets (Zechariah 7:12).

Scripture: Zechariah 7:8-14
Song: "Jesus, the Truth and Power Divine"

I've heard that "a wise man learns from his mistakes, but the *wisest* man learns from the mistakes of others." And I believe this is true. The only problem is that many of us apparently struggle with implementing this nugget of wisdom.

I remember when I was just a child, my dad purchased my first minibike. It was shiny and spotless, and I was going to give it a "test run" in a vacant lot. Actually, the lot wasn't *completely* vacant—a telephone pole stood in the middle of the mostly open space. So there was only one rule: *stay away from the pole.*

I'm sure you already know what happened. As I putted around the lot on my little motorcycle, I circled closer and closer to the pole . . . until . . . I finally collided with it! My handlebars slammed into the tank and dented my new, prized possession before I even took it home.

The prophet Zechariah warned of severe consequences for ignoring God's rules. The good news is that this same God—the Father of our Lord Jesus Christ—is patient and merciful with us. Thus we can grow in wisdom even if it's learned from tough times or poor driving.

O Lord, I confess that I have turned a deaf ear to Your wisdom many times. But I thank You for Your mercy. Please soften my heart to be tender to Your touch and to extend that same warm mercy to others. Through Christ I pray. Amen.

Read the Owner's Manual?

Show me your ways, LORD, teach me your paths. Guide me in your truth and teach me, for you are God my Savior. . . . My eyes are ever on the LORD (Psalm 25:4, 5, 15).

Scripture: Psalm 25
Song: "Teach Me Thy Way, O Lord"

I recently reread Lord Byron's classic poem, "The Destruction of Sennacherib," a vivid account of the siege of Jerusalem under that Assyrian king, as chronicled in 2 Kings 19. When Sennacherib arrived in Jerusalem, ready to lay siege, the Lord stopped him cold. The angel of the Lord destroyed 185,000 Assyrian soldiers in one night — that's three Vietnam wars in one night. The king survived, limping home to Assyria in shame.

Byron's poem, faithfully committed to memory by British grammar-school students even today, commemorates this tremendous slaughter and God's awesome power. It opens with the familiar line, "The Assyrian came down like a wolf on the fold" and ends triumphantly with, "The might of the gentile, unsmote by the sword, hath melted like snow in the glance of the Lord."

Byron includes details of the debacle that would be lost on most Christians today. Likewise, for many of us, our grasp of Scripture leaves much to be desired. Yet our prayer, like that of the psalmist, implores God to teach us His ways. Is that Your prayer as well today?

Lord, teach me Thy ways. Give me a renewed hunger for Your Word. I need to get to know You better. In Christ's name I pray. Amen.

August 24–30. **Paul Tatham** has been a Christian school administrator and teacher for more than 40 years and is currently serving at the First Academy in Orlando, Florida.

I Could Have Saved More!

We make it our goal to please him. . . . For we must all appear before the judgment seat of Christ, so that each of us may receive what is due us for the things done while in the body, whether good or bad (2 Corinthians 5:9, 10).

Scripture: Matthew 7:7-14
Song: "Must I Go, and Empty-Handed?"

The cinematic masterpiece *Schindler's List* is a moving, true account of one story amidst the Holocaust—the systematic mass slaughter of European Jews in Nazi concentration camps during World War II. The hero is Oskar Schindler, a German industrialist who gradually becomes concerned for his Jewish slave workforce after witnessing their oppression by his Nazi compatriots. Pangs of empathy build in him, and finally he decides to use his wealth to purchase the freedom of his workers by bribing Nazi officials.

With the war drawing to a close and his bank account drained, Schindler anguishes over the conviction that he could have done even more. He frantically thinks of possessions he can sell in order to purchase the freedom of even more than the thousand Jews he's already redeemed.

At the judgment seat of Christ—Heaven's awards ceremony for believers—I'm sure there will be laments and regrets like that, similar to Spielberg's depiction. There will be much rejoicing, to be sure, but it will be tempered by a lot of eye-dabbing.

Lord, it's sobering to contemplate eternity and realize that we will someday be present with the Lord. On that day of my homecoming, I'll give account as to my use of Your gracious gifts. Help me to prepare well, right now! Amen.

Are You a Hall-of-Famer?

A scroll of remembrance was written in his presence concerning those who feared the LORD and honored his name (Malachi 3:16).

Scripture: Malachi 3:11-18
Song: "Precious Memories"

Many countries of the world have one particular sport at which its citizens excel and is the focal point of their national pride. For many, it's soccer. Others may dominate in wrestling, basketball, weight-lifting, distance running, speed-skating, or auto-racing. They each seem to be "really good" at something.

As a kid growing up in Canada, I knew our national sport was ice hockey. It provided bragging rights to a vast but sparsely populated land known for its long winters. Youngsters were expected to strap on skates as soon as they could walk and spend their Saturdays practicing their stick-handling and body-checking skills. Those who showed promise were mentored into adulthood where, it was hoped, they'd one day catch the eye of a pro scout. The goal? A spot in the much-revered National Hockey League. NHL standouts were assured of immortality at the NHL Hall of Fame, Toronto's shrine to all things hockey.

The underlying purpose of any such hall of fame, of course, is to inspire the next generation to carry on the torch. A Christian hall of fame, per se, does not exist. But we can all draw inspiration from those, great and small, who made an impact on us and nudged us to greater godliness.

Lord, I want to make my life count for time and eternity. I want to play my part in shaping the next generation for You—for Your glory, not mine. In Jesus' name, amen.

I Got Away with It! (Really?)

Swing the sickle, for the harvest is ripe. Come, trample the grapes, for the winepress is full and the vats overflow—so great is their wickedness! (Joel 3:13).

Scripture: Joel 3:9-16
Song: "Rescue the Perishing"

"You won't believe what I got away with last weekend!" I overheard one of my students whispering to another. "My grandfather gave me $50 for my birthday, and I told him I had spent it on new shoes. And he bought it!" She went on to explain to her classmate that she had actually spent the money on alcohol and was quite pleased at duping her grandfather so easily.

As a teacher for the past 44 years, I've been privy to a multitude of such conversations. Many have involved high-schoolers gloating over the fact that they'd honed duplicity into a valued life skill. And, indeed, if asked, they would unashamedly rattle off several accounts to prove it. "Best of all," they'd say, "I got away with it—which proves it mustn't have been wrong in the first place." Otherwise, in their thinking, someone—parents, grandparents, the cops, or God himself—would have intervened to bring their little charade to an abrupt stop.

Much of the world operates under a similar mind-set. They see the heavenly Father more as a heavenly grandfather—old, mellow, senile, viewing sin with an uninvolved boys-will-be-boys attitude. They fail to realize that He is very much concerned. Furthermore, He's keeping books that will one day be opened.

Lord, someday You will utter haunting words, "I never knew you. Away from me" (Matthew 7:23). Give me a renewed burden to rescue the lost. Through Christ, amen.

Testing Your Mettle

I have made you a tester of metals and my people the ore, that you may observe and test their ways (Jeremiah 6:27).

Scripture: Jeremiah 6:26-30
Song: "Something for Jesus"

January 9, 1956, is a date etched into the memories of many evangelical Christians. Opening their newspapers that morning, they were shocked to read of the martyrdom of five missionary men in Ecuador, South America, the day before.

A few weeks earlier, the five had finally managed to make contact with the primitive Auca Indians, a tribe untouched by civilization or the gospel. After a few gift exchanges on the banks of the Curaray River, they felt they were making headway. Perhaps it was only a matter of time before they could share Christ's love with these indigenous people. But misinterpreting the missionaries' intentions, the Aucas suddenly turned on the outsiders and speared them to death.

Amazingly, the surviving wives didn't abandon the mission begun by their husbands. Instead, they carried on the work and won many Aucas to Christ. Their mettle had been tested, and their true character demonstrated.

Jeremiah was a metal tester, from which the expression "show your mettle" is derived. His mission was to evaluate the true worth—the true character—of God's people. So, if Jeremiah were to test us, how would we fare? Would we flee the mission?

Lord, there is an old saying, "When the going gets tough, the tough get going." But in my case, I'm more apt to hail a cab and leave town! Strengthen me, Lord, and bolster my resolve to remain firmly planted in the face of testing. Through Christ, amen.

Only a Matter of Time

Is it not because I have long been silent that you do not fear me? (Isaiah 57:11).

Scripture: Isaiah 57:10-21
Song: "Sinner, Come to Jesus"

Several years ago, I had a dream about the frightful amount of crime afflicting our nation. Saved from this nightmare by my morning alarm clock, I set about writing an article that offered suggestions for stemming the rising tide of lawlessness.

A small local newspaper published it. The article, "America's Crime Problem Could Be Solved in One Month," was a rather hyperbolic claim that, in essence, recommended a good dose of Old Testament justice that was long on punishment and short on mercy. I knew my suggestions had precious little hope of implementation. But just the act of putting pen to paper was personally satisfying.

One of my recommendations was to dramatically fast-forward the time lapse between the commission of a crime and its resolution in court. Far too many crimes languish for years in a tedious judicial system that provides little deterrent to crime.

At times, God's judicial system doesn't strike us as much better. Someone persists in sin that seems to go unnoticed by Heaven. We wait for the heavenly shoe to drop, and nothing happens. But let's not mistake God's forbearance for forgiveness, His silence for sympathy. It's only a matter of time before He demands accountability.

Lord, I can become complacent about the consequences of sin. Sober my thinking and give me a healthy sense of fearful reverence. In Jesus' name, amen.

Willing to Make God's Day?

Test me in this ... and see if I will not throw open the flood-gates of heaven and pour out so much blessing that there will not be room enough to store it (Malachi 3:10).

Scripture: Malachi 3:1-10
Song: "The Windows of Heaven"

One of the most memorable movie catchphrases of all time has to be Clint Eastwood's character, San Francisco police inspector Harry Callahan, saying: "Go ahead, make my day." Through clenched teeth and in his characteristic raspy grumble, Eastwood utters the line when he confronts a hostage-taker bent on shooting his victim. Instead of backing away, Callahan unholsters his own .44 Magnum revolver, unflinchingly points it at the criminal's head, and dares him to make his move.

But our God used such a line centuries before Hollywood ever thought of it. He throws down the gauntlet in Malachi 3 by daring His followers to put Him to the test. He asks us to go out on a financial limb by supporting His work—the only time in Scripture, by the way, that God asks us to test Him.

For many of us, reaching for our wallet may require even more chutzpah than reaching for a .44. We're willing to do almost anything for God other than that.

But to those who do manage to take God at His word, confidently relying on His promise, they find that He not only meets their needs but opens the floodgates of Heaven.

Lord, I bow before You, admitting my own reservations in trusting You with my money. It boils down to a matter of faith—whether I can really rely on You or not. Grant me the boldness and the peace to take You at Your word. Through Christ, amen.

Clara's Song: Knit One, Pray Two

This, then, is how you should pray: "Our Father in heaven, hallowed be your name" (Matthew 6:9).

Scripture: Matthew 6:9-15
Song: "Praise to the Lord, the Almighty"

A few knitters in our church enjoy making prayer shawls. Each shawl is a simple stole, created for someone who is grieving, ill, or in need of comfort. Prayer shawls have proven to be extremely helpful in physical and psychological healing.

I felt blessed and grateful when a shawl was presented to me. My shawl is a soft, sky blue. I drape it over my shoulders when I'm feeling chilly and snuggle with it during my devotional time.

Although I am not an accomplished knitter, I decided to try to knit a prayer shawl for someone else. How to begin? I mentioned my idea to my friend Clara. She piped up, "All right, you buy three skeins of homespun yarn and size 13 circular needles. Cast on 60 stitches, and just knit. When the shawl is 62 inches long, I will show you how to crochet the edges."

Don't you love it when God works in this way? Exact instructions, plus help from a friend. All of this reminds me: Jesus instructs us to begin our prayers with praise to God. Today I am praising Him for friends like Clara. The next time we met, she untangled the "mistakes" I had made. I know I will finish the shawl because Jesus put Clara in my corner.

Almighty God, You are an awesome God, and hallowed be Your name. Accept this my joyful praise! In Jesus' name, amen.

August 31. **Anne Collins** lives in Venice, Florida. Her interests are faith, family, friends, food, flowers, fitness, and fabrics.

DEVOTIONS®

SEPTEMBER

> They never stopped teaching and proclaiming the good news that Jesus is the Messiah.
>
> —*Acts 5:42*

Gary Wilde, Editor   **Margaret Williams,** Project Editor   Photo Brand X Pictures | Thinkstock®

Norm's Legacy

You are not the one to build the temple, but your son, your own flesh and blood—he is the one (2 Chronicles 6:9).

Scripture: 2 Chronicles 6:1-15
Song: "Now Thank We All Our God"

We need to remind ourselves, and others, that our life on earth is short. Our "big picture" life plan, all we set out to accomplish, is likely to be interrupted by death. But God reminds us that our legacy lives on in our loved ones.

Our daughters and their spouses, our beautiful grandchildren, all were washed, combed, and shiny in their church clothes. Bursting with pride, they lined up right in the front pews, glowing, standing in the sunbeams filtered through stained glass. They assembled to share seemingly small—but hugely important—ways in which life is forever better because of their dad, their dad-in-law, and their Grandpa Norm.

Next, there were Norm's "prodigies"—youngsters who had worked for and learned from Norm over the years. Five of these, now successful young men, had followed in Norm's footsteps in choosing their own careers. Each stood up to share his memories and gratitude, even telling how Norm had been like a father to them. And they have been, really, like sons to us.

My friend Marietta said it perfectly, "There stands Norm's legacy, right here in front of us. He must be so very proud."

Thank You, **precious Lord,** for loving us. Thank You for the part we get to play in God's big picture. Teach us how to play and be grateful. In Your name, amen.

September 1-6. **Anne Collins** lives in Venice, Florida. Her interests are faith, family, friends, food, flowers, fitness, and fabrics.

Jennifer's Song

Sorrowful, yet always rejoicing; poor, yet making many rich; having nothing, and yet possessing everything (2 Corinthians 6:10).

Scripture: 2 Corinthians 6:1-13
Song: "Take My Hand, Precious Lord"

Jennifer showed unusual maturity, confidence, creativity, and outstanding leadership qualities. She was one of my former students, a 9-year-old fourth grader. Her big, struggling, non-church-going family would probably have been labeled "dysfunctional." Her parents divorced when Jen was 10, and her mom began moving all over the country with the kids, facing one derailment after another.

Oh, by the way—God chose Jennifer to be one of His co-workers! Jen became a Christian, and this spring she graduated from the University of North Carolina. Now she's working toward her master's degree in theology.

She writes to me: "I just got a new job working for a study-abroad program out of the university called the Atlantis Project. The program allows students to gain work experience in medical or education fields in the Azores, a group of islands off the coast of Portugal. I will be organizing student internships and events. And I could not be more excited! This is quite an unexpected but blessed opportunity. God has done amazing things in my life since graduation, and I feel so blessed to follow Him."

Dearest Father, I fill up with joy and gratitude when I witness Your loving hand leading a precious child into Your service. Thank You for allowing me to share the very beginning of Jen's amazing story. In Jesus' name, amen.

Anne's Song

I will do whatever you ask in my name, so that the Father may be glorified in the Son (John 14:13).

Scripture: John 14:11-13
Song: "Thank You, Lord"

The boy I married 53 years ago was becoming a stranger, fading into a world of physical disability and dementia. And I wasn't ready to accept the situation. Praying for strength and understanding, I was led to accept Jesus' total presence in my life and to accept my own vital role as Norm's caregiver. Gradually I learned to accept the facts too: *Norm's illness is terminal. It will get worse. It won't be pretty.*

Yet Jesus taught me to accept help. Resources presented themselves: kind doctors and caring neighbors, our daughters and their families, our church and local fire and rescue personnel. All, in a sense, came to my rescue. Then there were the physical therapists, the hospice volunteers, and the people who would call — or just show up — exactly when their help was needed.

Specialists installed safety equipment in our home. The Senior Friendship Center offered caregiver support classes. I was blessed to meet people facing situations similar to ours. It became clear that we could give Norm the loving care he needed. One day at a time, we did just that.

Eventually, Norm passed away, peacefully, in our living room, surrounded by his family. We accept, and we are grateful for, God's peace. As I look ahead, I will do whatever He asks.

Heavenly Father, I am blessed just now with an overwhelming love for Norm, for my precious family, and for Jesus my Lord. In His name, amen.

Mary's Song

It is by the name of Jesus Christ of Nazareth, whom you crucified but whom God raised from the dead, that this man stands before you healed (Acts 4:10).

Scripture: Acts 4:1-12
Song: "O Bless the Lord, My Soul"

My dear friend Mary is a talented, beloved, first-grade teacher in Michigan. Mary started a prayer group for our school staff, and we'd meet briefly every Wednesday morning before the school day began. We'd pray with and for each other, and about whatever school issues might be bubbling up. We'd praise God, then go about our week feeling blessed, refreshed, and confident.

One day Mary couldn't figure out how to drive home. *Glitch.* The next day, she couldn't read the clock. *Ooops.* Her doctor found a dangerous brain tumor, with surgery required.

But Mary wasn't afraid. She'd given her life to Christ years ago and looked forward to going to Heaven some day. So off she went to the hospital. The rest of us weren't taking it lightly. We prayed: for Mary, for the doctors, for a miracle. We couldn't live without her. *Don't call her home now. Please, God.* Weeks of uncertainty followed.

Then Mary breezed back to school, glowing, more beautiful than ever, a pretty scarf tied around her head. She's been in remission for 12 years.

Teaching is both an art and a craft. Mary is an artist and a craftswoman. She does it for Jesus.

Thank You, **Lord,** for life. Teach me, and all of us, to discover our spiritual gifts and to do our crafts for Jesus and His kingdom. In His name, amen.

Diana's Song

As for us, we cannot help speaking about what we have seen and heard (Acts 4:20).

Scripture: Acts 4:13-22
Song: "Come, Holy Spirit, Heavenly Dove"

My friend Diana calls it "living in expectation." When she and I make eye contact, we quietly open our palms to the heavens and spontaneously break into smiles of recognition and joy. It's sort of like a secret between friends. But it's not a secret. We have developed the habit of looking forward to witnessing miracles that happen every day.

It requires awareness, though—awareness of, and acceptance of, each blessing. Then I find myself saying "Thank You, God," or "Thank You, Jesus," many times each day.

Continually expressing gratitude has increased my awareness of the work of the Holy Spirit. This morning I phoned my new friend, Judy, to invite her to my quilting circle meeting. "Oh, my, yes!" she exclaimed. "I'm so happy. I can't wait to show you my quilts." (I'd had no idea Judy was interested in quilting.) And over coffee that afternoon, my friend Rosario delighted me with wonderful stories of her childhood in Mexico.

Working in my kitchen, I recently found my engagement ring that I had lost—52 years ago! And tonight, on the anniversary of first receiving my ring, our daughter invited me to dinner. I would have been alone—how did she know?

Thank You, **God,** for the miracles You offer to our view every day. When I look, let me truly see Your hand at work, in me, in the friends around me, and in the world at large. May I live in expectation this day. In Jesus' name. Amen.

Norm's Song

"Sovereign Lord," they said, "you made the heavens and the earth and the sea, and everything in them" (Acts 4:24).

Scripture: Acts 4:23-31
Song: This Is My Father's World

My husband told delightful stories of his childhood in western New York. His family lived in a sparsely populated, wonderfully scenic, rural region near Lake Erie. There Norm and his brother explored nearby farms, hills and valleys, lakes and forests, wetlands, rock formations, and waterfalls. Norm and Donnie were brave little explorers, even experts, immensely knowledgeable about local plants and wildlife habitats.

Recently I was delighted to discover that the hymn "This Is My Father's World," was penned by a man who lived in the exact area of western New York that Norm knew so well.

Maltbie Davenport Babcock (1858 – 1901) was a popular young minister in the village of Lockport, and his favorite getaway was to enjoy walking the local terrain. He would tell his young wife that he was "going out to see the Father's world." Babcock was also, rather secretly, a poet. After his death, his verses came out in a little book called *Thoughts for Every-Day Living*.

This is my Father's world: I rest me in the thought
　　Of rocks and trees, of skies and seas;
His hand the wonders wrought.

Thank You, **Creator God,** for the wonders You have wrought. Teach us to treasure and cherish, nurture and protect, Your creation, as we would a newborn babe. In the name of my Lord and Savior, Jesus Christ, amen.

Keep the Channel Open

Rescue the weak and the needy; deliver them from the hand of the wicked (Psalm 82:4).

Scripture: Psalm 82
Song: "Deeper, Deeper"

Sandy Pond is a sheltered bay located due east of Lake Ontario. To access the lake, boaters must steer through a narrow channel dividing the pond from the larger body of water. Over time sediments, weeds, and debris accumulated within the channel, making it shallow and narrow. While small watercraft could get through, larger power boats and fishing vessels found it increasingly difficult to navigate through the opening. So every year the town brings in a dredger to scoop out the unwanted accumulation, clearing the channel and allowing the water to run deep and wide once again.

In our reading today, a warning comes to those who would disrupt and choke off access to the truth and righteousness of God. While the psalmist directs his words to the leaders of Israel, the message applies to each of us who bear the name of the Lord. One day God will come and judge the earth, dredging up and casting off offenders.

Left undisturbed, sin becomes like waterway debris, choking off access to God. By repentance, we excavate offenses as they occur, ensuring a wide channel of communication with God.

Heavenly Father, I give You thanks for providing a means of open communication between us through the sacrifice of Your Son for my sins. Through Christ, amen.

September 7–13. **Judyann Grant,** of Mannsville, New York, writes an inspirational column that appears in four secular newspapers.

Clear Vision, Going Forward

Test me, LORD, and try me, examine my heart and my mind (Psalm 26:2).

Scripture: Psalm 26
Song: "Day by Day"

In our farmhouse we have 35 windows. The smallest, two dormers, measure a mere 20 inches across. The largest—a picture window in the living room—measures a whopping expanse of nine feet. The remainder of the windows fall somewhere in between. Along with the windows we have five doors, each with varying amounts of glass.

I love seeing the sun shine through all the windows on cloudless days, but it takes work. The windows don't clean themselves, despite advertisements that make window cleaning look like a breeze. If I tried to tackle them all in one day, the task would be overwhelming. So I break up the chore into manageable increments. As I wash each pane, cleaning away dust and cobwebs, I think ahead to the beautiful view that's coming.

Becoming Christlike doesn't come easy or naturally, either. There is no way to become more loving, faithful, and kind in one day. It takes daily commitment, being faithful in big and small matters, and living each moment with Heaven in mind.

Washing a few windows each day helps me stay on task. So, too, walking daily in faith with God helps me better handle the big challenges and tough choices that always come along.

Dear Lord, I long to walk close to You every day. Speak to my heart, and help me daily to keep the windows of my heart sparkling clean so that Your love might shine through me to others. I ask this in Christ's name. Amen.

The Lure of Gossip

Give the enemy no opportunity for slander (1 Timothy 5:14).

Scripture: 1 Timothy 5:11-19
Song: "Holy Spirit, Be My Guide"

As I waited in the checkout line, my eyes scanned the large selection of impulse buy items that lined both sides of the aisle: candy bars, gum, breath mints, beef jerky, mini-flashlights, and batteries. Taking up the most space, however, were a variety of celebrity magazines. Each cover abounded in full-color photographs and large headlines declaring news.

Randomly, I flipped one of them open, and it contained lots of photos of celebs in less-than-flattering attire. These were accompanied by articles that were nothing more than gossip and innuendo. Disgusted, I stuffed the magazine back into the rack.

The lure of gossip began when the serpent in Eden's garden first spread distorted information about God's command. After thousands of years, gossip remains one of the ways Satan sows discord among believers. I, myself, have been guilty of trying to disguise it as a legitimate prayer concern.

As we kids headed out the door each morning, our father's parting advice was, "Keep your nose clean." That is, don't go poking it into others' business. It's still good advice. By looking well to our own affairs, we have no time to spread rumors that only cause heartache.

Lord God, I realize that gossip is a pothole along the pathway into which any of us can fall. But may the Holy Spirit bring my every thought, word, and deed into submission with Your will and Your plan for my life. In Your name I pray. Amen.

Foxhole Religion?

When you spread out your hands in prayer, I hide my eyes from you; even when you offer many prayers, I am not listening (Isaiah 1:15).

Scripture: Isaiah 1:15-18
Song: "Just a Closer Walk with Thee"

Sitting in the dentist chair, waiting for my twice-yearly cleaning, I look at the tray of metal instruments waiting close by. While the dental hygienist pulls on rubber gloves, I pray she will find no cavities. As she picks up the sharp-pointed, double-bladed hand scaler, I silently vow to floss daily and never let decadent sweets touch my lips—ever again!

Within an hour the ordeal is over, and I'm on my way home. In less time than it takes to say "come back in six months," I have brewed a cup of enamel-staining tea and opened a bag of cavity-causing chocolates. My dentist-chair prayer? Forgotten.

Weren't the people of Judea like that? When their land was laid waste by their enemies, they desperately pleaded for God to save them. They offered sacrifices while their hearts remained distant. And they constantly returned to old, rebellious ways.

God wants our whole hearts, but not just in times of trouble. He knows when we're sincere. He desires that we settle the matter, once and for all: If we are not for Him, we are against Him. Without a complete turning away from wrongdoing, our "foxhole" prayers won't even hit the ceiling.

Dear Father in Heaven, I know old habits die hard, but I also know that, with an honest commitment, great change is possible. Please help me to change any attitude or action that isn't pleasing in Your sight. In Jesus' name I pray. Amen.

Steadfast Faith

Do not be anxious about anything, but in every situation, by prayer and petition, with thanksgiving, present your requests to God (Philippians 4:6).

Scripture: Philippians 4:1-14
Song: "Jesus Is Lord of All"

On this anniversary of the attack on the World Trade Center, my thoughts travel back to that day. I had just gotten our first grandchild down for a nap when my husband called from work. His words tumbled out, "Have you heard? Turn on the television." As the picture came into view, I saw the south tower exploding into a cascade of fire and smoke. Tears filled my eyes as I feared war had been declared on our country.

I looked at the peaceful, sleeping form of our baby granddaughter. What kind of world had she been born into? Would she even have the opportunity to grow up? The uncertainties threatened to overwhelm me, and I turned to prayer. During those dark and somber days, and many bleak days since, Philippians 4:6 sustained me.

Two years ago our family visited the 9-11 Memorial. The hustle and bustle of the city faded away, until only the waterfall was heard. Tears again filled my eyes as, together with my now teenage granddaughter, we read the names of those who lost their lives. Our grandchildren are inheriting a broken world, but they have a loving Father who can calm their uncertainties.

Father God, help me remember that You will never abandon or forsake me in this imperfect world. May I keep my eyes on You and not just on my circumstances today. In Your Holy name, I offer my thanks. Amen.

Stealing the Glory?

I baptize you with water. But one who is more powerful than I will come . . . He will baptize you with the Holy Spirit and fire (Luke 3:16).

Scripture: Luke 3:10-16
Song: "Give Him the Glory"

"Look what the rooster did!" our young visitor exclaimed. Rita held two warm brown eggs in her small hands. "He left these in the box!" The little girl had never been around chickens before. When she entered the coop, Billy, our big, red rooster, was standing in a nesting box, flapping his wings and crowing loudly. When Billy saw her, he jumped out of the box and ran out the door—like a big "chicken." That's when Rita saw the eggs in the nest.

When we fail to acknowledge the Lord's working in our lives, we mislead people into believing that our accomplishments happen by our own efforts. We bask in the praise of people instead of giving the glory to God.

John the Baptist was neither imposter nor chicken. A popular preacher, he proclaimed Christ at every turn. He knew Jesus was the real thing. When people wondered if John were the promised messiah, he set them straight. He used every opportunity to proclaim Christ—eventually at the cost of his life.

I wonder how it is for God when He sees us running around, crowing about our accomplishments, stealing His glory.

Father God, forgive me when I take credit for what You have done in my life. Take away any foolish pride in me, that I may give You all the glory. In Your precious name I ask. Amen.

Share Your Resources

From time to time those who owned land or houses sold them, brought the money from the sales and put it at the apostles' feet, and it was distributed to anyone who had need (Acts 4:34, 35).

Scripture: Acts 4:34—5:10
Song: "Make Me a Blessing"

Our church donates items to our community's Friendship Shop. The volunteer-operated store sells the items and uses the money to aid folks facing financial hardship. It's a win-win situation as our trash becomes someone's treasure.

When I did my September spring cleaning, I tossed several items into a pile to donate. One was a flannel shirt my husband had never worn—and with good reason. The gaudy shirt was covered with large black and yellow checks. It looked like something a lumberjack would wear.

A few weeks later, when it came time to dress my autumn scarecrow, I made a quick stop at the Friendship Shop. I found a perfect shirt and plunked down two dollars for it.

When my husband came home, he thought Mr. Scarecrow looked quite dapper in the black and yellow-checked shirt. He laughed when I told him I had given it away, only to buy it back. But after all, the whole idea of the thrift store is to raise money to help those in need. When I put the scarecrow away for the winter, I again donated the shirt. And now that autumn is coming, I just may check to see if the shirt is still there.

God, I give thanks for people who work to help those in need. May I always do what I can to help ease the financial burdens of others. In Jesus' name, amen.

A Love Song, but Not Silly

Your throne, O God, endures forever and ever. You rule with a scepter of justice" (Psalm 45:6, *New Living Translation*).

Scripture: Psalm 45:1-7
Song: "O, How I Love Jesus"

I couldn't get the Paul McCartney tune out of my head that talked about people who wanted to fill the world with "silly love songs" and asks "What's wrong with that?"

For one thing, it was annoying. McCartney is singing a silly love song about silly loves songs. But he does answer the question, "What's wrong with that?" (Answer: "Love isn't silly"). So the question is answered and explained. That's the basic flow of McCartney's silly lyrics. Yet there's really no need to *explain* when we sing our love songs to God, as the psalmist did. He uses the king as an example, because the king is God's servant. In the New Testament, Hebrews 1:8, 9 quotes Psalm 45:6, referring to Christ.

Have you written a love song lately? Or at least sung one in your heart? A Bible study teacher I know suggested that we pause regularly during our day and lift up this song, "Lord, I love You." While we may not sing the words, we can at least say them. How much sweeter when we say them as a sincere prayer.

Lord God, words cannot express my love for You. My heart truly overflows, and so do my tears of joy for knowing You. Thank You for first loving me! I pray this prayer in the name of Jesus, my Savior and Lord. Amen.

September 14–20. **Jimmie Oliver Fleming** is enjoying her new home and new neighbors, where she lives and writes in Chester, Virginia.

Ruled by Anger . . . or No Regrets?

People with understanding control their anger; a hot temper shows great foolishness (Proverbs 14:29, *New Living Translation*).

Scripture: Proverbs 14:22-29
Song: "Love Lifted Me"

Many tragedies have occurred because of a hasty temper. And I can vouch for that, firsthand. Yet in some cases, my hasty temper can be rightly directed toward me, Jimmie. For instance, I've never forgotten the time when I let a gem of an opportunity slip away because I thought it was "too good to be true." Now I get angry every time I think about it, because moving forward on this wonderful opportunity could have saved me a lot of money and a lot of trouble too. That anger is good motivation to learn and to do better next time.

The old saying "Don't cry over spilled milk" has to overcome my constant regret, though, if I'm to move forward with joy. I'm learning to hand the past over to the Lord.

Bottom line: Thank the Lord for second chances.

And third and fourth chances too! And fifth and sixth.

Well, I think you get the idea. We might need to let anger do its work in us for a season. Then we simply must find ways to let it go. Usually, the best way is to take all that pent-up energy and—rather than directing it at a *person*—point it like a laser beam at a *problem* to be solved.

O God, I'm so thankful that You are in control of all the circumstances in my life, especially my anger. Thank You for lifting me in love. Nothing else could have helped. Having tried other methods, I know this for sure! In Jesus' name, amen.

Home Sweet Home

Jesus returned to Galilee in the power of the Spirit, and news about him spread through the whole countryside (Luke 4:14).

Scripture: Luke 4:14-19
Song: "Jubilee"

A long day at the office can often make you utter the words "home sweet home." Yet in some instances, you may dread going home. What if you don't get the welcome you expect? Or what if you're greeted by the ton of work you left behind? Or how about having to face the guests who came visiting? (On that note, it has been said that the one thing you should never tell your guests is "make yourselves at home").

Unlike us, Jesus was prepared for all circumstances. Before arriving in Nazareth, His boyhood home, He'd become well known throughout the surrounding country. His time of teaching in the synagogue brought praise from everyone. And He continued teaching in His hometown, proclaiming the good news to an enslaved and downtrodden people.

Like Jesus, we can be instruments of spreading good news. There are so many enslaved and downtrodden people around us today, in any hometown! (Think of the addicted—or the financially struggling.)

We are expected to give as Jesus did. We've received redemption, release from captivity to all lesser gods. Now we can be a light of God's grace in our hometown, and everywhere we go.

Thank You, **Father,** for sending Your Son to make it possible for us to be at home with You for eternity someday. May we show others the way "home" also. Amen.

Run for Your Life!

Pursue righteous living, faithfulness, love, and peace. Enjoy the companionship of those who call on the Lord with pure hearts (2 Timothy 2:22, *New Living Translation*).

Scripture: 2 Timothy 2:14-16, 22-26
Song: "More Like the Master"

There's a time to stand still and a time to run. Depending on the circumstances, you may find yourself literally running for your life. However, if you are in the presence of those with impure hearts, this would also qualify for a time to run. It can be the case, whether you're young or old.

I have had to run or stand still by not making a particular phone call. In other cases, I have phoned friends and gotten their answering machines and have been highly thankful that I did. Listening to their greeting message gives me a way out. And if I leave a message at all, I make sure that it's a positive one, and one that reflects the principles in our Scripture today.

For example, I'll say, "Hi, Leticia. I'm just checking to see how you and John are doing. Have a great day." Another time I might say, "Oh, hello, Mrs. White. Sorry I missed you. I just wanted to say 'Happy Thursday morning.'"

Pursuing faith, love, and peace truly works. When you do so from the beginning, you're less likely to have to run for your life. (Still, I think it's a good idea to keep those running shoes handy.)

Lord, thank You for Your Word. Thank You that Your thoughts are not my thoughts, as the prophet Isaiah proclaimed. Yet I know I can remove my impure thoughts with Your help! Through Jesus my Savior, I pray. Amen.

Stopping the Curse

No longer will there be a curse upon anything. For the throne of God and of the Lamb will be there, and his servants will worship him (Revelation 22:3, *New Living Translation*).

Scripture: Revelation 22:1-7
Song: "Follow the Lamb"

One definition of "curse" involves the ideas of *pain* and *trouble*. A certain home on the market was said to be cursed, so the real estate agent decided to pass on that one. Besides, she had an inkling that word had gotten around and that house would probably be on the market for a long time.

On the other hand, she knew from experience that the house she had finally landed as her own dream home had been on the market for five years. Even though newly built and conveniently located by two major interstates—and dozens of area merchants—no one had ever purchased it. She had decided that it was just meant for her.

However, she soon changed her mind. Lots of repairs were needed—so the house was actually a pain. She couldn't stop this pain (or curse), however; she simply had to live with it.

Down here on earth, we all have to live with a certain amount of daily pain and trouble. Yet in Heaven, we'll have no more curse, no more pain, no more trouble. Let us follow the Lamb now, so we'll be perfectly comfortable living with Him in eternity.

O God, I've experienced much pain and trouble and suffering in this world. Yet I know You have prepared a better place for me. Worshipping You faithfully down here means worshipping You always in Heaven. Thank You, in Jesus' name, amen.

A Name That Really Counts

Salvation is found in no one else, for there is no other name under heaven given to mankind by which we must be saved (Acts 4:12).

Scripture: Acts 4:5-12
Song: "The Name of Jesus"

"What is your nickname?" a man once asked me. "I'm just curious." I wouldn't share it with him (nor with you!). My real name, Jimmie, is more important.

In fact, names, in general, are very important. This applies to the brands of the things we buy for our households. For example, some people will buy only name brand products. Nothing else will do.

And consider the famous celebrity names. Many are instantly recognizable, even as first names only. Oprah, for example, means only one person in your mind, right?

But what about the rest of us, with no name recognition? Or whose names have questionable reputations attached to them?

Jesus came to give hope to such people. This is why His name is above all other names, even on the refrigerator. My granddaughters Yelena and Ngozi illustrated this one day when they rearranged some magnets on my refrigerator, making sure the one with the name Jesus on it went at the top.

That name will remain permanently affixed on my refrigerator. What a glorious name to remember each day!

Thank You, **dear Jesus,** for being my Savior. How blessed I am to be able to claim Your name. I know that only You can save me. And only You can keep me safe, now and forever. Thank You, once again, in Your precious name. Amen.

Rejoicing in Suffering

The apostles left the Sanhedrin, rejoicing because they had been counted worthy of suffering disgrace for the Name (Acts 5:41).

Scripture: Acts 5:27-29, 33-42
Song: "Were You There When They Crucified My Lord?"

Peter and the other apostles set an example for moving forward in faith and witness for the Lord. They even rejoiced in the disgrace that came to them for bearing Jesus' name—and believed that suffering for Him was somehow a badge of worthiness in God's eyes. It mattered not what the world thought of them. They rejoiced and continued to teach every day, publicly as well as in their homes.

Hopefully I will take hold of this example and do more teaching in my home. Some of my family members are quick to criticize me for my beliefs (and I do suffer for this). However, I know that they need to hear the all-important and life-saving message, "The one you are looking for is Jesus."

When I think of the troubles and sufferings any of us disciples will encounter because of our faith, I recall some words of a famous nineteenth-century minister, Henry Ward Beecher. May they bless you, as well: "Affliction comes to us all, not to make us sad, but sober; not to make us sorry, but to make us wise; not to make us despondent, but by its darkness to refresh us as the night refreshes the day."

Heavenly Father, thank You for keeping me strong when so many things try to creep in and get me offtrack in my service to You. I know that I can go through whatever is necessary, and even rejoice, through Your strength. In Jesus' name, I pray. Amen.

God Keeps Covenant

The LORD your God, He is God, the faithful God, who keeps His covenant and His lovingkindness to a thousandth generation with those who love Him and keep His commandments (Deuteronomy 7:9, *New American Standard Bible*).

Scripture: Deuteronomy 7:1-11
Song: "Ah, Lord God"

The man came out of Vietnam wounded in body and soul, crushed in every way. He, like Ishmael, was a wild man—against everyone, with everyone against him. No one could speak to him about God without being cursed by him. One day, while on his motorcycle, he was hit by a huge truck. His body was now as mangled as his heart; he would never walk again.

As I sat by Bush's bedside, I prayed, "Lord, give me the words You would say." I began, "There were two men on crosses beside Jesus. They were not religious, they didn't know any theology, never studied Scripture. One cursed Jesus, and one asked to be with Him in paradise. That second man is you, Bush. Only now it is God who is calling *you* to be with *Him.*" I went on to tell him that God didn't care so much about his past as what he would decide about his future. Would he trust God with it?

I had prayed many years for my brother Bush. And that day he became a child of my covenant-keeping God.

Thanks, **Lord,** that You keep covenant with Your children. You have been faithful to my family and me from generation to generation. Praise You, in the name of Jesus, Lord and Savior of all. Amen.

September 21–27. **Marty Prudhomme,** of Mandeville, Louisiana, is a mom, grandmother, and great-grandmother. She teaches Bible studies and leads an evangelism ministry called Adopt a Block.

No Disappointment Here

Incline Your ear to me, rescue me quickly; be to me a rock of strength, a stronghold to save me (Psalm 31:2, *New American Standard Bible*).

Scripture: Psalm 31:1-5, 19-24
Song: "Praise You in This Storm"

At 13 years of age, Michelle suddenly fell into a coma. Her family was devastated to learn she had fluid on the brain. The doctors didn't know why it happened, but they quickly inserted a drain tube to relieve the pressure.

The family began a prayer vigil in Michelle's hospital room, asking friends to help. I too sat with her and prayed Psalm 31 aloud each time I would visit. Her parents and I prayed many times, "Lord, in You we have taken refuge, incline Your ear and rescue Michelle. She is Your child; we put our hope in You."

Two months passed, and then Michelle suddenly woke up. She immediately began to sit up, talk, and walk with very little help. It seemed to us that God had fought her battle when she wasn't able to help herself. Today Michelle is a wife and mother with children of her own.

Often we find ourselves in situations that are totally out of our control. We feel helpless and may become frustrated. These are perfect opportunities for us to trust the Lord. God will be a stronghold for those who call on His name and place their trust in Him. I firmly believe He will not disappoint us.

King of glory, I put my trust in You. You are my rock of strength. Help me to be strong and courageous, even when things look hopeless. In the holy name of Jesus, my Lord and Savior, I pray. Amen.

My Delight

If Your law had not been my delight, then I would have perished in my affliction (Psalm 119:92, *New American Standard Bible*).

Scripture: Psalm 119:89-94
Song: "Thy Word Is a Lamp unto My Feet"

The love of my life had grown cold—I wanted a divorce. He and I were very different, we clashed at every turn, and the fighting seemed endless. Things would certainly be difficult, and my prayer was, "Lord, please don't let this hurt my children."

A group of ladies at my church were praying for me and invited me to their Bible study. I'd never been to a Bible study, so I was willing to see what it was all about. The ladies showed me how to study the Word for myself—and it was so exciting and challenging to discover God's will for my life. Soon I began to realize what God was saying about marriage in the Scriptures.

I'd prayed for an easy divorce (as if there were such a thing). Instead, God gave me a hunger for His will and taught me to trust in His ways. He revived my love for my husband as I walked in obedience to biblical precepts.

All of this happened 40 years ago. My husband and I have been married now for 45 years, and I have never regretted following God's plan. When we surrender to Him, He revitalizes parts of our lives that we'd thought were lost forever.

Almighty and most merciful God, You are full of lovingkindness and patience. I would have been lost and unhappy in my affliction without Your precepts. Please continue to teach me Your Word and give me grace to keep Your commands. In the precious name of Jesus I pray. Amen.

God Equips Us

In everything you were enriched in Him, in all speech and all knowledge (1 Corinthians 1:5, *New American Standard Bible*).

Scripture: 1 Corinthians 1:1-9
Song: "You Raise Me Up"

My husband, Bill, is an electrical engineer and computer specialist. He's your guy for any kind of technical job. When Bill gave his life to the Lord, he worried about how God could possibly use his abilities. He would ask me, "I can't preach, teach Bible studies, or sing. How can I be of use to the Lord?"

Bill soon discovered that God had already equipped him with every gift he needed. His first opportunity to use his talents came when Bill met a minister in our community who was building a church. The minister was in a financial bind and asked Bill to design the wiring for his church. Since that time, Bill has developed church websites, designed sound systems, and planned various types of audio/video setups for Christian ministries and missionaries.

At one large church he developed a video ministry, even training the volunteers in using the cameras. Singers and teachers abound, but very few people have Bill's much-needed skills.

Many of us may wonder, "How can God use me?" Through his letters to the Corinthians, Paul reassures us that God has given each church what it needs to grow and thrive. Each of us has a spiritual gift to contribute to the cause.

Dear God, thank You for equipping our churches with the spiritual gifts we need to serve You and one another. I ask that You would continue to use me for Your glory, as I eagerly await Your glorious return. Through Christ, amen.

Another Opportunity to Trust?

Examine everything carefully; hold fast to that which is good (1 Thessalonians 5:21, *New American Standard Bible*).

Scripture: 1 Thessalonians 5:16-25
Song: "Rejoice in the Lord Always"

The doctor said I would be like "the guy on the golf course" — who dies quickly from a heart attack. Surprisingly, I wasn't frightened, because the Lord whispered to me in a still small voice, "You are in a win–win situation." If I died, it would be quick. And if I lived, it would be God's will. I thought to myself, "win–win." I was amazed that I could rejoice in the Lord.

There were three choices: quench the Spirit, panic, or choose to rejoice and give thanks that God's will ruled over my life. In fact, I found tremendous comfort in knowing God would make the final decision. Rejoicing lifted my spirit and calmed my emotions.

Fifteen years have passed since that time, and my heart is ticking just fine, perfectly normal for my age. The Lord taught me to listen to His voice, to examine everything carefully, and to cling to what is good.

I suppose it always comes down to trust or don't trust, doesn't it? We face difficult choices daily. We can receive God's wisdom and peace or refuse it. The thing is, it takes practice to learn how to put our full weight in His arms. Maybe that's why He allows the constant procession of opportunities to do it.

Dear Lord, give me a greater sensitivity to Your Word, and help me yield to Your will. Teach me to trust more. I want to cling to what is good and continually rejoice in Your goodness. I pray in the name of Jesus my Lord. Amen.

Full of Grace and Power

Stephen, a man full of God's grace and power, performed great wonders and signs among the people (Acts 6:8).

Scripture: Acts 6:7-15
Song: "No Chains on Me"

My friends Gail and Greg were American missionaries working in various churches in Costa Rica. The power of the gospel message was spreading, and the Lord's signs and wonders became evident to many people. On the front lines of the gospel's advance, when the message would encounter pagan beliefs or even demonic influence, it seemed the Lord worked in special ways. There were physical healings, for instance, and many new churches sprang up overnight.

However, before long, some ministers became jealous of the churches that were growing. Lies began to spread, saying Gail and Greg were false teachers. Eventually the leadership of the churches called them in to accuse them. This action hurt Gail and Greg deeply, but they didn't argue with the leaders; instead, they trusted the Lord to defend them.

One by one, the lies of their accusers came to light. The couple continued to minister in Costa Rica, Panama, and Guatemala. My friends were not the only ministers to experience the revival that swept Costa Rica and most of Central America in the 1970s and 80s. When God's Word is preached—the kingdom of God increases.

O Lord, You are my Savior, Redeemer, and healer. I pray that You will use me to bring the good news of Your gospel to many people. I want to follow You and be a witness to others of Your great love and goodness. I pray in Jesus' name. Amen.

He'll Rescue You

[God] rescued him from all his troubles. He gave Joseph wisdom and enabled him to gain the goodwill of Pharaoh . . . So Pharaoh made him ruler over Egypt (Acts 7:10).

Scripture: Acts 7:2-4, 8-10, 17, 33, 34, 45-47, 52, 53
Song: "My Deliverer"

The Lord rescued my grandson Scott by sending him to prison. He was a drug user who became a dealer in order to pay for his habit. But while in jail, he fully committed his life to the Lord and was healed from many old wounds.

Scott learned obedience to the Lord through many trials as he remained in prison. He worked diligently to get a welding certificate, took two years of business college, and gained a sign-language certificate. Soon he moved into the deaf dormitory where he led many prisoners to the Lord and helped others with their paroles.

Scott was greatly persecuted for his faith, but he found favor with the warden, his teachers, and many ministries in the prison community. God heard his groans and the prayers of his family. He gave Scott favor in the midst of his own personal Egypt. Yesterday Scott phoned; he was with his Gramps on the way home. They wanted to surprise me—he'd been released three months early. And the man who'd taught him sign language is the translator for the governor of Louisiana. He has a job waiting for Scott.

Dear Lord, You have seen my oppression, heard my prayers, and rescued me out of the hand of my enemies. You are my deliverer and have shown me great favor. I pray for Your continued protection. In Jesus' name. Amen.

The Guest List

LORD, who may abide in Your tabernacle? Who may dwell in Your holy hill? (Psalm 15:1, *New King James Version*).

Scripture: Psalm 15
Song: "More Holiness Give Me"

Our granddaughter was making a list of family, friends, and coworkers for her wedding. She pictured the people as she wrote their names. The guest list grew as she thought of the people who had been a part of her life for 22 years. Customers she waited on weekly, at the restaurant, were also included.

Her fiancé had a list, but there were some questionable people on it from his past years, before he'd become a Christian. They decided to invite those with good character, not those who were known for questionable behaviors or causing dissension.

The details of the wedding were meticulously planned, the right colors blending with the theme set by the bride. She wanted everything to be as perfect as possible. On her wedding day, she would be transformed from the friendly waitress to the beautiful bride.

I want to be on the guest list of the Lord and be a person of good character. What is a person of good character? David gives us the answer in this short psalm. Won't you join me in taking it to heart today?

Lord, thank You for showing me what's required to be on Your guest list. Help me to have a strong, good character. I want to dwell with You in eternity. I seek to please You in my days on earth. Guide me, in Jesus' name. Amen.

September 28–30. **Beverly LaHote Schwind** retired to Tennessee and teaches at a rehab mission. She is the author of five books, as well as being a Senior Olympics medalist.

One Life

Keep your lives free from the love of money and be content with what you have, because God has said, "Never will I leave you; never will I forsake you" (Hebrews 13:5).

Scripture: Hebrews 13:5-10
Song: "Unsearchable Riches"

Charles Thomas Studd, known as C. T. Studd, became a Christian when he was 18 years old in 1878. This wealthy young man attended Trinity College in Cambridge, England. He ended his school career in a blaze of glory as a cricket player (still considered best in the world). Fame shadowed his commitment to Christ until his brother became very ill. This caused C. T. to realize how unimportant fame, glory, and wealth were.

He stunned the world by leaving it all behind, and with a passion became one of the "Cambridge Seven" that followed a missionary calling to China in 1885. His motto was: "If Jesus is God and He died for me, then there is no sacrifice too great for me to make for Him."

This makes me think of the rich young ruler in Luke 18. Jesus told this young man to sell all he had and distribute it to the poor; he would have treasure in Heaven. Then Jesus invited the man to follow Him. But the man couldn't bring himself to give his possessions away, as he was very rich. He allowed his treasures to keep him from following Christ (see Luke 18:18-23).

But what did C. T. Studd say? "Only one life, 'twill soon be past. Only what's done for Christ will last."

Dear Lord, thank You for the blessings I enjoy in my life. Help me to control my finances and not let them control me. In Jesus' name, amen.

Hunting Season

Take the helmet of salvation, and the sword of the Spirit, which is the word of God (Ephesians 6:17, *New King James Version*).

Scripture: Ephesians 6:14-18
Song: "God's Got an Army"

"Where's my hunting vest?" I heard my husband mumble to himself as he and our son organized their equipment. Our son had come from out of state to go hunting with his dad. Neither of them had ever gone turkey hunting before, but they'd talked about it for a few years and read much about it. Now they'd been invited to hunt on a wooded property.

I took pictures of them. They had on their hunting hats, camouflaged vests, buckled up boots. They had their ammunition belted, and they carried their guns. "It looks like you're going to war," I said as I snapped the picture.

"We are, against the turkeys," they laughed.

Spiritual battles need their equipment too. We can equip ourselves in the same manner as the hunter or soldier—but against the spiritual forces of darkness. The spoken Word of God, empowered by the Holy Spirit, will help attract the sincere seeker of truth. Also, when we have our armor on, we can stand against all manner of fiery temptations.

I'm not good at memorizing, so I write encouraging Scriptures on index cards, and I put them on my refrigerator door. Thus I "put on" God's Word, and it becomes my daily armor.

Dear Father, I thank You for Your Word. As I dress each day, I want to be reminded to put on that special armor You have provided. In Jesus' name, amen.

My Prayer Notes

DEVOTIONS®

OCTOBER

The righteous are as bold as a lion.

— *Proverbs 28:1*

Gary Wilde, Editor **Margaret Williams,** Project Editor Photo Blend Images | Thinkstock©

DEVOTIONS® is published quarterly by Standard Publishing, Cincinnati, Ohio, www.standardpub.com.
© 2014 by Standard Publishing. All rights reserved. Topics based on the Home Daily Bible Readings,
International Sunday School Lessons. © 2012 by the Committee on the Uniform Series. Printed in
the U.S.A. All Scripture quotations, unless otherwise indicated, are taken from the *HOLY BIBLE,
NEW INTERNATIONAL VERSION®. NIV®.* Copyright © 1973, 1978, 1984, 2011 by Biblica, Inc.®
Used by permission of Zondervan. All rights reserved worldwide. *New American Standard Bible®,*
(*NASB*) Copyright © 1960, 1962, 1963, 1968, 1971, 1972, 1973, 1975, 1977, 1995 by The Lock-
man Foundation. Used by permission. (www.Lockman.org). *Holy Bible, New Living Translation*
(*NLT*), © 1996, 2004, 2007. Tyndale House Publishers. Scripture quotations marked (*NKJV*) are
taken from the *New King James Version®.* Copyright © 1982 by Thomas Nelson, Inc. Used by
permission. All rights reserved. *The Living Bible* (*TLB*), © 1971 by Tyndale House Publishers,
Wheaton, IL.

Joy in the Cottage

The disciples were filled with joy and with the Holy Spirit (Acts 13:52, *New King James Version*).

Scripture: Acts 13:52–14:3
Song: "Jesus Saves"

"Jim, can you meet me at the Sullivan cottage? I'm working there tomorrow morning." The phone call was from my husbands' friend Stan, who was struggling with some problems in his life. Jim had advised Stan at times in the past, also sharing how his own life had changed after his baptism into Christ.

Stan and Jim spent the morning in the empty cottage, talking things over. Stan wanted some changes in his life. They shared and prayed, and then Stan asked the Lord to forgive him and come into his life. It happened 25 years ago, and they still talk about it with great joy. In fact, Stan gets teary every time he talks about the day in the cottage story.

The bond between these two men is strong even though they live states apart. A marriage was saved—and other issues handled—when Jesus was invited into the situation.

Telling someone about the Lord is exciting, but sometimes we may just plant the seed of faith, knowing that someone else will actually witness the results. This brings joy to the messenger and the convert. It is a joy that lasts—an everlasting joy.

Lord, thank You for the joy that comes into our hearts when we tell others about Your plan of salvation for them. Nothing else can measure up to that joy! In Christ, amen.

October 1–4. **Beverly LaHote Schwind** retired to Tennessee and teaches at a rehabilitation mission. She is the author of five books, as well as being a Senior Olympics medalist.

Joy in the City

The believers who had fled Jerusalem went everywhere preaching the Good News about Jesus! (Acts 8:4, *The Living Bible*).

Scripture: Acts 8:1-8
Song: "I Love to Tell the Story"

"It's a boy!" I watched on TV as joy spread through the city of London. Kate and William, the Duke and Duchess of Cambridge, had a baby boy. When the couple first arrived at the hospital, the crowd waited outside for hours to be the first to hear the news. The media waited with the crowd, interviewing various people and repeating the same reports over and over.

It was good news that an heir to the throne was born, healthy and whole. And that news rippled through the world in myriad languages.

There was other news that week, news of disaster to airlines and forest fires raging in the West. But the good news of what had happened in England seemed to take priority. Well-wishers went back to their homes and countries full of joy. They will pass the story to future generations: *We were at the hospital the day the prince was born!*

The believers who heard about Jesus left Jerusalem, and their joy was much greater than their fear. They had witnessed miracles, and they couldn't contain what they'd seen and heard. That's just how it is when the world changes for the better.

Jesus, I pray that the good news of Your birth and resurrection be proclaimed to the world. Fill me, Lord, so that I may share this message with others and tell of Your goodness in my life. In Jesus' name I pray. Amen.

What a Trough!

Then Phillip said, "If you believe with all your heart, you may." And he answered and said, "I believe that Jesus Christ is the Son of God" (Acts 8:37, *New King James Version*).

Scripture: Acts 8:26-40
Song: "Come, Now Is the Time to Worship"

Nine girls in orange scrubs walked into the jail garage. Their faces showed fear, anxiety . . . and yet . . . there was an air of excitement. White towels draped about the necks of some, while others clutched their towels like a pacifier.

A large metal trough for watering animals stood in the middle of the room, and the minister stood waiting to baptize the women and then the men. They'd given their hearts to Christ.

The guards stood at the door as the names of the women rang out. No choir sang as they walked forward. Having been taught week after week about the love of Jesus, they had said, like the eunuch, "I believe and want to be baptized." Next, the group of men that had also asked to be baptized came into the garage and nervously awaited their turns.

I thought about how Christ was born and laid in a feeding trough. And now these men and women in jail were baptized into His family . . . in a watering trough. As their teachers, we applauded them all and hugged each one, grateful to be a part of their entrance into the kingdom of God.

Dear Jesus, thank You for the gift of eternal life through baptism! As Phillip brought understanding of Your salvation to the eunuch, help me to shine forth Your saving love in all I do and say. I am so grateful for Your mercy and grace. In Your holy name I pray. Amen.

Real or Fake?

Peter said to him, "May your silver perish with you, because you thought you could obtain the gift of God with money!" (Acts 8:20, *New American Standard Bible*).

Scripture: Acts 8:9-24
Song: "All Who, with Heart Confiding"

When I was 12, I was baptized with a class of others, because that is how they did it in my church. Everyone presumed that I knew who Jesus was, and I thought I did too. I received a Bible, a cross, and a certificate.

I thought I was a Christian. I sang all the songs and sat in church almost every Sunday. From my outward appearance I *was* a Christian. I went to Bible camp when I was in my teens and saw a passion in people that I did not have. Many of them were thrilled with reading the Bible.

I was hungry for what they had, and finally I was able to hear with my heart what the Lord was saying through the good teachers around me. I suppose I could say the Holy Spirit ministered to me; I do know that Jesus became real to me.

Any of us could buy a T-shirt with a Christian emblem on it. We might purchase a beautiful silver cross and wear it every day. We may look the part, but none of this would produce a genuine faith. Faith is a matter of the heart—not merchandise. In other words, the stark message of Peter to Simon is applicable to us today.

Dear Lord, thank You for the free gift of salvation that You offer to all people. You alone were able to purchase it—with precious drops of Your own blood. In light of Your great sacrifice, I wish to give my whole life to You. In Jesus' name, amen.

Really Clean?

The LORD has rewarded me according to my righteousness, according to the cleanness of my hands in his sight (Psalm 18:24).

Scripture: Psalm 18:20-30
Song: "Cleanse Me"

Training my 2-year-old son to wash his hands has been an adventure. Usually he's more interested in splashing the water out of the sink than onto his hands. I let him participate in the process, but I help him scrub his chubby digits to make sure they actually get clean. Even though I'm doing most of the work, I lavish praise on my little guy for a job well done.

God rewards those whose hands are clean in His sight. As Christians, we know we're saved by God's grace, not by works (see Ephesians 2:8, 9). When we receive that gift of salvation, God sees Christ's righteousness in us rather than our sin. Our hearts and hands are not yet fully clean on their own—they are soiled by our sin—though the process of cleansing has begun. But they are clean in His sight, purified by Jesus' blood.

What a loving heavenly Father we serve! Even we, as sinners, know how to give good gifts to our children. How much more gracious is our God for cleansing us through the blood of His Son and by the work of His Spirit in our hearts.

Lord, thank You for justifying grace, Your declaration of righteousness. And thank You for the sanctifying process of cleansing that continues in me daily. One day I will stand before You, perfectly clean in every way. Praise You, through Christ! Amen.

October 5–11. **Lisa Earl** writes from her home in western Pennsylvania. She enjoys spending time with her husband, two young sons, and cream tabby cat.

A Legacy of Faith

Surely the righteous will never be shaken; they will be remembered forever (Psalm 112:6).

Scripture: Psalm 112:1, 2, 6-9
Song: "Faith of Our Fathers"

I've recently started making family collages for my children. Two of my grandparents and my uncle recently passed away, and I want the kids to remember these beloved family members. But when I realized I'd have to label each photo, it became a much more complicated process than I first envisioned.

Then it hit me: as our children and future grandchildren—and even our great-grandchildren—branch out on their own, these ancestors will be long forgotten, and so will I. It's inevitable. Who knows anything about their great-great-great-great grandparents? Such things are easier today with digital photography, but eventually we will all be forgotten. Only one legacy can be left behind permanently: The person of Jesus Christ, and His gracious offer of adoption into the Father's family.

My children may not know that my grandma went to church every Sunday or that her favorite hymn was "How Great Thou Art," but they will know that gospel message. They may not remember that my mom sang Vacation Bible School songs with me on the swing set, but they will know the gospel. I may not remember my great-great-great grandparents, but surely some of them loved the Lord. Their legacy of faith lives on.

Dear God, please help me to share Your truth with my children, grandchildren, or other young people You place in my path. May the truth of Your gospel endure from generation to generation. In Jesus' name, amen.

Paranoia Needed?

Since you call on a Father who judges each person's work impartially, live out your time as foreigners here in reverent fear (1 Peter 1:17).

Scripture: 1 Peter 1:16-19
Song: "Guide Me, O Thou Great Jehovah"

My husband and I decided to spend a week in Prince Edward Island, Canada, a few years ago. As a lifelong fan of the Anne of Green Gables books, I couldn't wait for this adventure to begin.

We signed up for an official tour of the area, riding in a van with a tour guide. As we rumbled over country roads, some made only of tightly packed red dirt, I started to become a bit paranoid. Here we were, far out in the country—in a foreign country—with just our tour guide and a retired English couple. Our cell phones didn't work. We had no idea where we were going or how to get back to our inn. An uncomfortable feeling set in: We were at the mercy of this guide.

Likewise, as Christians, we are foreigners on this earth. We don't know where life will take us next. The road might be smooth for a while, but often we're led through rough patches: illness, injury, financial problems, relational conflict.

We are at the mercy of Jesus, our guide, to help us find our way back home to Him. Thankfully, we know that Jesus is a kind, gracious, perfect guide, and He will never abandon us or lead us astray. No need for the slightest paranoia.

Dear Lord, help me to follow You in every area of my life today. As You keep my focus on Heaven, my ultimate destination, may I be a good ambassador of Your love right here until I arrive home. In Jesus name, amen.

The Wisdom Before Us

The Queen of the South will rise at the judgment with the people of this generation and condemn them, for she came from the ends of the earth to listen to Solomon's wisdom; and now something greater than Solomon is here (Luke 11:31).

Scripture: Luke 11:30-37
Song: "Eternal Wisdom, Thee We Praise"

A former university professor and gay activist recently published a book titled *The Secret Thoughts of an Unlikely Convert*. In this memoir, she writes about her conversion to Christianity after receiving a thought-provoking letter from a local minister. She sought godly wisdom by meeting with the minister and his wife in their home. After coming to Christ, she left her former community and lost many friends and colleagues.

Today's passage warns us against ignoring God's revelation. The queen of Sheba came to Solomon, the king of Israel, because she had heard of his godly wisdom. This was long before Jesus, the greatest revelation, came to earth and died on the cross for our sins.

I've gone to church all of my life, and I've believed in Jesus for as long as I can remember. I don't want to take that for granted. So I must ask myself: How am I allowing the truth of the gospel to transform my life? Am I truly seeking God's wisdom? Let us daily recognize the privilege of having the greatest wisdom right before us: the message of Christ crucified, risen, ascended, and coming again.

Father, thank You for the privilege of knowing You and Your Word. Help me to become more and more thankful for the precious gift of Your Son. In His name, amen.

The Blink of an Eye

For three days he was blind, and did not eat or drink anything (Acts 9:9).

Scripture: Acts 9:1-9
Song: "I Waited Patient for the Lord"

Recently, Google engineers discovered that Internet users won't even wait 400 milliseconds—literally the blink of an eye—for a website to load. Software developers seek to make websites work faster and faster as people search for information from computers, smart phones, and other devices that connect to the Internet.

Today's passage tells us that Saul waited three days before he received the Holy Spirit and began preaching. After he heard the voice of the risen Jesus on the road to Damascus, he was blind and had to be led by his companions the rest of the way.

The biblical time frame of three days is powerful. Abraham was commanded to sacrifice his son, Isaac, and he set out on a three-day journey. Jonah languished in the belly of a fish for three days. Jesus rose from the dead on the third day.

Sometimes God's plan requires patience. In a culture that can't even pause for the blink of an eye, let us fix our eyes unflinchingly on Jesus, the pioneer and perfecter of our faith (see Hebrews 12:2). Then we will be able, in quietness and confidence, to discern His will for our lives. And we will be able, with wisdom and grace, to share the gospel with those He places in our paths.

Lord Jesus, I fix my eyes on You today. Free me from distractions, doubts, and fears. In the name of the Father and of the Son and of the Holy Spirit I pray. Amen.

Recharging Through Fellowship

After taking some food, he regained his strength (Acts 9:19).

Scripture: Acts 9:10-19
Song: "What a Fellowship"

My husband and I live several hours away from our families and the friends we knew in childhood. We both moved from rural areas to a midsized city to attend college and find work. Most of our college friends left the area after graduation, leaving us feeling isolated.

A few years after we were married, we joined a church dinner group that meets in each other's homes. Each family brings a food item to share, and we simply eat and enjoy the company of friends. The four families in the group have all had children at the same time, and we now strive to raise our children in the fear and admonition of the Lord. We encourage one another.

The idea isn't all that new. The apostle Paul was the most powerful missionary in Christian history. It would make sense that, once he received the Holy Spirit, he'd jump up and immediately begin preaching. Nevertheless, he took time to eat and then spent several days with the disciples in Damascus, sharing in fellowship and gaining strength for the work ahead. He too needed the support and encouragement of other believers.

Let us never be afraid to take time simply to enjoy the fellowship of other believers. How refreshing it can be—and how essential for a powerful witness to the world around us.

Dear Lord, help me connect with others in Your body, the church. Place people in my path with whom I can serve, grow, and share. In Jesus' name, amen.

Keep the Main Thing, the Main Thing

Living in the fear of the Lord and encouraged by the Holy Spirit, it increased in numbers (Acts 9:31).

Scripture: Acts 9:19-31
Song: "Great Is Thy Faithfulness"

A blog called "The Christian Pundit" recently noted a trend among young evangelicals: they're flocking to more traditional congregations that emphasize liturgy and church history. Blue jeans are out, and more formal church clothes are in. This seems to be reversing the trend of a generation ago, when 20-somethings opted to worship in a more casual, contemporary setting.

It can be hard to keep up with the trends. One minute hymns are out, and then, all of a sudden, everything old is new again. How should we reach others with the gospel? Should we focus on the musical style or vestments, or should we bring in the latest celebrity preachers?

Today's verse reminds us that the power of the Holy Spirit will grow the church, not our efforts alone. Our main focus should be on faithfully proclaiming the gospel and living in the fear of the Lord. Trends will come and go, but one thing never changes: the invitation to repent and receive forgiveness in Christ.

While God may call different congregations to reach different groups of people through different worship styles, we can never go wrong if we remain focused on the main thing: that God was in Christ reconciling the world to himself. Let that message be our theme as we seek to reach the world for Him.

Gracious God, thank You for Your faithfulness in building Your church. Purify me by Your Holy Spirit, so I can reach others for You. Through Christ, amen.

Victory Redefined

Can anything ever separate us from Christ's love? Does it mean he no longer loves us if we have trouble or calamity . . . ? (Romans 8:35, *New Living Translation*).

Scripture: Romans 8:31-39
Song: "O the Deep, Deep Love of Jesus"

It didn't feel like a victory. The words to "O the Deep, Deep Love of Jesus" didn't arouse warm feelings when the soloist sang it. My daughter had committed suicide, and I was attending her memorial service. I stood at the starting point of a long, difficult journey of healing. I didn't feel comfort, love, victory, or hope—but I knew such things existed. That hope was the knot at the end of my rope, and I clung to the lifeline.

The next year tested the truth of my favorite Bible verse, "Can anything ever separate us from Christ's love?" (Romans 8:35, *NLT*). That is, do you still believe God loves you when you're in deep trouble? When you're poor and hungry? (I could have added: when your daughter commits suicide?)

Paul's conclusion confounds me: "Despite all these things, overwhelming victory is ours through Christ, who loved us" (v. 37, *NLT*) Despite evidence to the contrary, I do know God loves us. He promises not a victory won by the skin of our teeth, but an overwhelming victory. Such love wins through, even as hope lies shattered on the floor.

Loving Father, Your love is inscrutable, yet limitless. Teach me to trust it amidst the most trying times. Come with Your healing comfort, even now. Through Christ, amen.

October 12–18. **Darlene Franklin** lives in a retirement home in Purcell, Oklahoma. The author of 25 books, she continues to write full-time.

The Son of God . . . for You?

Then those who were in the boat came and worshiped Him, saying, "Truly You are the Son of God" (Matthew 14:33, *New King James Version*).

Scripture: Matthew 14:22-33
Song: "You Are God Alone"

GODISNOWHERE. Our worship leader wrote those capital letters jumbled together on a blackboard and asked us what we saw. Despair or hope? God is *nowhere*, or God is *now here?*

That simple sermon has stayed with me more than any other Christmas message. For the first time, I understood why Christians put so much emphasis on Jesus' birth: He is Immanuel, God with us.

God is now here! God, all of God, the one who created the earth and stopped the Red Sea is with us. God is now here. He is also all man, all here, all of God bound up in a helpless infant.

That was my aha! moment when I worshipped: Truly this man is the Son of God, in my heart as well as my head.

Today's Scripture describes an aha moment for the apostles. Others—Jesus' family, demons—had called Jesus the Son of God. Before this time, the disciples had called him Master. What opened their eyes—Jesus walking on water? Saving Peter from drowning? Stopping the storm as soon as He climbed in the boat? And for that matter, what has made you say: "Jesus is the Son of God"?

Lord, You are God. I see You in the world You created. You reveal yourself in Your Word. And I know You in my heart. May I live each moment of my life with the confidence that You will help me walk on rough waters daily. In Jesus' name, amen.

Something Greater Here

I tell you that something greater than the temple is here. If you had known what these words mean, 'I desire mercy, not sacrifice,' you would not have condemned the innocent. (Matthew 12:6, 7).

Scripture: Matthew 12:1-8
Song: "Sanctuary"

One year, my family made a whirlwind trip from Oklahoma to Ellis Island in a week. We drove past miles and miles of crops in the state of Illinois. To commemorate the occasion, we stopped and took a picture of our two preschoolers hiding in the cornstalks.

When I read about Jesus and His disciples walking through wheat fields, I remembered that day. Hungry and tired, the disciples didn't think about Sabbath rules. They saw a food source and took advantage of it. So the religious leaders pounced.

Something greater is at work here. Worship was never the sum of the law. Rather, the law pointed to deeper truths: Mercy, not sacrifice. People, not rules.

On our trip, we didn't make it to church. But we had many opportunities to worship. We saw the God who gave us food and carved caves into the mountains. We thanked Him for our country at the Statue of Liberty. He joined in our fellowship with friends. Worship doesn't depend on time and place. It depends on our hearts.

Lord of the Sabbath, You still desire mercy and not sacrifice. When my shortsighted heart focuses on unimportant details, correct my vision to see people as You see them. Then make me a conduit of Your mercy. In Jesus' name, amen.

By No Means

Peter said, "By no means, Lord, for I have never eaten anything unholy and unclean" (Acts 10:14, *New American Standard Bible*).

Scripture: Acts 10:1-16
Song: "I Surrender All"

Due to a recent health crisis, I've moved from my house to a retirement home. In doing so, I had to downsize my belongings to what I most wanted to preserve. At the top of my list, right after the books I've written and my family pictures, were my Christmas ornaments. The collection tells my family's story, and I collected them based on many cherished memories.

Unfortunately, my collection came into conflict with my son's point of view about Christmas. He chooses to celebrate only the religious observances mentioned by name in the Bible, which shuts out the word *Christmas*. (This, of course, is clearly a minority opinion!) When he refused to keep my ornaments, I wasn't so much surprised as disappointed.

Did God feel the same when Peter said, "By no means, Lord"? Did the disciple hesitate before he uttered the words that contradicted each other? (If Jesus was his *Lord*, Peter shouldn't have said *no*.) Our arguments today may still hinge on food and holidays. Or they might go on to differences in church ordinances or worship styles. In such gray matters, let us be careful not to say "by no means, Lord" when He says to "get up and eat."

O God, how many times have I called You "Lord" and yet have refused to obey? Forgive me. Tame my pride when I have looked down on others who don't worship as I do. Let me never say no when You are urging me to say yes. In Jesus' name, amen.

From Doubt to Certainty

Arise therefore, go down and go with them, doubting nothing; for I have sent them (Acts 10:20, *New King James Version*).

Scripture: Acts 10:17-23
Song: "O Hope of Every Contrite Heart"

Six-year-old Ruby Bridges performed one of the bravest acts in the history of the United States. She simply attended her first day of first grade in 1960, in New Orleans. She was the first and the only black student in this all-white school. In many ways, she symbolized the wave of school desegregation that was changing the landscape of American education.

The Bridges family attended church while they debated the wisdom of pitting their daughter against centuries of ingrained racial hatred. But when the government—dare we say God?—sent federal marshals, they allowed Ruby to go with them. Did they make the decision without reservations? I doubt it.

Peter stood at such a crossroads between faith and doubt. Was the message of salvation for the Jews only—or for all the people of the earth? But God said: "Go with them. Don't doubt."

A risky faith acts in spite of doubt. I may doubt that I will succeed. I may doubt my own strength. But I place my hope in the God who gives me everything I need and who makes me strong.

A new school—a new church—a new job. Wherever God leads, we can move forward with Him in confidence.

Almighty and everlasting God, sometimes You lead me to do things that frighten me. Shine Your light on my path, that I may follow You step by step, day by day. May I discern the difference between dreams sent by You and my own selfish desires. In Jesus' name I pray. Amen.

Eyes to See

God raised Him up on the third day and granted that He become visible, not to all the people, but to witnesses who were chosen beforehand by God (Acts 10:40, 41, *New American Standard Bible*).

Scripture: Acts 10:39-48
Song: "Open My Eyes"

When my family went traveling, three of us kids crowded into the back seat. As the trip stretched to long hours eating up the highway between Kentucky and Wisconsin, we played games. One involved spotting letters in alphabetical order. Some were easy to find. Others, like a *Q* or a *Z*, rarely showed up on billboard signs. That's when we scouted license plates.

Sometimes my brother found a letter that I missed. When I claimed I saw it, my dad told me, "No, you didn't." I pouted. I had no chance to win if I had to wait for the next time a *Q* showed up on a road sign.

I had missed letters hidden in plain sight. Something similar to that happened at Jesus' resurrection. Not everyone saw Him. The soldiers guarding the tomb? They slept through the most momentous event of their lives. The priests? By the time they were called to the tomb, Jesus had gone.

God handpicked the witnesses to Jesus's resurrection. He became visible when He chose—without benefit of special effects. Even so today God has given us eyes to see, eyes of faith, a heart-vision granted to us from Heaven.

Light of the World, as those disciples of old told the story of Jesus' resurrection, let me also bear witness to what I have seen and heard. Through Christ, amen.

Guess Who Moved?

Now we are all here in the presence of God to listen to everything the Lord has commanded you to tell us (Acts 10:33).

Scripture: Acts 10:24-38
Song: "In the Garden"

"Eighty percent of success is showing up," said Woody Allen. Every month, I receive a calendar of daily activities at the home where I live. All I have to do is show up to have popcorn and a movie, get my hair cut, or sing hymns with a visiting church.

Excuses abound for not attending, though. I might not receive help in time. My therapist arrives to work with me. I forget.

Most disappointing, sometimes the people who promise to come . . . *don't!* That happened last Sunday when the local church group didn't show up. Their pianist was unavailable. Even worse, some weeks I just choose to remain in my room. What would the church be like today if Cornelius hadn't sent for Peter, or if Peter had refused to go?

When we do gather together, God descends on that lonely lobby. We sing the familiar hymns of our childhood. Unable to sing, I cry at God's beauty.

Even when alone, God invites me to come into His presence, be it by reading the Bible on the computer, by singing hymns and praise songs, or by silent prayer. God meets me there.

I cannot hear what God has to say if I don't take the time to listen. As someone has said, "If you feel far from God, guess who moved?"

God, You invite me to worship, whether on my own or with others, in the silence of nature or in the symphony of music. When You call, may I respond. In Christ, amen.

Default to God

I will also make you a light for the Gentiles, that my salvation may reach to the ends of the earth (Isaiah 49:6).

Scripture: Isaiah 49:5-7
Song: "Make Me a Servant"

At the end of our horse pasture, there's an old cedar tree whose branches formed perfect junctures for a tree house. With our kids, we spent an afternoon rounding up old boards from the barn, a discarded telephone cable reel, rope, and nails.

We measured and sawed the boards to make a square frame that would fit between the branches. We disassembled the cable reel, converting it into a floor to wedge within our framework. Using a ladder and rope, we hoisted the foundation pieces upward, then nailed everything together in the crooks of the tree.

Our tree house hosted many adventures, and even served as a hideout. Little Marci found refuge there when she ran away from home with a jelly sandwich, a copy of *Little House on the Prairie,* and her stuffed rabbit. Now, 20 years later, our little tree house, with steps nailed into the trunk and rope to swing out with, still serves as a treasured setting for pursuing God's heart.

Isaiah poised himself to seek God. He listened as the Lord shared His vision for his life. God designed Isaiah to be a servant and commissioned him as a catalyst for restoration.

Dear Father in Heaven, I'm grateful for Your purposeful design—from houses to hearts. In any creative endeavor, may I look to You for the meaning and purpose to infuse it. In Jesus' name I pray. Amen.

October 19–25. **Vicki L. Hodges** lives in the mountains of western Colorado with her family. She's a high school Spanish teacher who loves to travel.

A Grooved Heart

Whoever drinks the water I give them will never thirst. Indeed, the water I give them will become in them a spring of water welling up to eternal life (John 4:14).

Scripture: John 4:3-14
Song: "Springs of Living Water"

In today's verses, we meet a Samaritan woman who encountered the Lord at Jacob's well. After an intensely personal conversation, He talked with the woman about living water and eternal life. She was forever changed.

Hand-dug wells in ancient Israel were deep, sometimes with depths of 60 to over 100 feet, depending on the water table level. People fastened a bucket or clay jar to a rope and lowered it into the well, allowed the container to fill, then heaved it up. Over time, friction from the rope's sliding carved deep grooves into the well's "curbs," its top edges.

When I was in college, I was involved with a campus ministry whose director, Ron, was a man of great spiritual stature. He so enjoyed encouraging believers in their spiritual growth and relished helping them become disciple-makers.

Because of Ron's passion for people and God's Word, in a process of disciple-multiplication, countless people around the world are now walking with Jesus. The curbs of Ron's heart contain deep grooves from constantly drawing the living water of God's Word and sharing its truths of eternal life.

Lord, I'm thirsting for You. Would You fill me with a conscious awareness of Your presence and with a passion for Your living Word? Please wear a groove in my heart as I draw in Your life-giving water. In Jesus' name, amen.

Prepared, Not Frightened

In your hearts revere Christ as Lord. Always be prepared to give an answer to everyone who asks you to give the reason for the hope that you have (1 Peter 3:15).

Scripture: 1 Peter 3:13-18
Song: "The Battle Belongs to the Lord"

Our dream vacation to Sitka, Alaska, quickly approached, and we discussed itinerary options with Mark and Hedy. Hedy, proud of her Alaskan native heritage, wanted us to visit her parents and experience her rich Tlingit culture. When she suggested hiking, she casually referenced the abundance of sporting goods stores that sold pepper spray.

Steve and I exchanged glances. "Hedy, why did you mention pepper spray?"

"Well, it would only be necessary if bears attack us."

Bears! What would we do? flee? scream? spray ourselves with pepper? Hedy informed us that young school children receive extensive training for living in bear country. Adequate education, preparation, and a tranquil spirit are essential.

Perhaps one of our greatest privileges is sharing our faith with others. During any given conversation, such an opportunity may arise. Sometimes I am prepared to share and do so with confidence. Other times, my instinct is to flee. I lose my nerve and forget that God has empowered me. In His strength I can speak of Him with grace, love, and all humility. (Preparation and a tranquil spirit are essential.)

Father, thank You for the reliable, relevant truths in Your Word. The hope of the gospel is the encouraging message I want to share. In Jesus' name, amen.

Fire and Rain

His purpose was to create in himself one new humanity out of the two, thus making peace (Ephesians 2:15).

Scripture: Ephesians 2:11-22
Song: "My Faith Has Found a Resting Place"

"The fire stopped 500 yards from my apartment." Aimee's words flooded us with peace. Our daughter had evacuated twice from the 2012 Waldo Canyon fire in Colorado Springs. Tearfully, from her front porch, Amy viewed once lovely homes now standing as smoking hulks, with blackened vegetation replacing verdant wildlife habitats.

"I'm in the middle of a flash flood warning!" A year later, Aimee's words blazed through the phone. She had received numerous calls urging her to be prepared to move to higher ground. Midsummer cloudbursts assaulted the charred, eroded terrain. Forests no longer restrained rushing water. Once again, the elements were at odds with humanity, potential enemies of the land, poised to cause devastation.

Despite reseeding efforts and the installation of massive drainage systems, threats still existed. Similarly, Paul declared that many live as enemies of the cross of Christ—and their potential destiny is devastating. But for followers of Jesus, our citizenship is in Heaven. We are part of an eternal reclamation project!

Thank you, **Lord,** for Your sacrifice on the cross. Because of Your shed blood, I have forgiveness and am no longer an enemy, but a member of Your family. Thank You for the peace that passes understanding. I'm grateful You are transforming me into the likeness of Christ. In Your holy name I pray. Amen.

The Please Car

Join together in following my example, brothers and sisters, and just as you have us as a model, keep your eyes on those who live as we do (Philippians 3:17).

Scripture: Philippians 3:17-21
Song: "There Is a Redeemer"

"Imitation is not just the sincerest form of flattery, it's the sincerest form of learning." The second half of George Shaw's statement appears to agree with the apostle Paul's advice in today's passage. Paul modeled a reproducible lifestyle because the one he followed was Jesus Christ, who lived a perfect life.

Mark and Hedy are teaching modes of transportation to 20-month-old Jason. They tell him about a vehicle's name and offer some accompanying representation of it. So, when he sees a type of vehicle, he names it and makes an association.

Recently, Mark displayed a picture of a fire truck, and Jason muttered something vaguely resembling "fire," and then blurted, "Truck! VROOM!" While chasing Daddy in the front yard, a jet flew over, and Jason screeched to a halt. Pointing to the sky he said, "Plane! Fly!" He was definitely learning to imitate his parents' examples. Later that evening, I showed him a picture of a police car, and he rubbed his chest in a circle with a flat palm (sign language for "please"), voiced "Car," and made sounds like a siren! Like followers of Jesus, sometimes Jason can produce an accurate imitation, and other times, he's derailed.

Jesus, thank You for keeping all the commandments perfectly on my behalf—and for offering the perfect sacrifice for my sin. Now help me live for You by following in Your footsteps. Praise Your holy name. Amen.

The Band-Aid® Box

When he arrived and saw what the grace of God had done, he was glad and encouraged them all to remain true to the Lord with all their hearts (Acts 11:23).

Scripture: Acts 11:19-26
Song: "He Ransomed Me"

"What's so special about a Band-Aid® box?" When Steve's dad initially showed him the container, Steve didn't comprehend its importance. The rusty metal box, tied to a fence post, stood at the end of their graveled county road. His dad opened the tin, revealing a crumpled paper containing neighbors' names.

Each neighbor owned shares of irrigation water and notified the ditch company when they intended to utilize it. They received permission to divert water into their ditches on requested dates. The "ditch rider" added their names to the box.

Seven years ago, Steve and I assumed the responsibility for irrigating Dad's property. After our attempt at ordering water, we sprinted out, eager to route the first gushes. We encountered a dry channel. "Where's our water?"

Our parched ditch still thirsted at 8:00 a.m. so we drove to the Band-Aid® box. The document lacked our name! Steve contacted the ditch rider about our negative water flow.

When early believers shared the gospel of Jesus Christ, mercy met grace. Many added their names to the registry of those who draw living water.

Lord, even at my best, I'm unworthy. I'm thankful for Your sacrificial death and resurrection so I could have citizenship in Heaven. Please write my name in the Lamb's book of life for all of eternity. In Jesus' name, amen.

Head Toward That Rock!

The Spirit told me to have no hesitation about going with them (Acts 11:12).

Scripture: Acts 11:1-18
Song: "Be Thou My Vision"

Goal! Celebrating another beach soccer victory, our teenaged students plunged into the ocean, splashing near the shoreline. Without warning, a flash rip current seized Andrew and Tyler, dragging them out to sea. Chaperones ordered everyone back to land, then scaled a nearby boulder. Andrew swam parallel with the beach, escaping the grip of the rip.

Whitecaps volleyed Tyler from boulder to boulder, adjacent to the headland. Luigi shouted, "Relax!" while Tyler wrestled for his life. As waves dragged Tyler around the corner of the cliffs, concealing him from sight, he hollered, "I can't keep swimming!" We prayed.

Suddenly, Tyler reappeared. Luigi bellowed, *"Head toward that rock!"* Tyler paddled forward and, finally, crawling onto the rock, gripping securely, he embraced safety. Seconds later, the sea scraped him off, plunging him under. When he surfaced, powerful waves blasted him near Luigi, now close enough to toss a boogie board. Tyler clutched it while Luigi hauled him in.

Peter listened carefully to ensure He heard God correctly. Then, convinced of God's instructions, he proceeded without hesitation. That is always the way to service . . . and safety.

Lord, when You show me what to do, I want to respond immediately. Give me a heart that listens to You and a willingness to act without hesitation. Remove any excuses I allow to stand in the way of Your will. In Jesus' name, amen.

Delivered from Death

In my distress I called to the LORD; I cried to my God for help. From his temple he heard my voice; my cry came before him, into his ears (Psalm 18:6).

Scripture: Psalm 18:1-9
Song: "A Mighty Fortress Is Our God"

Talk about rip currents! Here's another item: A 12-year-old boy struggled in potentially deadly tide waters. Nicole, also 12 years of age, turned her boogie board toward the deeper water and headed out to help. She reached Dale and got him onto her board. As they headed in, a fierce wave knocked them off the board, and other rescuers had to wade in to help pull Dale out. But without Nicole's initial efforts, it is doubtful Dale would have been saved.

How grateful would you be to someone who saved your life? Psalmist David expresses his gratitude to God for repeated moments of deliverance. In vivid terms, he describes what one might express today as "my life flashing before my eyes."

I love the way David connects his prayer to God's response. The Lord is roused . . . and rises to the rescue.

Were it not David we might think the writer is a bit conceited. How can he be so sure that God, in His temple, hears his prayer? But this is the God that all of His children serve. He hears our prayer and rises to rescue us in all our times of need.

Lord, I'm not in such distress and danger as David faced. But I thank You that even if my life were threatened, I could count on You to be there with me. In Christ, amen.

October 26–31. **Dan Nicksich** and his wife, Donna, live in Grant, Michigan, where Dan is senior minister of the Northland Church of Christ.

Seek and Go

Let your hand rest on the man at your right hand, the son of man you have raised up for yourself (Psalm 80:17).

Scripture: Psalm 80:1-3, 7, 17-19
Song: "All Hail the Power of Jesus' Name"

Holly was in tears. She and her boyfriend had fallen to temptation. Her family's negative feelings toward this relationship intensified, and Holly had left home for a long time. Now she sought reconciliation with God and her parents.

Israel, represented by Ephraim, Benjamin, and Manasseh sought reconciliation with God. In a surprising twist, the Psalm writer turns the focus of restoration to the "man at [God's] right hand, the son of man" in fact.

Whether it's to ancient Israel or to us today, God's offer of reconciliation comes through this same Son of man, the one seated at His right hand. The New Testament is clear: this man is Jesus, the only means of peace between sinful humanity and a holy God. There's no other possibility for reconciliation.

Holly's willingness to confess her sin, coupled with her tears of regret, suggest a level of repentance that touches the heart of God. What remains to be seen: Will her parents welcome home a prodigal daughter?

Is there anyone in the church with whom you are at odds these days? Seek the reconciliation that only Christ can bring. Go to your brother, your sister, without delay.

Heavenly Father, how difficult it can be to forgive those who sin against us. How difficult to forgive those who defy us. It helps me, even more, to appreciate the depth and breadth of Your forgiveness toward me. Thank You, in Jesus' name. Amen.

Grab My Hand!

At the first light of dawn, the king got up and hurried to the lions' den (Daniel 6:19).

Scripture: Daniel 6:19-24
Song: "Leaning on the Everlasting Arms"

Dan's wife and daughter were about to head out in their kayaks when Dan noticed a man in the water nearby. He was struggling to stay afloat while two frightened children clung to him. Dan edged out into the water and extended his hand. He was about to slip into a hole when he heard a voice behind him, "Grab my hand." Together they pulled the three to safety—and soon Dan waved goodbye to his wife and daughter as they paddled downstream. Later that evening, Dan commented on his daughter's strength. "But Dan," his wife said, "Sue was already in her kayak alongside of me."

"Well, who was it that grabbed my hand?" Dan asked.

"There was no one there; it looked as if you reached back to balance yourself and, next thing we saw, you were pulling them in." Had Dan been helped by an angel, a ministering spirit?

We know the biblical Daniel was helped that way! Though some seem to doubt the presence of angels, or even the possibility of miracles, I'm thankful an ancient king ventured out to check on Daniel in the morning. Daniel didn't give up hope.

While we may not deliberately seek miracles or feel we must put God to the test, both Dan and Daniel can affirm: our God ministers to us through myriad ways.

Lord, I thank You that You have various ways to express Your omnipotent power and matchless goodness to us. Through Christ, amen.

Inspiring the King

I issue a decree that in every part of my kingdom people must fear and reverence the God of Daniel. "For he is the living God and he endures forever; his kingdom will not be destroyed, his dominion will never end" (Daniel 6:26).

Scripture: Daniel 6:25-28
Song: "Dare to Be a Daniel"

Jerry pedals his bike all over town delivering newspapers. To his customers, it seems as if he's been doing it forever. In fact, he started when he was 10 and will soon be 40. Jerry, you see, is someone we call "special needs." But his customers love him. You can always count on Jerry getting your paper to you. You can also count on his smiling face and a friendly greeting.

"What makes you so happy, Jerry?" one of his customers asked. Jerry answered without hesitation. "Jesus. He saved me, and someday I won't be like this anymore. I'll be just like everyone else when I'm up in Heaven with Him."

When his church was preparing for Friend Day, Jerry handed out invitations to any customer he happened to see. Several came to church that Sunday. "We're here because of Jerry," they said. But many still wonder if Jerry understands just how powerful his example has proved to be.

I may not inspire a king like Daniel inspired King Darius. I may not be delivered miraculously. But, like Jerry, I hope there are others who are moved to praise God because of me.

Lord, I am humbled by those like Jerry whose simple faith and trusting obedience bear such awesome fruit. As I learn from their example, I pray You will use me in similar fashion. In Jesus' name I pray. Amen.

I Told You So!

Do not be afraid, Paul. You must stand trial before Caesar; and God has graciously given you the lives of all who sail with you (Acts 27:23, 24).

Scripture: Acts 27:14-25
Song: "Soon and Very Soon"

Few things are as irritating as someone who likes to say, "I told you so." Perhaps it's different if the speaker is an inspired apostle of the Lord. For example, Paul had every right to say, "I told you so." He had offered advice against the timing of a ship's voyage. Now battered by an unrelenting storm, Paul addresses the fearful crew and passengers.

He didn't stop with, "I told you so," and I marvel at his calm, deliberate speech. After all, these are sailors he's talking to! Yet to a boatload of salty seafarers, hardened Roman soldiers, and other prisoners, Paul says there's no reason to worry. Why? Because an angel told him so! Would you be so quick to tell such a crowd about personal angelic visits? Paul didn't hesitate.

Apparently something about Paul inspired trust and serenity. Few men could speak as convincingly in such distressing circumstances but Paul pulled it off.

If you're going to say, "I told you so," think twice. Do you have words of assurance to follow up with? Do you have a solution to the problem, the issue being faced? If not, silence might be the preferred response.

Lord, I want to be the one lifting up prayer in distressing times, the one others look to for words of calm assurance. And may I always think twice when tempted to say, "I told you so." In the name of Jesus, amen.

Trust His Answers?

"You're out of your mind," they told her. When she kept insisting that it was so, they said, "It must be his angel" (Acts 12:15).

Scripture: Acts 12:12-18
Song: "Lord, Listen to Your Children Praying"

Martin always seems to struggle financially. His latest trial involved a car that would prove too costly to fix. "I'm praying for a new car," he said. "But money's very tight right now."

The next day Martin was unexpectedly called to work over-time. Then, he was surprised by a check in the mail for over $700. It was for excess escrow funds withheld by his credit union. "I knew God was going to provide. I just didn't know it would be this quickly." I've heard story after story like this. We pray for help yet are surprised when God provides it.

The church was praying for Peter. He was imprisoned by King Herod, who had recently killed James, his fellow apostle. But when angels release Peter, the servant girl is so excited at Peter's arrival that she forgets to unlock the door. The prayer meeting can't believe what they're hearing.

"What's that? Peter's at the door? It can't be; he's in prison!"

I wonder if any of them ever caught the irony of their belief-inspired prayer for Peter . . . coupled with their statement of disbelief when their prayer was answered?

I wonder how faithfully we are praying? Wouldn't it be great if, after praying, we simply trusted His answers?

Lord, thank You for hearing my prayers. My desire is simply to be a person of faith, always trusting as I await Your answer. In Jesus' name, amen.

DEVOTIONS®

NOVEMBER

Giving joyful thanks to the Father, ... he has rescued us . . . and brought us into the kingdom.

—*Colossians 1:12, 13*

Gary Wilde, Editor   **Margaret Williams,** Project Editor   Photo iStock | Thinkstock®

DEVOTIONS® is published quarterly by Standard Publishing, Cincinnati, Ohio, www.standardpub.com. © 2014 by Standard Publishing. All rights reserved. Topics based on the Home Daily Bible Readings, International Sunday School Lessons. © 2012 by the Committee on the Uniform Series. Printed in the U.S.A. All Scripture quotations, unless otherwise indicated, are taken from the *HOLY BIBLE, NEW INTERNATIONAL VERSION®. NIV®.* Copyright © 1973, 1978, 1984, 2011 by Biblica, Inc.® Used by permission of Zondervan. All rights reserved worldwide. *New American Standard Bible®, (NASB)* Copyright © 1960, 1962, 1963, 1968, 1971, 1972, 1973, 1975, 1977, 1995 by The Lockman Foundation. Used by permission. (www.Lockman.org). *Holy Bible, New Living Translation (NLT),* © 1996, 2004, 2007. Tyndale House Publishers. Scripture quotations marked *(NKJV)* are taken from the *New King James Version®.* Copyright © 1982 by Thomas Nelson, Inc. Used by permission. All rights reserved. *King James Version (KJV),* public domain.

Delivered!

Peter followed him out of the prison, but he had no idea that what the angel was doing was really happening; he thought he was seeing a vision (Acts 12:9).

Scripture: Acts 12:1-11
Song: "Faith Is the Victory"

In July of 2002, nine Pennsylvania coal miners were rescued after being trapped underground for more than three days. Some hailed it as a miracle after a team successfully drilled a rescue shaft down to the men. As the miners emerged, one by one in the rescue capsule most seemed dazed as if in disbelief.

Peter's rescue reads the same way. Released by an angel, he struggles with the reality of his escape. He thinks it's all a dream or a vision. King Herod had already killed James, a fellow apostle; surely Herod would kill him next.

We won't always know why some are rescued and some are not. There's no explaining why some are delivered and some are not. Miracles aren't always the order of the day; some continue to suffer at the hands of evil men.

It would seem that the best course is always to center ourselves in God's will. If rescues and miracles come our way, we accept them as opportunities to continue serving. If suffering is the order of the day, our faithfulness continues to point the way to Jesus.

Lord, Your will. Nothing more, nothing else, nothing less. Help me to see every situation that arises in the light of Your will for my life. In Jesus' name, amen.

November 1. **Dan Nicksich** and his wife, Donna, live in Grant, Michigan, where Dan is senior minister of the Northland Church of Christ.

Being There for One Another

I long to see you so that I may impart to you some spiritual gift to make you strong—that is, that you and I may be mutually encouraged by each other's faith (Romans 1:11, 12).

Scripture: Romans 1:8-15
Song: "The Bond of Love"

"Why did you let go of my hand?" Sitting in her living room only hours after her husband's death, I held her hand through the whole visit. But as soon as I let go, she wanted to feel that personal warmth again. The words, the laughter, the memories, and the tears flowed freely. But those things could have happened over the phone. She needed a comforting friend holding her hand, physically present in her grief.

We need the personal presence of people we love and people who love us. Four times in today's passage Paul explains to the Roman Christians how deeply he longs to be with them. Messengers were adequate. Letters were necessary. Hearsay was enlightening. But being in Rome with them would make encouragement and ministry to them more practical. So he prayed fervently for the opportunity.

That's why hospitals and military units have chaplains. It's why we wash feet and lay on hands to pray. The physical presence of other believers delivers tangible support, encouragement, and comfort to those who need it.

Emmanuel, give me the awareness to see those around me who need my physical presence. Then give me the grace to show up. Through Christ, amen.

November 2–8. **Matthew Boardwell** is an avid nonfiction reader and enthusiastic musician. He is husband to Pam, father of nine, and a church-planting missionary in the west of Ireland.

A Dose of Reality

You are a God of forgiveness, gracious and compassionate, slow to anger and abounding in lovingkindness; and You did not forsake them (Nehemiah 9:17, *New American Standard Bible*).

Scripture: Nehemiah 9:6-21
Song: "Come, Ye Sinners, Poor and Needy"

When I was a child, I used to sit upside-down on the sofa and imagine that the ceiling was the floor. In that world, I would have to step over door frames and around light fixtures. I would reach up to set out plates on the underside of the table. Sometimes I'd imagine that kids were in charge, too. Then parents would have to obey and do the chores; kids could just have fun. In other words, I imagined things were the opposite of reality.

What if God were the opposite of reality? What if He weren't a forgiving God, full of grace and kindness? What if He were quick to anger and meager in love?

Certainly, that sort of God would have abandoned Israel in the desert. After all their rebellion and obstinacy, He would have washed His hands of them. He would have let them hunger, thirst, and perish. In fact, He might have abandoned them to slavery in the first place.

Wouldn't He have done the same with us in that topsy-turvy, imaginary spiritual landscape? Instead, He loves and forgives us, shows us patience and grace, and calls us His treasured children. Sometimes, it takes a prayer of confession to remember it.

Father, I'm humbled when I remember who You really are. Forgive me for projecting onto You my own inconsistent love. Today I gratefully receive Your grace and kindness. It covers my sin and nudges me to righteousness. In Christ, amen.

Solving the Mystery

Now to Him who is able to establish you according to my gospel and the preaching of Jesus Christ, according to the revelation of the mystery which has been kept secret for long ages past but now is manifested (Romans 16:25, 26, *New American Standard Bible*).

Scripture: Romans 16:25-27
Song: "O Come, O Come, Emmanuel"

Don't you love a good mystery film? There's the challenge of figuring out the puzzle. There's the tension of suspense. There are all the clues, obvious and obscure. And of course, there's the satisfying conclusion when all the clues come suddenly together.

Paul writes that his good news was the ultimate in mysteries, a secret kept hidden and finally revealed in Jesus Christ. In fact, for generations there were clues. Prophecies pointed to a certain kind of messiah, coming from a specific place, doing a particular work. According to these clues, God would personally come to the rescue. The Savior would live and die not only for His own nation, but for the Gentiles as well. Then everyone could be aware of the secret plans of God to save the whole world.

Throughout his letter, the apostle revealed how these pieces fit together. Overjoyed, he concluded with ecstatic praise to the God who designed and carried out such a magnificent plan. And we—if we could identify with those first Christian hearers, we too would marvel at and proclaim the revealed wisdom of God.

Eternal God, You could have left us in the dark, surrounded by questions. But You are the God who reveals himself. One step at a time You have shown Your plan to the world. And by Your mercy, You revealed yourself to me too. Through Christ, amen.

Coming Out of Hiding

Nothing in all creation is hidden from God's sight. Everything is uncovered and laid bare before the eyes of him to whom we must give account (Hebrews 4:13).

Scripture: Hebrews 4:12-16
Song: "Search Me, O God"

Joe has an unusual pain in his side. It's never bothered him before, but it's pretty intense these days. He figures it will go away, but when it doesn't he still won't see a doctor. You see, he doesn't want to know for sure whether something is wrong (even though he knows for sure that something is wrong). So he puts up with pain. He puts off the tests. When it can no longer be avoided, Joe will find out what he has suspected all along. He has a serious cancer . . . that's no longer treatable.

Ever since Adam and Eve covered themselves with fig leaves to escape the piercing gaze of God, human beings have specialized in covering up their sin. Hebrews tells us how useless these efforts are. The razor of God's Word slices right through our evasions, getting to the heart. Every effort to obscure or deflect God's notice proves futile. There is nothing He cannot see and eventually, we must face Him.

The cure for our sin is the mercy and grace of a sympathetic Savior. Jesus has all the mercy we need. But first we must submit ourselves to His soul-deep examination. Exposure is the way to healing.

Gentle Healer, I humbly offer my heart to You with all its broken pieces and dark sin stains. Apply Your grace and forgiveness to each flaw. Remake me in the image of Jesus. I know that He understands where I am. In Christ I pray. Amen.

God Wants to Be with Us

Look! God's dwelling place is now among the people, and he will dwell with them (Revelation 21:3).

Scripture: Revelation 21:1-5
Song: "The Kingdom of God"

Many people believe that if there is a God, He is indifferent to us. All they need to do is read the first and last chapters of the Bible to see how laughable that is!

God wanted a walk *together*. He wanted human fellowship. He offered humans His tangible presence and personal interaction. The only thing that impeded Adam and Eve being with Him was their own shame. Still, even their shame didn't keep God from pursuing them or addressing their need. Even in their sin, He wanted them. He still sought and found them. He still provided for them and promised a rescue.

One day, He will build His children a new Heaven and a new earth. He will scrape off the old and lay down the new. He will wipe every tear away and banish death and pain. He's moving history toward that final chapter. It's what He's always wanted.

He still offers His permanent presence. His tangible lasting friendship is there for all who will receive it. He is preparing a future set free from heartache. When we arrive, we will discover that His longing has always been what we've wanted most. Belonging with Him — being home.

Father, what a joy it will be when I am finally gathered home where I belong. With the rest of Your children I look forward to a sin-free, sorrow-free, sickness-free future with You. As much as I long for that, it is a thrill to know that You want it even more. I praise You, through the precious name of Jesus. Amen.

Welcomed In

He redeemed us in order that the blessing given to Abraham might come to the Gentiles through Christ Jesus (Galatians 3:14).

Scripture: Galatians 3:6-14
Song: "Room at the Cross for You"

Have you ever been left out? The third wheel in a friendship? The new kid who can't find his way into a clique? An outsider painfully aware of how much she doesn't belong?

What does it take to belong? You can crash your way into the circle. Sometimes that works, but most of the time the circle becomes more irritated than welcoming. What works better is for someone in that friendship to reach out to you—and the more important the person, the better the reception of the others.

During Jesus' earthly ministry, many assumed that the kingdom of God was just another way to describe Israel. Sure, a non-Jew could convert, but very few would ever bother. So the circle was small, as small as a small nation. It would take divine intervention to invite the rest of the world in.

One of the two in this relationship between God and Israel reached out to us. The most important one took the initiative to bring us in. He reached out to us, Jew or Gentile, who were excluded. He died for the sin of everyone, Jew or Gentile. With no other sacrifices or ceremonies needed, He made us all children of Abraham.

Lord, You welcome the stranger and outcast. You welcomed me. Where would I be without Your love? For taking the initiative to find me and invite me in, I worship You. Grant me a love that welcomes others who are alienated too. In Jesus' name, amen.

Too Heavy for Our Brothers

Why do you try to test God by putting on the necks of Gentiles a yoke that neither we nor our ancestors have been able to bear? (Acts 15:10).

Scripture: Acts 15:1-12
Song: "Jesus Paid It All"

When we go grocery shopping for our family of 11, we usually fill a car. When it's time to unload, the kids come out to help. Our 4-year-old can carry a couple loaves of bread. The older teens can carry a few gallons of milk. I can usually manage a half-dozen sacks on my own. But no one can carry the whole load alone. To try (or expect someone to try) is foolishness.

Maybe that's how Peter felt when some early Jewish Christians wanted new Gentile Christians to obey the law of Moses. The Gentiles could come in, but they'd have to comply.

This approach troubled Peter because he knew the Jewish experience personally. Once in a while, someone could get it right. They could follow the law, keep the feasts, maintain ritual purity, and do it all with a good heart . . . for a while. Before long, though, they would stumble into sin. The law was just too heavy for even the strongest to carry.

Peter also knew Jesus personally. He watched Him live. He heard His teaching. He remembered His death. He experienced Him alive. And he knew the law was no match for the freedom of salvation by grace through Him.

Dear Lord, thank You for lifting my heavy load for me. I never could have been disciplined or faithful enough to measure up to the law's exacting standard. So You measured up for me. Thanks be to You, through Your holy name. Amen.

Danger Ahead, Turn Back

Perhaps they will listen and each will turn from their evil ways. Then I will relent (Jeremiah 26:3).

Scripture: Jeremiah 26:1-6
Song: "Turn Your Eyes upon Jesus"

The man stood in the fork of the highway. He wore a khaki shirt rolled up at the sleeves and a pair of faded blue jeans. He carried a shovel, which he was waving to get our attention. Although he wasn't wearing his uniform, my father recognized him as a U.S. Forest Ranger. Rangers working a fire line or other forest-related emergencies seldom dressed in their traditional hats or uniforms. Dad immediately brought our Chevy Suburban to a stop.

The officer told us we needed to turn around and go back the way we came. The river had washed out the road to the campground, and if we continued, the rocks and potholes would damage our vehicle. With his message delivered, he rushed back to warn two more approaching cars. They ignored him and continued down the road. He just shook his head in disbelief.

Likewise, Jeremiah tried to warn the people of Judah about their current path. By not listening to God or heeding His messengers, Judah was heading toward a judgment they would bring upon themselves. Our God has the same message of concern for the people our generation.

God, I want to walk only the pathway of Your will. However, if I am heading the wrong way, please stop me and point me in the right direction. In Jesus' name, amen.

November 9–15. **Charles Earl Harrel** was in church ministry for more than 30 years before stepping aside to pursue writing. He enjoys photography and playing the 12-string guitar.

Unsearchable Treasure

Unto me, who am less than the least of all saints, is this grace given, that I should preach among the Gentiles the unsearchable riches of Christ (Ephesians 3:8, *King James Version*).

Scripture: Ephesians 3:7-12
Song: "My Precious Bible"

In 1847, John Sutter, a former artillery captain in the Swiss army, collaborated with James Marshall, a skilled carpenter, to build a sawmill along the South Fork of the American River in California. The mill, however, had a design flaw: the ditch that drained water from the waterwheel was too shallow.

It wasn't until Mr. Marshall decided, in January of 1848, to let the rushing current cut the mill's channel deeper that he discovered something entirely unexpected: gold.

"Unsearchable" normally means unreachable or beyond comprehension. However, some treasures only *appear* unsearchable—not because they're unreachable—but simply because we must dig deeper to find them. Such is the case with the unsearchable riches of Christ. The apostle Paul realized these boundless truths were searchable, after all. In fact, he not only preached them, he wrote about them in his epistles.

As you read the Scriptures each day, allow the Spirit of God to flow over your soul like living waters, opening a deep channel in your heart. Let Him wash away the familiar and uncover the unexpected. The Holy Spirit, who is our divine teacher, wants to reveal the richness and the depth of Christ's love.

Precious Lord, please open the treasure house of Your presence and draw me closer. Let me uncover all the riches hidden in Your Son. In Jesus' holy name, amen.

First, Remove the Stone

I will give you a new heart and put a new spirit within you; I will take the heart of stone out of your flesh and give you a heart of flesh (Ezekiel 36:26, *New King James Version*).

Scripture: Ezekiel 36:22-30
Song: "Change My Heart, O God"

Daisy Lane was a great place for children to play. Our private street had endless potholes, a huge rock in the middle of the road, and plenty of untrimmed bushes to hide behind. It was also one of the last dirt roads in the city of La Cañada.

After years of costly repairs for their washed-out road, the residents of Daisy Lane, which included my family, decided to pave the old road. Everything went according to plan until the paving company tried to remove the rock. It wouldn't budge. They tried chipping away at it with a pick and a sledgehammer. Both tools bounced off. Even with a jackhammer, the rock remained intact. Finally, the supervisor called in a large bulldozer and backhoe. After hours of digging and pushing, the stone released its hold on the old road—and the paving began.

Before God can put a new spirit within us, He must remove the heart of stone in our lives. Spiritually speaking, a stony heart is a hindrance that makes us unteachable. Once removed, a heart of flesh, one that's responsive, sensitive, and compassionate, can be implanted. Such excavations are a specialty of the Holy Spirit. Just ask Him to renew a right spirit within you.

Mold me, **Lord,** into the servant You want me to be. If my heart has become hardened, then take out anything that hinders my Christian walk, give me a heart of compassion, and refresh my parched spirit. In Jesus' name, amen.

Are You Willing?

"Teacher, I will follow you wherever you go" (Matthew 8:19).

Scripture: Matthew 8:18-22
Song: "I'll Go Where You Want Me to Go"

For two months I had been attending a little church in the farming town of Reedley, California. It was the last night of their 1972 missionary convention. My wife and I sat in the back row next to the center aisle. I don't recall the missionary's name or the country where she served. The "call," though, I remember in vivid detail.

After the speaker finished her talk, she asked everyone to bow their heads and close their eyes. Then came the first of two questions: "How many here tonight are willing to follow the Lord into the harvest field?" Being curious, I peered through half-closed eyelids. Most of the people raised their hands. Next, she asked, "But how many are willing to go wherever He calls you . . . or, if necessary, stay, wherever He wants you to stay?" Still peeking, I saw many of those hands lowered.

After the closing prayer, those who had carefully considered her questions went forward to the front of the church. My wife and I decided to join them. We realized that evening: to follow Christ requires a solemn, unwavering commitment.

God wants our help to bring in His harvest. Although He is understanding and compassionate, He's not interested in our excuses, only our sincerity and willingness.

Dear Lord, please forgive me for all the times I promised to follow You, but instead I charted my own path. If You still want me, I am Yours. In the holy name of Jesus, my Lord and Savior, I pray. Amen.

In His Name

He turned around and said to the spirit, "In the name of Jesus Christ I command you to come out of her!" At that moment the spirit left her (Acts 16:18).

Scripture: Acts 16:16-24
Song: "We Rest on Thee"

The village elder, one who practiced sorcery, controlled the people of his African village by claiming to know the future. Among other things, he predicted the yield from future crops, the success of hunts, and the gender of unborn children.

Always nervous, the man twitched his head back and forth, never standing still, even for a moment. If a village member disagreed with him, he or she often became sick; some even died. Threatening retribution, he warned his villagers against accepting the newly appointed missionary. Anyone listening to Melvin's teachings about Jesus the Savior would surely perish.

When Melvin conducted church services, the village elder would attend, trying to disrupt them. Finally, Melvin told the spirit that controlled the man: "Be gone, in the name of Jesus!" The man ran off screaming, heading toward his nearby cave.

The next morning, the elder returned to the village square. He looked happy, no longer a bundle of nerves. He knelt down in front of the young missionary in the presence of the entire village and gave his life to Jesus. Other villagers followed. The name of Jesus Christ can save, heal, and deliver. Early Christians never hesitated to use it. And neither should we.

Heavenly Father, thanks for sending Your Son into this world and for giving us believers a name that is higher than any other name. Through Christ's name I pray. Amen.

Some Are Listening

Paul and Silas were praying and singing hymns to God, and the other prisoners were listening to them (Acts 16:25).

Scripture: Acts 16:25-40
Song: "I Will Sing of the Mercies of the Lord"

Carl shuffled down Division Street in Portland, Oregon, his mind clouded, confused. He was looking to score again. He hated using drugs, but somehow, he could no longer say no. Maybe someone in the homeless camp, hidden on the nearby hillside, would help him out.

Carl turned left at the church property. The congregation was conducting its evening service. Mumbling to himself, "That's funny—the church should have dismissed by now—it's almost 10:30 p.m.," he decided to hang around to beg for some cash.

Meanwhile, the singing continued. "Why haven't they stopped yet?" Carl moved closer. "What's happening in there?" Now he could hear people praying inside. A divine compulsion slowly drew him through the front doors—and that's when he felt a warming presence. He dropped to the floor and wept for what seemed like hours. When Carl stood again, his life had changed; he would never abuse drugs again.

Most of the time, we don't consider prayer and worship as being witnessing tools, but they are. They can influence those who are listening in, and in some cases, might even inspire people to a brand new faith in God.

Dear God, I love praying and singing praises to Your name. It draws me close to You, and I can feel Your presence. If seekers can feel Your presence as well, then may I pray and worship everywhere I go! In Jesus' name, amen.

Help Wanted

A vision appeared to Paul in the night. A man of Macedonia stood and pleaded with him, saying, "Come over to Macedonia and help us" (Acts 16:8, 9, *New King James Version*).

Scripture: Acts 16:1-5, 8-15
Song: "The Vision"

While in prayer one evening, Melvin heard the word *Africa* whispered in his ear. A few months later, he saw a vision of an outreached hand and heard the same voice saying, "Take my hand, and I will lead you to a place where you are needed." That's when Melvin began to seek divine guidance about going to Africa as a missionary.

He applied to the mission board of his church, and they assigned him to the Gold Coast, in Africa. However, before Melvin could begin his term, the missions department halted all outgoing missionaries due to financial concerns.

When the money crisis eased, they reassigned Melvin to India. His heart sank, because this change contradicted his call and vision. Nevertheless, he accepted the appointment and started raising funds. Just before his departure in 1955, the mission board switched his assignment again. They had an urgent need for someone in the Gold Coast.

God calls every Christian to minister somewhere. He may use a dream, a vision, an inward voice that speaks to our spirits — and sometimes, even a daily devotional reading.

Dear God, I realize the harvest is plentiful and the laborers are few. I am open to Your call and ready to serve as one of those laborers. Please show me where my help is needed the most. In Your name, I pray. Amen.

The Greatness of Our God

I will proclaim the name of the LORD. Oh, praise the greatness of our God! (Deuteronomy 32:3).

Scripture: Deuteronomy 32:1-12
Song: "I Could Sing of Your Love Forever"

Hooked up to tubes and monitors, my grandson Luke lay motionless in his little bassinet in the Neonatal Intensive Care Unit (NICU). He was born without a diaphragm, and doctors gave him only a 30% chance of surviving. Parents and grandparents took turns holding his tiny hands and praying before and after surgery—a procedure to move his liver and intestines down into the abdominal area and install an artificial diaphragm.

Doctors and nurses worked around the clock. They relied on modern medicine and equipment. Some babies didn't go home from NICU, but I prayed as if Luke's life depended on my prayers.

When we brought our baby home from the hospital, I felt like Moses when he sang, "I will proclaim the name of the Lord. Oh, praise the greatness of our God!"

Moses experienced God's miracles through a 40-year journey in the wilderness. My family continues to witness the miracles of Luke's life, 10 years after his difficult birth. He is a constant reminder to us of how God drew us closer to himself and to each other.

Thank You, **Father God,** for never leaving me to suffer alone. It is wonderful to know You are with me in troubling times. I proclaim Your greatness, through Christ. Amen.

November 16–22. **Sue Tornai** lives with her husband, John, and dog, Maggie, in Carmichael, California. They enjoy vacationing at Lake Almanor in Northern California.

Our God Is Near

I have set my rainbow in the clouds, and it will be the sign of the covenant between me and the earth (Genesis 9:13).

Scripture: Genesis 9:8-17
Song: "It Is Well with My Soul"

On March 11, 2011, Japan suffered a massive earthquake—of 9.0 magnitude—that triggered a 23-foot tsunami. The waves swept away homes, cars, boats, and trains, and caused the meltdown of two nuclear power plants. It took more than 16,000 lives and left nearly 6,000 people injured. Many who could return to their homes were afraid of contamination.

Scenes of the disaster made me wonder what it might have looked like when waters covered the earth in Noah's day. God promised that He would never again destroy the earth with water; He put His rainbow in the clouds to remind us of His vow.

People might have questioned whether God would keep His promises when the waves washed away so much property and life. The cost of damages (more than $300 billion) was the most in world history. But by the end of 2011, the spending involved in Japan's recovery increased its economy by 6.2%.

Even though it appeared as if the water might wash the country away, it didn't. God kept His Word. The rebuilding and restoration we have seen shows the resilience of people made in God's image. He doesn't abandon us human beings, but is with us through the storms and the reconstruction. He is as close as the cries of our hearts.

Father, You are worthy of praise, and I praise You. Thank You for being with me, even when I least expect it. Thank You for keeping Your promises. In Jesus' name, amen.

Awesome God

I will make you into a great nation, and I will bless you; I will make your name great, and you will be a blessing (Genesis 12:2)

Scripture: Genesis 12:1-4
Song: "Our God Is an Awesome God"

No medicine or supplies arrived at Rwanguba Hospital for more than six weeks. Dr. Filipe could not give aid to the refugees who came from Rwanda. He thought he would have to close the doors. Against all odds he knelt and pleaded with God, "O Lord, I cannot look into the empty, longing eyes of people I am unable to help. Please send us a miracle."

Like Abram, Dr. Filipe trusted God . . . because he *had* to. Abram had no clue where he was going when he left Haran, but he believed God, and it was credited to him as righteousness. Dr. Filipe had no one else to turn to, so he turned to the one who had the answer.

A plane landed on an open field near the hospital the next day. The rugged-looking pilots jumped to the ground. "We found these boxes filled with medical supplies on our docks," one of the men said. "We didn't know what we were supposed to do with them, but we thought of you and the hospital."

Zana, the doctor's wife, smiled. "We serve an awesome God." Without delay, she and Dr. Filipe carried the boxes to the hospital and began giving the patients their treatments.

Thank You, **Precious Lord,** for the miracles of our faith. Thank You for the example of Abram, whom You honored as righteous. Help me to trust You as he did. In the name of Jesus, my Savior, I pray. Amen.

His Inescapable Presence

What is mankind that you are mindful of them, human beings that you care for them? (Psalm 8:4).

Scripture: Psalm 8
Song: "How Majestic Is Your Name"

It was a Saturday night, and I drove to a nearby bakery, thinking a piece of French silk pie would ease the pain of my loneliness. When the perky waitress said, "We're fresh out," I couldn't keep the tears from rolling down my cheeks. "I'm sorry," she said. "We have other delicious choices."

Embarrassed, I later realized I'd tried to meet a spiritual need with a physical solution. Back at my apartment, I cried out to God, "I don't want to go on anymore!"

It was as if the Father met me at the point of my deepest need, wrapped His arms around me and whispered, "Could you make it another day if I stay with you?"

I felt His amazing love surround me. "I guess so," I whispered. I dusted off my Bible and began to read. Every word seemed to speak directly to me and melt my heart.

Soon I was reading the Bible and praying every morning before I went to work. Sometimes I didn't know what to pray. All I could say was, "Thank You, Jesus. Thank You, Jesus for loving me."

Many times I've wondered to myself, *Who am I that the God of creation would care for me?* I am glad He does.

Thank You, **Father God,** for surprising me with Your amazing love. Thank You for loving me when I didn't love myself. It means so much to know You are always with me. In the precious name of Jesus my Lord. Amen.

Blessing in Disguise

We wait in hope for the LORD; he is our help and our shield (Psalm 33:20).

Scripture: Psalm 33:13-22
Song: "Count Your Blessings"

My friend Carol suffered through the last days of her husband's ill health and subsequent death, and she often left the hospital in tears. But one afternoon she did something she normally wouldn't do. She drove through an intersection on a yellow light. That is not what the citation read. It said the light was *red* and it included a picture, a $750 fine, and a court date.

Carol held the ticket in her hand a few days after her husband's funeral, tears streamed down her face. Where would the money come from? She bowed her head and prayed Psalm 33:20, with first-person pronouns, "I wait in hope for the Lord; He is my help and my shield."

Carol trusted God through those dark hours. Since she had never been in trouble, the courtroom frightened her. God provided a police officer to speak for her before the judge, someone she refers to as "the angel in blue" to this day. In light of all Carol had been through with the loss of her husband, the judge forgave her the fine . . . if she would do community service.

Carol agreed and served in a nearby church. The work gave Carol the break she needed from her grieving. "That ticket must have been sent from Heaven," she says.

Thank You, **Lord,** for Your faithfulness, counsel, and powerful presence. I couldn't make it without Your love surrounding me and holding me as I walk through difficult days. In the name of the Father and of the Son and of the Holy Spirit, I pray. Amen.

Praising God

Clap your hands, all you nations; shout to God with cries of joy (Psalm 47:1)

Scripture: Psalm 47
Song: "Everybody Clap Your Hands"

I had to tell Mama, who lay in a hospital bed with a terminal illness, that my 3-year-old grandson was rushed to the hospital for emergency surgery. "I wish I could hold him," she said. "I wish I could do something, but I can't even help myself."

"Luke needs your prayers," I said.

"I *can* pray," Mama replied. Lying in her hospital bed, trapped in her helplessness, she prayed, "Lord, who else can we turn to? You are the Great Physician, and we put our hope in you alone."

During the weeks that followed Luke's surgery, I prayed with Mama on the phone. When the doctor finally said we could bring him home, I couldn't wait to tell her. I heard her shout, "Praise God! Hallelujah!"

The next morning the nurses found Mama sitting up in bed, with her legs hanging off to the side—something she hadn't done for a long time. "What are you doing?" asked the nurse.

"I just want to dangle my feet," Mama said. No more earthly cares. No more pain and suffering. It was as if Mama was home, splashing her feet in a heavenly river. Then she lay back on her pillow. In that moment God did carry her home to be with Him forever.

Praise God! Hallelujah! You are a great and awesome God. Thank You for Your presence. Thank You for always being with me, especially during challenging times in my faith. Through Christ, amen.

Life in Christ

"In him we live and move and have our being." As some of your own poets have said, "We are his offspring" (Acts 17:28).

Scripture: Acts 17:1-4, 10-12, 22-25, 28
Song: "In Christ Alone"

Dennis rode his bike into the country with only a sandwich and a Bible in his backpack. On a patch of grass under an old oak tree, he spent the day crying out to God because he didn't like his hippie lifestyle anymore. Yet, he had no clue what to do next. The words "follow the manufacturer's instructions" popped into his head, and he wondered why he heard those particular words.

Since he didn't know where to start reading, he opened the Bible to the center. His eyes fell on the words of Psalm 25:4. "Show me your ways, Lord, teach me your paths." That's what he wanted—to give up his crazy parties and live for the God of his youth.

When he went home, he told his wife the decision he'd made, and together they knelt in their living room and prayed a prayer of repentance and surrender to God.

Dennis says that he would not be living for Christ if his neighbors hadn't first showed him what that looked like. They had never judged him for the way he lived, but they'd certainly prayed for him regularly. And they had invited him to their church, where he found God's love at work in His people.

Thank You, **Lord God Almighty,** for not giving up on me. Thank You for second, third, and fourth chances. I invite You to live and move and have Your being in my life. I pray this prayer in the name of Jesus, my merciful Savior and Lord. Amen.

Teachable?

He guides the humble in what is right and teaches them his way (Psalm 25:9).

Scripture: Psalm 25:8-12, 20, 21
Song: "O Master, Let Me Walk with Thee"

Nursing instructors sometimes prefer students who are a little apprehensive and who have no experience, as they begin the practical portion of their education in a hospital setting. Now working with real people in a dynamic setting, the eager students use their "book learning" as the foundation for "hands on" application. When they lack any previous experience, they're usually more *teachable*. Those with some background experience may not be as receptive to on-site instruction.

Jackie, a nursing instructor, told one of her students that she should take a particular newborn's temperature by placing the thermometer under the patient's armpit. One of her new students challenged Jackie. "When I worked as an aide in another hospital, the nurses always did this differently."

But Jackie clearly explained her reasons in the case of the infant before them. And, though obviously skeptical, the student nurse did what she was told to do.

Throughout His ministry years, our Lord encountered experts in religion who refused to be teachable. Yet any human being can only grow spiritually through an attitude of humility.

Lord, give me an attitude of humble expectancy each time I open Your Word. I want to grow in Christlikeness, ready to listen and to obey. In Jesus' name, amen.

November 23–29. Married for over 35 years, **Katherine Douglas** and her husband like to try something new each year. This year it's growing heirloom vegetables in their small garden.

Waiting Without Whining

Wait for the LORD; be strong and take heart and wait for the LORD (Psalm 27:14).

Scripture: Psalm 27:4, 5, 8, 9, 11-14
Song: "Everlasting God"

Do you ever mumble or talk out loud when you're alone in the car? I do. It usually goes something like this: "Come on! The traffic light isn't getting any greener, my friend . . . Are you blind? Hey, get going!"

Of course, the person in the car ahead of me isn't my friend, because I don't know her. And we both know the traffic lights have three colors and not several hues. Fortunately, she can't hear my impatient "reminders." I work hard at keeping my hand off the horn (admittedly, not always successfully).

Waiting on, or for, something or someone often translates into more than inconvenience. So many times we must await medical test results or wait to hear news of friends ministering in dangerous places. Clearly, the Lord gives me—gives us all—ample opportunity to develop the virtue of patience.

The Lord tells us through David that we're not only to wait *on* the Lord, but we're to wait *for* Him too. "Be still before the LORD and wait patiently for him" (Psalm 37:7). Paul tells me as Christians we're "waiting for the coming of our Lord Jesus Christ" (1 Corinthians 1:7, *KJV*).

Whether I'm waiting *for* others or *on* them, I want to do it as unto the Lord, with calm kindness. No whining or fretting.

Lord, help me wait patiently on others as well as You. I pray to make the best use of waiting times and waiting rooms, as You work patience in me. Through Christ, amen.

Woman with the Answers

The wise in heart are called discerning, and gracious words promote instruction (Proverbs 16:21).

Scripture: Proverbs 16:19-24
Song: "How Great the Wisdom"

Kristin, who once taught in elementary school classrooms, now zeroes in on helping children who struggle with reading. As a public school reading specialist, she has learned what books are particularly effective in creating a love of reading. She begins with books that kids want to read again and again.

One of those books for preschool children is titled *Don't Let the Pigeon Drive the Bus!* by Mo Willems. Kristin gave it as a gift (along with some other books) to our grandsons when she met them for the first time. My daughter, who plans on home schooling her sons, questioned Kristin on several topics related to schooling and learning. After Kristin left, our daughter was still marveling at my friend's wealth of knowledge and insight. "She's like the answer woman, isn't she?"

The truths of Proverbs continue today. Have you ever had a speaker regale you with his funny stories or delight you with an object lesson? If you're like me, you may often remember the object lesson or the funny stories, but . . . not the point made!

Words spoken graciously and with straightforward wisdom—like those of my friend—stay with us long after theatrics and object lessons have faded from our minds.

God of grace and glory, thanks for the wise counsel of friends. And I praise You too, for those You bring into my life who help me to be more discerning. Give me Your wisdom this day and always. Through Christ I pray. Amen.

Water and the Word

Therefore go and make disciples of all nations (Matthew 28:19).

Scripture: Matthew 28:16-20
Song: "Holy, Holy, Holy, Lord, Thy Disciples"

For years Doug and Karen have worked among the poor in the arid country of Burkina Faso in west Africa. In addition to sharing the gospel message, this couple has also been involved in digging village wells. Once this basic need is met, they often find listeners willing to receive the story of Christ, the one who offers living water (see John 4:10).

During a recent trip to check out a site for a well in a poor village, this missionary couple was unable to stay and do any teaching. With heartache they wrote in an e-mail, "The village chief was disappointed. He wanted us to stay right then and tell his people about Jesus." Though water was needed, this chief had a greater burden for the spiritual thirst of his people.

I aspire to be like that man. I want to share the gospel with my friends and neighbors. Physical needs are many and can overwhelm us all, but may I keep in view the greatest need of all: that people hear the glorious, saving message of forgiveness of sins in the cross of Christ. Since "All authority in heaven and earth has been given" to Christ (v. 18), I know I don't have to be a foreign missionary to participate in making disciples. I can do that important work right where I am.

Use me, **Lord,** not only as a disciple, but as a disciple maker. I pray for the leading of your Holy Spirit in doing my part in mentoring others. I pray this in the name of Him who has all authority, the Lord Jesus Christ. Amen.

How Do You Spell That?

I know you by name and you have found favor with me (Exodus 33:12).

Scripture: Exodus 33:12-17
Song: "He Knows My Name"

Ted came across a former acquaintance on the street. The man greeted him by name and began asking him about his family and other mutual friends. As Ted stood there answering his questions and asking some of his own, he knew he was stymied. *He simply could not remember the man's name!*

Is this a member from one of my previous churches? Do I know him from the gym? From my high school days? Lord, please don't let him be one of my wife's bazillion relatives!

Ted decided to ease his way out of the situation with a trick he learned as a minister. Before they went their separate ways, he asked, "How do you spell your last name again?"

The man's face contorted slightly. "S-m-i-t-h."

Ted has not used that little "trick" again.

Our great God never has to ask our names. And, thankfully, Jesus tells us that our Father knows far more than our names. He knows us so well that the hairs on our head aren't just counted for a grand total. God has actually *numbered* each one (see Matthew 10:30). Whenever we feel as if we're "just a number," or a faceless person in the crowd, we can know that the one who created us remembers our names—and a whole lot more.

Thank You, **Father,** that I'm Your child and that You know me by name. Thank You for the assurances from Your Word that I'm valuable to You. In the name of Him whose name is Wonderful, amen.

Elder Care—for the Younger Ones

They invited him to their home and explained to him the way of God more adequately (Acts 18:26).

Scripture: Acts 18:24-28
Song: "Tell Me the Story of Jesus"

When we hear the phrase "elder care," most of us think about caring for the aged. Yet there may be another kind of elder care that benefits younger generations more than the older generation.

Betty used to host backyard barbecues in the summer months, and she served up cocoa and cookies in the wintertime. She invited young teens, most of whom had just come to trust in Christ for salvation, to her home for food and fun. Yet her primary purpose was to expose these young people to the application of the Word of God to every area of their lives.

Dick did a similar thing. He led Bible studies in the homes of young couples so they might get established in the Word. He encouraged his students to study the Bible so they wouldn't be duped by religious charlatans or messages of "name it and claim it" for material prosperity. Dick, like Betty, was an elder in the faith and cared deeply about helping new Christians grow in the faith of the Lord Jesus.

Some of us may be called upon to provide elder care for an aging parent. Yet opportunities surround us now for encouraging and mentoring those younger in the faith than we are. As the elders, we must care for them.

Father, I want to be an encourager. Use me to lovingly and kindly mentor those younger in the faith, especially those in my own family. In Jesus' name, amen.

Dive In!

Paul lived and worked with them, for they were tentmakers just as he was (Acts 18:3, *New Living Translation*).

Scripture: Acts 18:1-11, 18-21
Song: "Your Mission"

Anna and her husband, Mike, recently relocated to another country as international workers. Planning to work in their outreach center in the heart of a coastal city, they thought everything was in place for them. But then the government began making changes in the rules for expatriates.

If the couple wanted to remain, they'd have to contribute more to the local economy in other lines of work. Anna was granted permission to help in women's ministries at the center, but Mike must work elsewhere—and he found just the thing: training nationals in scuba diving and snorkeling.

As an experienced scuba instructor, Mike could start this new venture. And by establishing a new business, he'd help the local economy while gaining new opportunities in ministry and outreach.

Centuries ago, Paul the apostle used his secular training to help supplement his income and to avoid stressing his struggling young churches any further. Today missionaries are doing it throughout the world. My part is to prayerfully encourage and monetarily support, those on the front lines of gospel proclamation.

Father, I pray for those who minister throughout the world—many of them in dangerous places—as they preach the good news of salvation in Jesus. Give them courage and wisdom as they often work in hostile cultures. Through Christ, amen.

Out of Nothing at All?

[God] rested from all the work of creating that he had done (Genesis 2:3).

Scripture: Genesis 1:28–2:3
Song: "Creator of the Earth and Sky"

Christians have always affirmed that what God did "in the beginning"(v. 1) was *ex nihilo*, "out of nothing." There is a clear distinction between making and creating something. To *make* is to gather existing materials and form something different. But to *create* is to bring about something more than just different. What comes to be, from God, is what has never been before.

Do you believe only God can accomplish such a feat? Or could it be that humans will be able to pull off an *ex nihilo* exploit?

God was once approached by a scientist who says, "God, we've decided we don't need You anymore. These days we can clone people, transplant organs, and do all sorts of miraculous things."

And God says: "Suppose we have a man-making contest'"?

"You're on!" replies the scientist.

"Well, now," says the Lord. "We'll do it the way I did it with the first man, Adam, OK?"

"Fine" agrees the scientist as he bends down to scoop up a handful of dirt.

"Whoa!" says God. "Not so fast. You get your own dirt."

Lord God of Creation, I am so thankful that You are omnipotent and sovereign, not only in the universe but in my life. Keep me walking according to Your will and rejoicing in Your power to guard my soul until the last day. Through Christ, amen.

Nov. 30. **Gary Wilde** is a minister living in Venice, Florida, with his wife, Carol. His twin boys were both recently married.

My Prayer Notes

DEVOTIONS®

DECEMBER

For you have one Teacher, and you are all brothers
. . . you have one Father . . . you have one
Instructor, the Messiah.

—Matthew 23:8-10

Gary Wilde, Editor   **Margaret Williams,** Project Editor   Photo Digital Vision | Thinkstock®

DEVOTIONS® is published quarterly by Standard Publishing, Cincinnati, Ohio, www.standardpub.com.
© 2014 by Standard Publishing. All rights reserved. Topics based on the Home Daily Bible Readings,
International Sunday School Lessons. © 2012 by the Committee on the Uniform Series. Printed in
the U.S.A. All Scripture quotations, unless otherwise indicated, are taken from the *HOLY BIBLE,
NEW INTERNATIONAL VERSION®. NIV®.* Copyright © 1973, 1978, 1984, 2011 by Biblica, Inc.® Used
by permission of Zondervan. All rights reserved worldwide. Scripture quotations marked (*NKJV*)
are taken from the *New King James Version®.* Copyright © 1982 by Thomas Nelson, Inc. Used by
permission. All rights reserved.   Volume 59 No. 1

Back to God

This shall be an everlasting statute for you, to make atonement for the children of Israel, for all their sins, once a year (Leviticus 16:34, *New King James Version*).

Scripture: Leviticus 16:29-34
Song: "Redeemed, How I Love to Proclaim It"

In *Les Miserables,* Jean Valjean is released from prison, and a bishop offers him shelter for a night. But Valjean steals silver plates from the bishop and flees under the cover of darkness. When he is caught, the bishop gives this felon even more silver!

Perplexed and moved, Valjean asks, "Why are you doing this?" With a piercing gaze of mercy in his eyes, the bishop answers, "Jean Valjean, my brother, you no longer belong to evil. With this silver, I bought your soul. I've ransomed you from fear and hatred. Now I give you back to God." From that point on, Valjean is transformed.

While no mere man can redeem anyone with silver, this story can illustrate how Christ ransomed us with His precious blood (see 1 Peter 1:18, 19). The elaborate sacrificial system of the Old Testament reminded the Israelites every year to reflect on God's redemption. All these sacrifices, however, foreshadowed Jesus' perfect sacrifice. He alone is our great high priest, "the Shepherd and Overseer" of our souls, who purchased us with His blood (see Hebrews 9:11, 12; 1 Peter 2:24, 25).

Father, may I never cease to praise You for purchasing me for yourself. You have given me eternal life and made me into a new creation, through Christ. Amen.

December 1–7. **Pete and Wendy Charpentier** live in Pineville, Louisiana. They enjoy serving in ministry together and spending time with their two sons.

Trust Me!

Trust in Him at all times, you people; pour out your heart before Him; God is a refuge for us (Psalm 62:8, *New King James Version*).

Scripture: Psalm 62:1, 2, 5-9
Song: "A Mighty Fortress Is Our God"

"Trust me!" Famous last words spoken right before the thrill of victory or the crash of defeat—all depending on whom you're trusting. There was my youngest son, little legs crossed tightly as he wiggled from the uncontrollable urge to go to the bathroom. He was trapped. He needed to potty, but the thought of using the "big" bathroom was more than he could handle.

You see, my son suffers from SIDDs, a sensory integration dysfunction disorder that overloads the brain with stimuli and makes the simplest tasks overwhelming. The only way to begin the process of helping him overcome his feelings of overload was to train him in complete darkness.

Walking toward the dark room, his hands shook as he labored to catch his breath. So I stooped down, looked into his eyes, and said, "Trust me." At that moment, he had to rest in Mom's love to protect him from what his mind told him was so dangerous.

Our heavenly Father does the same for us. As we walk through life, many things provoke fear. But the psalmist reminds us that God is our refuge and we can trust Him. It's as if the Lord stoops down, looks us in the eyes, and gently says, "Trust me."

Father, You are my refuge in every situation. I know that whether I walk beside still waters or trudge through shadowy valleys, You go with me. Thank You for always being there for me! Through Christ I pray. Amen.

No More Missed Opportunities

Today, if you will hear His voice, do not harden your hearts (Hebrews 4:7, *New King James Version*).

Scripture: Hebrews 4:1-11
Song: "Help Somebody Today"

In the movie *Radio*, "Coach Jones" befriends a handicapped man called Radio. But no one, except the coach, understands why the young man goes by that name. Coach just keeps on being Radio's friend, regardless of what others think and say.

Then, suddenly, Radio's mother dies. At this pivotal moment, Coach Jones shares a story with his teenage daughter, a story he'd never shared with anyone.

Jones tells about his paper route as a boy. One day on his route, he heard a strange noise coming from a house near some woods. There he noticed chicken wire stretched around the bottom of the porch—caging a boy like an animal! In shame, Coach Jones confessed that he continued his paper route for years, never trying to help that boy.

Jones's daughter finally understands her father's kindness towards Radio. He'd missed one opportunity, but he wasn't going to miss this one.

Hebrews challenges us to obey God's voice in faith . . . *now*. Yesterday may be gone, but today is open wide with opportunities to walk in faith and obedience.

Dear Heavenly Father, I want to thank You for Your great love and patience. I've missed so many opportunities to trust You, but I also know that every day is a new day in my spiritual journey. By Your grace may I forget what's behind me and reach ahead to what's before me. In Jesus' name, amen.

It's God!

God's dwelling place is now among the people, and he will dwell with them. They will be his people, and God himself will be with them and be their God (Revelation 21:3).

Scripture: Revelation 14:12, 13; 21:1-5
Song: *"We Shall Behold Him"*

The little girl, coming to worship with her parents, entered an enormous church. And all the sights and sounds of the sanctuary were more than she could absorb.

Since the sermon theme was "the presence of God," every song focused on God's closeness. The exuberant choir heralded His power in joyful anthems and invited His presence to saturate their gathering. Orchestral instruments swelled, seeming to usher each person into a special encounter with the Lord. Everyone was prepared to hear the sermon's glorious theme.

With wide eyes the little girl stretched on her tiptoes to catch glimpses of the worship leaders and musicians. Then, as the minister stepped into the pulpit, the little girl simply could not contain her excitement. "It's God!" she cried out. *"He's here!"*

Although this child made an honest mistake, the reality is that God's children will one day experience His full, undimmed presence in Heaven. This experience will be beyond description, and we will not be able to contain ourselves. On that glorious day, our faith will be sight, and we will thunder in rapturous praise, "It's God!"

Father, I thank You for Your presence in my life every day, and I long for the day when I will see You, face to face. I simply can't imagine how wonderful that will be. Yet, with gratitude, I receive it as the reality of my faith. In Christ's name, amen.

Perfect Provision

So it was, on the sixth day, that they gathered twice as much bread, two omers for each one. And all the rulers of the congregation came and told Moses (Exodus 16:22, *New King James Version*).

Scripture: Exodus 16:22-26
Song: "Trust and Obey"

Love and chicken—that's all Wendy and I possessed early in our marriage. We were teenagers, and money was sparse. I was a preacher, she was a bank teller. But we did have God and His gracious provision.

And the Lord began to show us His provision when we filed our taxes for the first time. We owed an overwhelming $1,500.00—basically, our entire savings.

Wendy wisely suggested we borrow against our own money. So we went to the bank, secured a loan, and drove straight to the post office to mail our check. That's when we also found a letter from a friend that explained how God wanted her to give us something—a check for $1,500.00. Standing speechless, we knew then that God would always meet our needs. The next morning we paid off our loan.

When God liberated the Israelites, they were free but didn't have much food. They lived on God's "love and chicken" in the form of water and manna. But God met their needs as He led them. Even for the day of rest, He gave them double on the day before. The hand that pointed the way provided the way.

Lord, You've taught me to ask for my daily bread, and I'm thankful that I can trust Your perfect provision every day. Thank You, in the precious name of Jesus. Amen.

Resting in Christ

In six days the LORD made the heavens and the earth, the sea, and all that is in them, and rested the seventh day. Therefore the LORD blessed the Sabbath day and hallowed it (Exodus 20:11, *New King James Version*).

Scripture: Exodus 20:8-11; 31:12-16
Song: "Rest for the Weary"

The soothing crackling of the campfire hardly reflected the state of my soul. My life was careening out of control, heading toward a cliff. Yet as I sat with Wendy in the flickering light, the Lord began to soothe my frayed emotions.

I'd been struggling under the weight of stress. In a short time, I had moved into the senior role of a thriving ministry—but amidst difficult circumstances. I left one postgraduate seminary program to complete another one, and I labored to finish a major ministry project.

As I shared these struggles with my wife, tears collected in my eyes. I realized my legs were buckling beneath me, and the bludgeoning of stress was creating a crisis in my life.

That night began a course-correction for me. Through prayer support and the practical application of God's truth, I started to learn how to rest in Jesus. I discovered my heavenly Father didn't want me to run and fret, but to rest in faith.

And why shouldn't that be so? After all, God himself is our greatest example of the sacred rhythm of work and rest.

O God, I know that when I don't rest in Christ, my life cuts against the grain of Your example and will for me. Teach me to rely on Your all-sufficient grace. I am weak, but You are strong. So I intend to lean on You today. Through Christ my Lord, amen.

A New Song

I waited patiently for the LORD; and He inclined to me, and heard my cry. . . . He has put a new song in my mouth— praise to our God; many will see it and fear, and will trust in the LORD (Psalm 40:1, 3, *New King James Version*).

Scripture: Psalm 40:1-8
Song: "Praise the Lord"

I remember when it happened. The day had caught up with me. I took a deep breath to yawn away the fatigue of the moment, and I heard it—SNAP! My jaw locked. No matter how I tried to manipulate my mouth, I could not completely open it.

Wendy, you're a singer! But with my jaw only opening a half-inch, I was no longer able to sing without pain. For years I asked God to deliver me from this "pit." His answer: "Trust me." Through the years, I learned that God's plan is good, even when it doesn't match mine. He taught me that my silent songs of the heart were beautiful to Him and that they were enough.

Like the psalmist, God inclined to me, heard my cry, brought me out of a horrible pit, and put a new song in my mouth. The pit was not that I could no longer sing aloud. My pit was the struggle to trust God with His plan for my life. When the day came that God graciously unlocked my jaw, I realized with the psalmist that the Lord had *already* delivered me.

Are you in a pit today? You can trust God in it.

O Lord God of every circumstance, please remind me that You hear my cries and You are with me through every struggle. Help me to embrace Your will each day, and give me a new song so that You may receive glory because of Your work in and through me. In Christ's name I pray. Amen.

Broken, Yet Stronger

My sacrifice, O God, is a broken spirit; a broken and contrite heart you, God, will not despise (Psalm 51:17).

Scripture: Psalm 51:15-19
Song: "He Touched Me"

Though my own expert diagnosis said otherwise, persistent pain led me to concede I might need a doctor. Sure enough—a broken bone . . . which now needed to be *re-broken* in order to heal properly. Fine. So I didn't get that one exactly right.

David, God's choice to reign over Israel, became a man of great power and great faith. Yet he sometimes fell victim to inherent human weaknesses. Having accepted the reality of his deficiencies, he sought the power of another physician. One of his songs, which is today's Scripture, reveals a key characteristic of his spiritual healing—and ours.

The lesson I learned from dealing with my injury had nothing to do with orthopedics. Mine was a lesson in humility. There's plenty in life that I can't handle alone. David had clearly accepted that same truth. He was, and we are, in need of God's continual guidance, redemption, and grace.

Is a broken bone once healed stronger than ever? Beats me. But David offered his "broken and contrite" heart in an attempt to receive God's forgiveness and a stronger faith. That's a treatment plan all of God's children would do well to follow.

Lord, You keep uncovering my perceived self-sufficiency. Today I lay my broken spirit at Your feet and rely upon Your unmerited grace. Through Christ, amen.

December 8–13. **Robert L. Stephens,** a retiree, loves spending time with family, freelance writing, and public speaking. He and his wife, Linda, travel frequently to national parks.

Got It? Live It!

When Jesus saw that he had answered wisely, he said to him, "You are not far from the kingdom of God" (Mark 12:34).

Scripture: Mark 12:28-34
Song: "The Gift of Love"

It was decades ago, and I recall his sermons being brief. But I can attest that those Sunday morning messages continue to rank among the most powerful I've ever heard. I always felt I "got it." Major William Livermon was a master at getting to the heart of the good news message, and I became quite interested in hearing what he had to say from week to week.

Jesus' replies to His inquisitors sparked a similar interest in one teacher of the law. "Of all the commandments, which is the most important?" (v. 28) he asked. Perhaps the teacher anticipated Jesus choosing from the commandments given to Moses on Mt. Sinai. What he got was clear, concise instruction on living a life pleasing to God. It's all about love. Love God. Love others. Period.

My time in William Livermon's congregation came to an end as I started a life of my own elsewhere. Even now, though, I count him among those responsible for enabling me not to just *get it* but eventually to seek joyfully to *live it*. The exchange that followed Jesus' answer to the teacher leaves little doubt — someone else had gotten it too.

Father, thanks for earthly saints placed along the pathway of my spiritual journey. Without them I would never have gotten this far. Most of all, I thank You for Your Son, Jesus, who continues to draw me ever closer to Your kingdom. In His' name, amen.

You've Got the Gift

We have different gifts, according to the grace given to each of us. If your gift is prophesying, then prophesy in accordance with your faith (Romans 12:6).

Scripture: Romans 12:1-8
Song: "Make Me a Blessing"

Every position I held during my 30-plus year career required, in varying degrees, written communication skills. Whether developing user manuals, updating company procedures, or simply corresponding, I was frequently at the keyboard, and I didn't mind one bit. It was as if I'd been made for it.

Paul made the idea clear to the Christians of Rome: God gifted each of them for a specific purpose—whether teaching, serving, giving, etc. In any particular congregation, no member was equipped to do it all, but everyone had been equipped to do something for the up-building of the body of Christ. Each member would ultimately decide whether or not to use his or her gift.

Paul's assurance of having been gifted by God applies to us down to this very day. Will we use the spiritual gifts that God has given us? Will we allow ourselves to be transformed into what He intended all along?

The world continues giving countless reasons just to go our own way. But I'm finding that the more I trust, the more I experience divine encouragement and direction. More and more, I see that God gives exactly what I need in order to do His will.

For the spiritual gifts You have given, **Father,** I offer my thanks. Grant me the courage to use them daily as You desire and the wisdom never to forget from whom they come. I pray in the precious name of my Lord and Savior, Jesus Christ. Amen.

That Says It All

Without faith it is impossible to please God, because any-one who comes to him must believe that he exists and that he rewards those who earnestly seek him (Hebrews 11:6).

Scripture: Hebrews 11:4-16
Song: "Faith Grasps the Blessing"

"Never leave home without it." What is it for you? Maybe it's your cell phone. For my grandson, it's his basketball. I don't recall him having one in the maternity ward, but beyond that . . . Well, you get my point. His passion for the game ultimately led to his playing college ball. He'd quickly tell you, however, that the key to success was unwavering determination and faith.

Scriptures abound with examples of faithful individuals: a man, who though far from any body of water, builds a huge boat; a woman in her 90s, having initially laughed at the mere notion, bears a child; a father who proves willing to sacrifice the son he had waited for all of his life. Faith surely abounded within them all—and the list could go on, as you know.

It delights me to hear my grandson say matter-of-factly that he always believed he would succeed at the sport he loves. Yet it's another profession of faith that fills my heart with indescrib-able joy: his faith in our God. As did Noah, Sarah, and Abra-ham, he believes in a Lord capable of making the ordinary ex-traordinary, the impossible possible. A sign often appearing at sporting events really does say it all, "You gotta believe!"

Precious Lord, I thank You for the faith of those who have gone before me in follow-ing You so faithfully. I know that only in believing can I realize my ultimate dream, a place by Your side. In the name of Jesus, amen.

My Father's Face

No one has ever seen God; but if we love one another, God lives in us and his love is made complete in us (1 John 4:12).

Scripture: 1 John 4:9-16
Song: "Lord, I Want to Be a Christian"

It's always been a source of pride for me, hearing others compare me to my father. It began as a young boy when I'd join my mother and sister at our small rural church. "How's little Bill today?" I loved it. My father, a merchant seaman often gone for months, held a place of honor in my mind exceeding even that of my TV western heroes. Hearing that I reminded others of Dad always brought a smile to my face.

The apostle John, in writing to Christian congregations, alluded to a characteristic that all God's children are to share with their heavenly Father—an attitude of love. It's been passed down to us just as surely as those physical features we share with our earthly parents. When first loved by our parents, we naturally reciprocated. Likewise, we're called to love God because He first loved us.

Truth be told, any resemblance to my father was limited to a few facial features. And though I had nothing to do with bringing that about, I was nonetheless thrilled to be identified as his son. Gifted with the Holy Spirit, we each have the capacity to grow in likeness to God the Father. How? John leaves little doubt. We resemble God when we love like God.

Dear Father, You unconditionally pour out Your love upon me, in spite of all my shortcomings. May I be equally as free in conveying that love to others. And, in doing so, enable them to see Your beautiful face in mine. Through Christ I pray. Amen.

Perfectly Possible

Do not bring anything with a defect, because it will not be accepted on your behalf (Leviticus 22:20).

Scripture: Leviticus 22:17-25, 31-33
Song: "Lamb of God, We Fall Before Thee"

True perfection. Entire lives have been spent in its pursuit, yet it remains quite elusive. A teen from Romania became the most famous gymnast in the world upon receiving a perfect score of "10" from Olympic judges. It's likely been the goal of every gymnast since. But is true perfection possible?

Moses may well have come away from his conversation with God, recounted in today's passage, wondering the same thing. The Lord made it quite clear: anything less than an unblemished sacrifice would be unacceptable, would in fact profane God's very name.

Yet who better than Moses to understand God's power to make the impossible possible? Having committed himself fully to being God's servant, he experienced that very thing on numerous occasions.

In our human folly we've reached a point where not even perfection is good enough. We're regularly urged to give 110% of ourselves to one cause or another. God, by comparison, asks simply for all we have . . . just as we are.

As for perfection, we needn't fret. God's got that covered.

Heavenly Father, in sending Your Son to walk among us, You allowed us to see what Christian perfection looks like. I ask, Lord, that You guide me on the path toward becoming more like Him until that day when by Your grace I too experience the impossible made into reality. Through Christ, amen.

Holiness: What a Project!

You must not live according to the customs of the nations I am going to drive out before you. Because they did all these things, I abhorred them (Leviticus 20:23).

Scripture: Leviticus 20:7, 8, 22-24
Song: "Whiter than Snow"

My favorite Bible character is Joseph. Having taught teenagers all my career, I offered Joseph as a fine role model. Despite spending his adolescence in Egypt, surrounded by all its pagan allure, this young man seemed to dodge every fiery dart hurled his way. Promoted from prison to palace, Joseph had at his fingertips all of Egypt's hedonistic pleasures. Yet he stood pure and undefiled, even with no fellow believer to buoy his willpower.

When Joseph's siblings later relocated to Egypt, then finally returned to Canaan, they found that land populated in their absence by tribes immersed in depravity. God commanded His returning people to have nothing to do with these folks. Indeed, the Israelites were even enjoined to exterminate them.

All of this shows how seriously God takes holiness. Even to this day, He invites us to be holy people as He pours His cleansing grace within us. It can be a difficult and painful process as we yield to Him, and it is the project of an entire lifetime. Yet the resultant blessing makes it all worthwhile: eternal joy in His presence.

Lord, You've promised that if I resist him, he will flee. Bring to my remembrance that promise the next time Satan makes his move. Through Christ, amen.

December 14–20. **Paul Tatham**, now retired, worked as a Christian school administrator and teacher for 44 years. Living in Orlando, he writes for Christian publications and leads Bible studies.

Brush It Off

The couriers went from town to town in Ephraim and Manasseh, as far as Zebulun, but people scorned and ridiculed them (2 Chronicles 30:10).

Scripture: 2 Chronicles 30:5-12
Song: "Am I a Soldier of the Cross?"

It happened again. Another customer was suing a fast-food restaurant because her spilled coffee was too hot. *What?* I thought. Coffee is supposed to be served piping hot, right? Odds are, though, this person will win a big court settlement.

Frivolous lawsuits have been part of our society for the past 50 years or so. It seems that when someone taunts us or makes fun of some quirk we may have, it can prompt us to burst into tears, gather up our toys, and scamper home in a huff. Much of the political correctness permeating our society today is a direct result of such behavior.

One biblical injunction conveys the idea that Christians are in a battle (see Ephesians 6). Perhaps we should get used to that. Those who go AWOL at the first sign of danger need encouragement to rejoin the kingdom campaign.

In today's passage, King Hezekiah reinstates the long-neglected Passover feast in Jerusalem. Both the northern and southern kingdoms are invited, but many spurn the call and ridicule the messengers. Hezekiah didn't let that bother him in the least. He brushed it off and soldiered on. What a lesson in spiritual tenacity!

God, grant me the fortitude to remain undeterred in the cause of Christ. In Jesus' name, amen.

Dedicated to the Ultimate Prize

[His] head is never to be touched by a razor because the boy is to be a Nazirite, dedicated to God from the womb. He will take the lead in delivering Israel (Judges 13:5).

Scripture: Judges 13:2-5, 24, 25
Song: "Jesus Loves the Little Children"

The minister called the new parents to come forward and face the congregation. One at a time, couples handed the minister their precious new bundle of joy, which he carefully cradled in his arms. After a prayer over the baby, he charged Mom and Dad to rear that infant in the nurture of the Lord.

Such a ceremony impresses upon parents the seriousness of their responsibility to steer a child "in the way he should go" (Proverbs 22:6, *NKJV*). A somber task, not to be taken lightly, the dedication includes the hope that the child go on to be baptized and make his or her life count for eternity. That, after all, should be the goal of all Christian parents.

As the life of that child unfolds, however, that lofty aim often fades. Sure, the church has received this child with open arms, but too often his or her career path is more focused on laying up treasure on earth. Like baby Samson, they may have been "dedicated to God from the womb" (v. 5) . . . but the counting-for-eternity part? Parents, let's reaffirm our duty to help our children focus on a life that has eternal worth.

Lord, I confess that as a parent I may have been more concerned with my children earning a comfortable living than with suffering loss for the sake of the gospel. It's often a lack of trust on my part. And I struggle to trust Your promise that all will be provided, if we seek Your kingdom first. Help, Lord, my unbelief! Through Christ, amen.

Lending to the Lord?

"So now I give him to the LORD. For his whole life he will be given over to the LORD." And he worshiped the LORD there (1 Samuel 1:28).

Scripture: 1 Samuel 1:11, 20, 24-28
Song: "Be Still, My Soul"

Sooner or later, most adults decide to take the plunge. After running the numbers, they figure it's time to sign up for a mortgage, often a 30-year commitment, and purchase a home. After all, we tend to view home ownership as the "American Dream."

Since most young marrieds lack the cash, they approach a mortgage company. The creditor, of course, expects to be repaid in full and has the debtor sign a mountain of paperwork to make it happen.

The typical loan involves the haves lending to the have-nots. But consider an interesting verse, tucked away in Proverbs that conveys just the opposite (19:17, *NKJV*). It talks about us actually lending to the Lord himself—"He who has pity on the poor lends to the Lord." In other words, if we do something noble for His sake, God, in a sense signs a promissory note and obligates himself to repay us—with ever-new opportunities for mission, perhaps?

Maybe this is how Hannah felt when she gave her miracle child Samuel to the Lord's work. No doubt she knew she could count on God to repay His loans.

O Lord God, I'm often reluctant to loan to You, even though I know full well that You always keep Your promises of blessing. I know that in my head, but I often can't actually bring myself to act upon it. Forgive my timidity! I pray in Jesus' name. Amen.

When I Look, Let Me Truly See

Send for him; we will not sit down until he arrives (1 Samuel 16:11).

Scripture: 1 Samuel 16:10-13
Song: "Pass Me Not, O Gentle Savior"

"Please send her in," I said to the receptionist. The young lady who appeared at my office door had graduated from our Christian school four years earlier and was now back applying for a teaching position. She was a beautiful girl who'd come close to being named homecoming queen in her senior year.

Before even beginning the interview, I was already thinking she'd make a fine addition to our staff. The students would love her, the parents would love her, and she'd likely have a good chance at achieving a Teacher of the Year award. All of this I surmised before she even opened her mouth!

Later I pondered how we are so swayed by what the Bible calls "the outward appearance" (1 Samuel 16:7). Psychologists call it *lookism*, a human idiosyncrasy ingrained in all cultures. Even infants tend to fixate on a photo of the more attractive person. Lookism is something we never outgrow, even when we're aware of its ability to unduly influence important decisions.

Tasked with anointing the next king of Israel, the prophet Samuel almost bypassed God's choice because of lookism. Lord, deliver us from that same trap.

Lord God Almighty, help me to look past the outward appearance and focus on inner beauty—just as You do. I want to make judgments about people based upon the things that really count, not just on my subjective impressions. Give me wisdom, in the name of the Father and of the Son and of the Holy Spirit. Amen.

The Non-Royal Treatment

If she cannot afford a lamb, she is to bring two doves or two young pigeons, one for a burnt offering and the other for a sin offering. In this way the priest will make atonement for her, and she will be clean (Leviticus 12:8).

Scripture: Exodus 13:13b-15; Leviticus 12:1-8
Song: "Away in a Manger"

The buildup started early, with the 2011 royal nuptials of Britain's Prince William to Kate, the newly named Duchess of Cambridge. The radiant couple was declared man and wife at London's Westminster Abbey, before a congregation of 1,900 and a worldwide television audience.

Once they had exchanged vows and the hoopla finally began to subside, it was promptly replaced by speculation over an heir. Then, after a two-year wait, Kate gave birth to Prince George, amidst the flourish befitting earth's most popular monarchy.

Another royal birth, two millennia earlier, was decidedly more subdued. Jesus, the King of all kings, took on flesh, humbled himself, and made His debut in a smelly stable in an insignificant village. A few local shepherds dropped in, but not one media outlet bothered to cover the story. No fanfare, no flashbulbs.

Later, at His dedication in Jerusalem's temple, Joseph and Mary could only give a poor person's offering. Yet salvation won at Calvary by Jesus isn't out of reach for the common man. It's not glitzy, and it's not expensive. In fact, it's free for the taking.

Father, I'm amazed afresh at the accessibility of Your saving grace. You died for everyone, even the least noteworthy among us, thus making Heaven available to all who will repent, believe, and ask. Thank You, through Christ the Lord. Amen.

Beam Me Up, Lord!

Sovereign Lord, as you have promised, you may now dismiss your servant in peace. For my eyes have seen your salvation (Luke 2:29, 30).

Scripture: Luke 2:22-32
Song: "I Want to Be Ready"

One of the most popular television shows of the 1960s was *Star Trek.* It offered up the exciting possibilities of space travel and quickly became a sci-fi cult classic.

Among the show's many futuristic devices was a beam of light that could immediately transport astronauts to the mother ship from any distant orbit. Captain Kirk used the device constantly, and "Beam me up, Scotty" became an instant catchphrase.

In a way, Simeon and Anna were ready to be "beamed up." A little over a month earlier, Jesus had been born in Bethlehem, and now his parents were in Jerusalem's temple for His dedication. Simeon and Anna, part of the faithful remnant of Israel eagerly awaiting the Messiah, frequented the temple and were providentially there at that very moment.

Simeon held the child heavenward in his arms and blessed God. He was so overcome with this momentous privilege that he stammered, "Lord, . . . now dismiss your servant in peace". In other words, "Beam me up, Lord, I'm ready to go home!"

It is good to ask ourselves occasionally: Am I ready to be beamed up at any time? Would I hear the Lord's "good and faithful servant" (Matthew 25:21, 23) commendation?

O Lord, keep before me the importance of making my life count for eternity. Today, may I focus on things that have heavenly value. In Christ I pray. Amen.

Newsflash: John Introduces Jesus!

"This is the one I spoke about . . . 'He who comes after me has surpassed me because he was before me'" (John 1:15).

Scripture: John 1:10-18
Song: "Rejoice, the Lord Is King!"

How exciting to be reunited with family and old friends! And what a privilege it is to introduce those folks to your *new* friends. There is pride and joy. You know the feeling.

Now, can you begin to imagine the excitement, pride, and joy that John the Baptist must have felt when he finally had the privilege of introducing Jesus? I wonder if it wasn't tinged with a bit of "showing off"—a sort of bragging—about knowing the Lamb of God?

Think about it: At that moment, John was the only human who could claim to know who Jesus actually was: "Listen! Pay attention! I'm going to tell you some really good news. This is the new guy. He is so great. He is awesome. He is so far above and beyond me that no words can express it!" What a privilege!

Do you suppose John also felt a sense of relief? (The Lord's promise is really coming to pass. *Finally!* Now I have my friend, my cousin, right here, working beside me.)

Could there have been an element of fear too? After all, John must have had some sense of what he and Jesus would be up against. Think about it.

Praise and thanks to You, great God and King! The world was about to change. The right to become children of God! What a privilege! Alleluia! Through Christ, I pray.

December 21–27. **Anne Collins** is a homemaker, retired teacher, and business owner. She lives in Venice, Florida. Her interests are faith, family, friends, food, fitness, flowers, and fabrics.

Grace and Mercy, All the Time

Because of his great love for us, God, who is rich in mercy, made us alive with Christ even when we were dead in transgressions — it is by grace you have been saved (Ephesians 2:4, 5).

Scripture: Ephesians 2:1-10
Song: "Amazing Grace"

Years ago, my mother tried to tell me that she couldn't accept God's grace. "I don't deserve it," she said. She didn't believe in Heaven or an afterlife, calling herself a "realist." Still, she demonstrated the qualities of grace and mercy in her own life — loving, caring, giving, forgiving, and generous.

I had chosen, on my own, at age 12, to be baptized and was overwhelmingly filled with joy and gratitude for the gift of Jesus in my life. "But Mom," I cried, *"no one* deserves it! Grace is God's gift to all of us." She didn't want to talk about it, though I desperately wanted her to receive God's gifts. How I prayed that she would.

Mom passed on almost 20 years ago. A very private person, stoic. As far as I know, she never accepted Christ. Might a failure of communication on my part have been somewhat to blame? If only words such as *grace* and *mercy* had been part of our family vocabulary. After all, they abound in the Bible.

But why are grace and mercy spoken of only in Bible studies and sermons? All the time, I feel a deep need to learn creative ways to share these concepts. Will you join me in that quest?

Dearest Lord, thank You for loving me. Help me so to love that I may never be afraid to tell others about Your love. Teach me more and more. Please grant me the courage and the words and the ways to share with others. In Christ's precious name, amen.

Dulane's Gift

Since you excel in everything—in faith, in speech, in knowledge, in complete earnestness and in the love we have kindled in you—see that you also excel in this grace of giving (2 Corinthians 8:7).

Scripture: 2 Corinthians 8:3-9
Song: "Teach Me, My God and King"

The mailbox in front of our house had been broken for over a year. The hinges were gone, and the door was sort of held in place by layers of duct tape I'd reapplied from time to time. I tried unsuccessfully to find the right mailbox (a neighborhood requirement) at our local home-improvement stores. It bothered me, because the box had been falling apart for a long time, it looked awful, and the mail carrier had to deal with it daily.

Yesterday I came home from work early. Lo and behold, our neighbor, Dulane, was parked in our driveway, back of his truck open, tools strewn about. He was putting finishing touches on my brand new mailbox!

I know he'd planned to be finished before I arrived home, never telling me who'd come to the rescue. But since I'd "caught" him, of course I exclaimed my surprise and gratitude, telling him that my whole frame of mind would be changed for the better. "Wow," I exclaimed, "*Where* did you find that?"

"Oh, it's a deep, dark secret," he said, quietly refusing my offer to pay for it.

Thank You, **Dear Lord,** for putting Dulane in our neighborhood. My friends and neighbors are so often my helping angels. Help me also to practice this same kind of grace-giving, through the power of Your love. In Jesus' name, amen.

Let the Gratitude Ring Out!

Let the message of Christ dwell among you richly as you teach and admonish one another with all wisdom through psalms, hymns, and songs from the Spirit, singing to God with gratitude in your hearts (Colossians 3:16).

Scripture: Colossians 3:12-17
Song: "Go, Tell It on the Mountain"

I have friends who will burst into song for no reason—other than for the pure joy of it. It may be an old popular song that pops into mind when we're having a conversation. "There's a song about that, you know." And we spontaneously start laughing and singing together. "Hey there, you with the stars in your eyes."

Sometimes it's a silly kids' song that suddenly pertains to something we're talking about. "The itsy, bitsy spider climbed up the waterspout." Or, we're pretend opera singers, performing "Santa Lucia." Often it's an old familiar hymn we love so much, such as "Go, Tell It on the Mountain."

The Holy Spirit brings this out in believers: singing to God with gratitude in our hearts. The psalms of David, for instance, are simply a songbook, the selections always meant to be sung.

In our church it's rare to merely recite a psalm's words; we're always singing them. But in any case, the key is heartfelt gratitude. So, dig into some psalms this week. Try singing them, even if you have to make up your own tunes. I have no doubt you'll feel the gratitude welling up within you.

Father, on this night commemorating Your Son's birth, how I thank You for psalms, hymns, and songs from the Spirit! In Christ's precious name I pray. Amen.

Susan's Gift

We have different gifts, according to the grace given to each of us (Romans 12:6).

Scripture: Romans 12:6-13
Song: "A Child Is Born in Bethlehem"

Our daughter Susan has a quiet, reflective, winsome way about her. Discernment is one of her spiritual gifts. Recently, in a letter I shared how much I'd enjoyed working with children at Bible school. She replied, "Working with children is very rewarding, isn't it, Mom? Just think, you and I were little children!" She went on to write, "Well, I'm like a little child even today. Sometimes I just like to sing silly songs and talk cat-language. Mom, what do you like to do for the child in you?"

Something shifted in my mind. She'd reminded me of something I believe: that everyone, at any age, on some level, remains a 10-year-old at heart. And that's a blessing.

Yes, I'm 73. But I dance around the kitchen. I yodel in the shower. I love riding my bike. I practice birdcalls. And I laugh about silly stuff.

Saved on my computer are old photos of Susie when she was a little girl. Here's the thing: We have very few pictures of her when she was *not* holding a cat in her arms. As a kid, she invented an entire cat-language that she still speaks to her current feline friends. By the way, Susie is 52 years old, a respected CPA, working in the financial district of Chicago. What a gift is Susie's—and what a gift is Susie!

Father, I thank You for the gift of Christmas Day, when I love to remember that Jesus too was a little child. Teach me to celebrate the child in me. Through Christ, amen.

Needed: No Trumpets, Just Kindness

When you give to the needy, do not announce it with trumpets, as the hypocrites do in the synagogues and on the streets, to be honored by others (Matthew 6:2).

Scripture: Matthew 6:1-6
Song: "Where Charity and Love Prevail"

I recently met a dedicated, compassionate woman named Lynette. She and her husband work tirelessly, with no desire for recognition, as they minister a unique church called Center of Hope. The congregation's full-time mission is reaching out to local homeless families.

Often, hungry children show up at the church's soup kitchen, while the parents are afraid to come in. Their families are hiding in the woods, or in cars, in store parking lots, as they avoid the authorities. Some fear being arrested on old warrants. Others can't obtain benefits because they have no government identification—but they can't get an ID without a mailing address.

Center of Hope offers food, new clothing, doctors and dentists, along with job-search help. All of this is good, but Lynette tells it like it is: "We need volunteers to help with everything: providing groceries, donating new underwear, answering phones, helping folks complete applications."

"But," she said, "the main thing we need is for you to come and just be kind."

Dearest Lord, I am saddened by the reality of Lynette's compelling story. Challenge me to step out of my comfort zone to find ways that I can help the needy. Teach me the way to go, so that my heartfelt impulse toward kindness may be used for practical mercies. Through Christ I pray. Amen.

Norm's Gift

Those who exalt themselves will be humbled, and those who humble themselves will be exalted (Matthew 23:12).

Scripture: Matthew 23:2-12; Mark 12:38-44
Song: "Lamb of God, I Look to Thee"

One day my husband, Norm, encountered my mom in the middle of her struggle with a bucket and brushes, ready to tackle the wall-to-wall linoleum floor in her basement. "Oh, hi, Mrs. Hatch. I'll be right back!" Norm turned on his heels, took off in his car, and quickly returned with a huge professional floor-cleaning machine he'd borrowed from his workplace.

Of course, Mom didn't trust that boy and his machine to clean the corners properly! But Norm had that figured out too. Soon the floor sparkled, and Mom had the day off.

Our tiny 10-year-old daughter loved playing the double bass fiddle in the school orchestra. Norm rigged a golf pull-cart for her, with a clever rack and bungee cords to hold the instrument. Now Susie could walk her huge fiddle to school. Neighbors got a kick out of waving at her as she pranced along, proudly wheeling her bass. "Nobody but your dad would ever have figured that out!" they would tell her.

Norman was strong, observant and insightful, creative and confident, yet humble. He would notice a need and jump in to do something about it right away, never wishing for anything in return. Our family loves to recall "Norm" stories, although we know he would say, "Sshhhh, stop!"

Thank You, **God,** for Norman, and for all those blessed with that endearing quality of showing up where there's a need, giving with a pure heart. Through Christ, amen.

Keeping Secrets

A talebearer reveals secrets, but he who is of a faithful spirit conceals a matter (Proverbs 11:13, *New King James Version*).

Scripture: Proverbs 11:9-13
Song: "They'll Know We Are Christians"

I still remember the day in third grade when one of the popular girls confided to me some negative secret about a classmate. What a thrill to be considered grown-up enough to be entrusted with gossip! From that day on, I had many opportunities to learn secrets, which I quickly relayed to interested friends. I was eager to share others' secrets, but didn't relish getting caught: *"Promise you won't tell anyone I said this!"*

Years later, when a good friend warned me that I should be praying for others instead of gossiping about them, I became indignant. By then, I no longer considered it gossiping—I was merely sharing my thoughts and insights about others. It took years, and a lot of Bible reading, before I began to appreciate my friend's warning and her wisdom. My habit of gossip, I now know, kept me from growing in Christ.

Today's Bible reading contrasts two types of people. On one side are the righteous, the upright, the understanding, those "of a faithful spirit" (v. 13). On the other side are hypocrites, destroyers with their mouths, the wicked, mockers, and gossips. May I stay on the right side today.

Dear Father, Your Word tells of Your blessings and tender mercies. You encourage and uplift. Help me, Lord, to be that kind of blessing to others. In Jesus' name, amen.

December 28–31. **Maria Anne Tolar** lives with her husband in Portland, Oregon, where they are members of a vibrant church. She is currently working on a historical novel.

Nothing but the Truth

Lying lips are an abomination to the LORD, but those who deal truthfully are His delight (Proverbs 12:22, *New King James Version*).

Scripture: Proverbs 12:19-26
Song: "O to Be Like Thee!"

When I was in the fourth grade, I had no athletic ability at all. But it wasn't my fault: I couldn't hit the ball because the pitchers cheated. If I ever did run the bases, someone always tried to trip me. I complained bitterly about it to my mother, until one evening, out of the blue she accused me of making things up, of lying. *My own mother!*

I remember not being able to sleep that night, thinking of Mom's shocking accusation. But as I continued brooding, I began considering how often I shaded truth, how I exaggerated to make the facts a little more interesting. And how my stories changed each time I told them.

I don't remember what happened next that night, but my mother sure did. I know it occurred, because even years afterwards she still mentioned it. Around midnight I shook her awake, sobbing, "Mom, wake up! I lied. The truth is, I just can't hit the ball!"

We live in a dangerous world, and if we don't treasure truth, if we don't stand for truth, we will fall for lies. Love of truth can help lead us to Jesus, the way, the truth, and the life.

Dear Lord, teach me to order my days that I may present to You a heart of wisdom. "Let the words of my mouth and the meditation of my heart be acceptable in Your sight, O Lord" (Psalm 19:14, *NKJV*). In Jesus' name I pray. Amen.

Seek True Wisdom

Through wisdom a house is built, and by understanding it is established (Proverbs 24:3, *New King James Version*).

Scripture: Proverbs 24:3-7, 13, 14
Song: "He Leadeth Me"

We don't talk about wisdom much these days or seek it out by that name. There's a shortcut called "self-help" and "how to" books. And there are always new titles, all promising that if we tweak our attitude or employ certain techniques, we too can find fulfillment and prosperity. We can attain our goals and accomplish our dreams just as the authors of all those books have.

Those self-help books are the modern equivalent of what the Bible calls wisdom. We want desperately to learn how to manage our lives, to get what we want, to develop the gifts we hope we have: to reach our destiny!

Until fairly recently, I often read self-help books. Then last spring I challenged myself to memorize 50 Scripture verses each month. Four hundred memorized verses later, I now realize that all the self-help instruction I'd ever needed had been in God's Word all along. I'd been wasting my time on questionable advice when what I needed was God's wisdom.

When we let the Lord's Word guide and direct our paths, we walk in heavenly wisdom. To His wisdom He adds His mercy and grace and joy, steadying us with strength and courage. In this way, we reach our true destiny to His glory.

O, Lord, teach me Your ways and Your thoughts. "For as the heavens are higher than the earth, so are My ways higher than your ways, and My thoughts than your thoughts" (Isaiah 55:9, *NKJV*). Thanks be to God! In Jesus' name, amen.

The Ministry of Truth

This is a faithful saying and worthy of all acceptance, that Christ Jesus came into the world to save sinners, of whom I am chief (1 Timothy 1:15, *New King James Version*).

Scripture: 1 Timothy 1:12-17
Song: "Sin, When Viewed by Scripture Light"

We're all in the ministry, even if we're not called to be apostles or write half of the New Testament, as Paul did. In one way we're just like Paul, though. Like him, we are all sinners.

I hate to remember who I once was as an adult sinner—a rebellious, chain-smoking mess with a chip on my shoulder when it came to the things of God. Yet He saved me as He found me, the least likely to succeed. It took—and still takes—God the Father, the Lord Jesus Christ, the Holy Spirit, and the Word of God, all working in my life, to continue transforming me.

Yet over time, even I can get so used to the light that I can't understand why some still sit in darkness, or why sinners keep willfully sinning. But we must never forget who we once were, where we came from. Paul mentions often in his letters how his life changed on the road to Damascus, and we need to remember the road we once traveled.

We don't have to be great evangelists or Bible scholars to be faithful witnesses to Christ. We can tell what it was like to be lost and what it is like to be found. Or, if we were raised in the church, we can convey with heartfelt gratitude how much pain the Lord allowed us to miss.

Heavenly Father, thank You for sending Your perfect, sinless Son to save me, help me, teach me, love me; and thank You for dying for me. I love You, Christ my Lord! Amen.